D1219203

THE GAME DEVELOPER'S DICTIONARY: A MULTIDISCIPLINARY LEXICON FOR PROFESSIONALS AND STUDENTS

DAN CARREKER

Course Technology PTR
A part of Cengage Learning

COURSE TECHNOLOGY
CENGAGE Learning®

Australia • Brazil • Japan • Korea • Mexico • Singapore • Spain • United Kingdom • United States

COURSE TECHNOLOGY
CENGAGE Learning

NOV 15 2012

The Game Developer's Dictionary: A Multidisciplinary Lexicon for Professionals and Students
Dan Carreker

Publisher and General Manager, Course Technology PTR: Stacy L. Hiquet

Associate Director of Marketing: Sarah Panella

Manager of Editorial Services: Heather Talbot

Senior Marketing Manager: Mark Hughes

Senior Acquisitions Editor: Emi Smith

Project Editor: Kim Benbow

Technical Reviewer: Ernest Adams

Copy Editor: Michael Beady

Interior Layout: MPS Limited, a Macmillan Company

Cover Designer: Luke Fletcher

Indexer: Kelly Talbot

Proofreader: Sue Boshers

© 2012 Course Technology, a part of Cengage Learning.

ALL RIGHTS RESERVED. No part of this work covered by the copyright herein may be reproduced, transmitted, stored, or used in any form or by any means graphic, electronic, or mechanical, including but not limited to photocopying, recording, scanning, digitizing, taping, Web distribution, information networks, or information storage and retrieval systems, except as permitted under Section 107 or 108 of the 1976 United States Copyright Act, without the prior written permission of the publisher.

For product information and technology assistance, contact us at
Cengage Learning Customer & Sales Support, 1-800-354-9706

For permission to use material from this text or product, submit all requests online at **www.cengage.com/permissions**

Further permissions questions can be emailed to **permissionrequest@cengage.com**

All trademarks are the property of their respective owners.

All images © Cengage Learning unless otherwise noted.

Library of Congress Control Number: 2011936042

ISBN-13: 978-1-4354-6081-2

ISBN-10: 1-4354-6081-2

Course Technology, a part of Cengage Learning
20 Channel Center Street
Boston, MA 02210
USA

Cengage Learning is a leading provider of customized learning solutions with office locations around the globe, including Singapore, the United Kingdom, Australia, Mexico, Brazil, and Japan. Locate your local office at: **international.cengage.com/region**

Cengage Learning products are represented in Canada by Nelson Education, Ltd.

For your lifelong learning solutions, visit **courseptr.com**

Visit our corporate website at **cengage.com**

Printed in the United States of America
1 2 3 4 5 6 7 13 12 11

This work is dedicated to my father,
who, in 1979, brought home
a TRS-80 computer with two games and said,
"If you want any more, you'll have to program them yourself."

He then provided me with all of the tools
I needed to make that happen.

FOREWORD

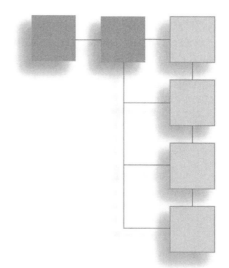

Video games have been surrounded by jargon since their earliest days, and their distinct vocabulary has permanently changed our culture. When the panicking Private Hudson shrieked, "Game over, man! Game over!" in the movie *Aliens*, the whole audience recognized that it was a video game reference. *Loading screens, levels, power-ups,* and *platformers*: these words are now part of our lives.

But those are just some of the words the general public knows. Behind the scenes, in the world of developers and publishers, there are thousands more—and that's not even counting the acronyms. To a newcomer, it can all be a little overwhelming. Worse yet, industry professionals don't always agree on what these terms mean.

Back when Andrew Rollings and I were writing our first book on game design, it worried us that there was no standard definition for a lot of game industry terms. We realized that if we wrote our book without explaining how we were using an important word, such as *gameplay,* our readers might not understand us. On the other hand, if we tried to provide a formal definition for everything, it would have taken up half the book. In the end we chose a middle way, defining a few words here and there. Neither of us was really satisfied with the result. The game industry needs a real dictionary, and at last, Dan Carreker has given us one.

It's a thankless job to be a lexicographer. Doctor Johnson, the greatest dictionary-maker of them all, complained that he was "exposed to censure, without hope of praise." When you write a dictionary, people often pick it up expecting to have their own viewpoint confirmed. If they agree with what they find, they put it down again with mild satisfaction, but if they don't, they send you outraged letters declaring you to be an ignoramus, or worse.

Dan has chosen to brave this predicament by giving us a large, interdisciplinary dictionary with hundreds of specialized terms, from the familiar (*game*) to the obscure (*traveler's dilemma*). Along the way, he covers aesthetic, technical, and commercial issues. He includes expressions that are theoretical (*zero sum*) and those that are practical (*screen space blurred shadow mapping*). Best of all, if a word is used in different ways by the game industry (*2.5D*), he gives all of the meanings.

This book is a useful tool for students and professionals alike. Keep it by you, and it will serve you well.

—Ernest W. Adams
November 2011

PREFACE

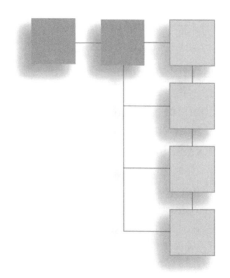

On the Need for a More Common Language

"I wish there was a dictionary…." I've heard this sentiment expressed several times as of late, but the first time I remember hearing it was several years ago. A few industry professionals and I had just spent a week arguing the importance of having a narrative within video games. Nothing uncordial, of course, but the participants had broken into two distinct camps and neither was willing to yield any points to the other. Baffled by the division, I finally asked people to define what they meant by the word "narrative."

By the time everyone explained what it meant to them (which varied from "dialogue" to "story arc"), we realized that there was no actual disagreement. In fact, we all had the same general point of view; it was simply the difference in how we defined that specific word that had caused the confusion. It was then that someone uttered the phrase "I wish there was a dictionary…." The next day, I decided to start a simple project, the results of which directly lead to the book you now have in your hands. I would create a list of the terms used in the industry and list, as plainly as possible, their commonly agreed-upon definitions. However, before I describe how that simple project developed into something not quite so simple, I think it prudent to explain why moments like the one previously described have become common.

The video game industry has evolved. What was at first hobbyists working in their spare time in school labs or converted garages has grown into veteran specialists working in high-rise offices and multimillion dollar studios. Some of these professionals came from those early days of video game development, but many emerged from other disciplines, including traditional game design, art, software programming, film animation, screenwriting, engineering, music production, and many more. Each of them brought along their own language—a collection of terms and definitions relevant to their fields—which filtered in and out of the industry as they did.

Games continued to change and so did the way we talked about them. Confusion inevitably arose as each discipline had, up until then, been largely independent and therefore had its own unique vocabulary. What was known as "value" by an artist would have been called "brightness" by a programmer (to whom "value" meant something else entirely). "Theme" had a different meaning to a game designer than it did to a writer. A common language had not, and still has not, developed—yet in order for the members of any multidisciplinary venture to communicate efficiently, a common language must emerge. Imagine an operating room in which the surgeon, nurse, and anesthesiologist all had something else in mind when they used the word "pulse." Such conditions would result in an inefficient work environment at the very least, if not something far worse.

The game industry is now facing that same problem. We have no common language. Instead, we speak to each other from our own semi-secluded area of expertise and muddle along hoping that those in other disciplines understand us. It was this problem I recognized in that moment a few years back when we argued pointlessly over something we all agreed on; it was a problem that I wanted to help solve.

When I began this project, I seriously underestimated the immensity of what lay before me. I asked myself, "How many words can there be?" In my mind I figured that the list of terms would be somewhere around 10 to 20 pages long; something that could easily be added to my website. Six months later, I found myself with just that: a 20-page list. Only I had not created any definitions yet. The list was composed entirely of words and terms still to be defined. In addition, each day I would discover another word or two to add to that list. I began to realize the task I had taken on was far more formidable than just a simple collection of a handful of words. It was becoming a fully developed lexicon.

It was at this time I began teaching. My class was composed of college freshmen who wanted to enter the game industry, and almost none of whom had any background or training in game development. The realization of just how much information they needed began to dawn on me. So much knowledge within the industry is handed down in a master-to-apprentice method and yet, as game development studies gain in popularity, that information is often absent from student textbooks or, at the very best, is spread out through dozens of different books on different subjects. While artists, for example, can certainly find much of the information they need on rendering techniques within their books, they have little-to-no exposure to production terms that may be bantered about on their first day on the job.

It became apparent that there was a need to not only help the existing professional but also the future professional. If the game industry is to utilize those who have been educated in game development programs, it is not unreasonable for them to expect the resulting prospects to not only be good at their job but also to communicate effectively in their new work environment. I added to my plans the goal of creating definitions that students in all disciplines could utilize—not to replace the encyclopedic definitions within their existing textbooks, but to complement their knowledge with simple and clear explanations of the terms they would likely encounter outside their field of expertise. I also recognized that having a definition wasn't enough; the reader would need an indication as to which field used the term in which way, so I added icons to each definition to represent just that.

With the help of two department chairmen at the school, Glenn Dunki-Jacobs and Mitchell Gohman, and several other members of the staff, I was able to put together a spiral bound version of the dictionary and bring it into the classroom. The students there provided me with not only a way to gauge the effectiveness of the work, but also with many suggestions and insights that served to make the dictionary stronger with each iteration. I am also thankful for the advice I received from several prominent authors of textbooks, including Ernest Adams and Ian Schreiber. The advice I received, from them and others, helped me produce something far greater than my original intent.

Once the dictionary had been refined, Cengage Learning expressed an interest in publishing it. With the help of several wonderful editors, including Emi Smith, Kim Benbow, and Ernest Adams, I was able to transform what started as a "simple" project into the reference work you are now holding. It is my hope that this dictionary will become an integral part of achieving the common language that the industry needs.

This book, of course, cannot actually create that common language. Only a consensus by the entirety of the game development industry, over time, will make that determination. What this book does, though, is collect the terms and phrases used within all avenues of game development, and defines them. The emphasis has been on creating an understanding between the disciplines; great care has been exercised to define terms in ways that someone outside the related area of expertise can easily grasp. Granted, some concepts lend themselves more easily to this task than others; however, the definitions were crafted as simply and clearly as possible to ensure that those professionals who are most unfamiliar with a term receive the greatest benefit from them.

At the same time, this work does not claim to establish any listed word or phrase as more relevant or authentic than another. The language used to describe games and the process of making them is still evolving and any attempt to set it in stone would not only be damaging to its growth but would also, eventually, fail. It is my desire, however, that the community of industry professionals gain an understanding of how we are currently using terms and phrases within the varied disciplines and thereby allow a more common language to emerge.

—Dan Carreker
December 2011

ACKNOWLEDGMENTS

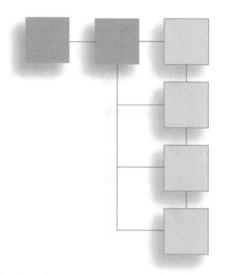

The author would like to thank the following people for their work and support in making this dictionary possible:

Sean Osborn, for his friendship and support throughout the years.

Glenn Dunki-Jacobs, Scott Russell, and Mitch Gohman, for their encouragement and assistance in bringing this book to the students of Mt. Sierra College.

Emi Smith and Kim Benbow, not only for their editorial expertise but also for making the whole process a pleasurable experience.

Ernest Adams, for his numerous contributions to the success of this project.

Shawna and Long Du, and Carolyn and Andre Kramer, for their encouragement, faith, and support.

Jim and Karen Carreker, for everything.

Ian Schreiber, for his advice early in the process.

Neil H. Weiss, for the inspiration to take on any challenge.

Violet Grundy and Rhinda Thomas, for their assistance in getting this book to my students.

Matt McClure and Bob McPherson, for providing me with the skills and knowledge I needed when I first entered the industry. I can't thank either of you enough.

And finally...

All of my students, who not only tested the book but who also continue to inspire me to explore the past, present, and future of this great industry that we are in.

About the Author

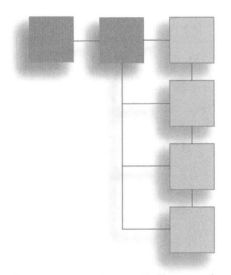

Dan Carreker currently teaches Game Development classes at Mt. Sierra College and has industry experience as both a Database Manager for Activision's Production/QA department and as a freelance game designer. He has published several articles including advice for Game Development students and how to break into the industry.

CONTENTS

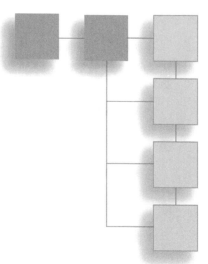

INTRODUCTION

How to Use This Dictionary
Headwords and Definitions

The headwords (or terms being defined) are listed on a separate line above the definition. These listings may be a word, abbreviation, or phrase. Each is listed using word-by-word alphabetization. Spaces are given the first spot in the order, followed by punctuation marks and symbols, numbers, and then letters in the order in which they appear in the English alphabet. Periods and slashes that are part of the headwords are ignored.

Definitions are listed directly beneath the headword or phrase, as in the following examples.

Act structure

A method of dividing a narrative into separate, recognizable units. ♪

Actants layer

The actions and reactions of the characters to the events within a story. Also known as the **Performance Level**. ♪

Action

1. A genre of video games that focuses on eye-hand coordination challenges. ♪

2. The events and movement within a story or game. ▣

Action-adventure

A genre of video games that combines the elements of traditional adventure games with combat challenges. ♪

Acronyms, Abbreviations, and Alternate Spellings

In cases where the listed entry is an acronym or abbreviation, the full word or phrase is written out in italics at the beginning of the definition.

RC

1. *Release candidate.* A build that is being evaluated for distribution. Also known as a **Code Release Candidate** or **Final Candidate**. ♪

2. *Release candidate.* The third phase of software development in which, traditionally, all of the features and assets have been tested and the emphasis is on confirming the fixes. Also known as **Code Release** and **Gamma**. ♪

In cases where the entry is the full word or phrase but is also commonly known by an acronym or abbreviation, the acronym or abbreviation is listed in parentheses immediately following the entry.

Technical Review Group (TRG)

A collection of employees tasked with the peer-review of a product or process. ♪

Also listed in parentheses are alternate spellings or pronunciations set in italic.

AAA

(*Triple A*) A game of the highest quality. See also **Topshelf**. ♪

Foreign Words

The literal translation of foreign words or phrases is included immediately before the definition in italics. The language they are translated from appears next to them in parentheses.

Deus ex machina

God in the Machine (Latin). A literary technique in which the resolution is reached by an unpredictable and improbable turn of events, such as the last-minute appearance of a powerful character that had not been previously introduced within the story. Named from the practice in Greek plays of having a god appear on stage to resolve the hero's problem. ⚓

Discipline Icons

As a multidisciplinary reference, this dictionary emphasizes how certain terminology is used differently, depending on the speaker's field of expertise. A series of icons are used to identify which disciplines are most likely to use the listed definition. One or more icons appear immediately after the body of the definition. These icons are as follows:

Game Design—Dealing with the creation of the features and mechanics within a game. ⊞

Production—Dealing with the business practices of creating, testing, and manufacturing a game. ♪

Programming—Dealing with the creation of the game's coded instructions. ▇

Sound Design—Dealing with the creation of the audio elements within a game. ♣

Visual Arts—Dealing with the creation of the visual elements within a game. ▝▍

Writing—Dealing with the creation of story, character, and dialogue within a game, and copy writing. ✍

The icons are listed in order of relevance with the discipline that utilizes the terminology most often listed first.

Cross-References

Entries related to other entries in the dictionary will list a cross-reference in boldface at the end of the definition.

"Also known as" signifies that the term being defined is also known by another name. Entries that can be cross-referenced this way will have exactly the same definition except in rare cases in which additional information is needed to explain a specific headword.

Positive testing
A QA philosophy in which the focus is on evaluating the software's ability to perform correctly when encountering anticipated situations. Also known as **Testing to Pass**. ♪

"See also" signifies the term relates to another term listed within the dictionary. The term may be a comparison, a contrast, or a closely associated term.

Ranged combat
Combat between units or characters that takes place while they are not adjacent to each other. See also **Melee**. ⊞

Reverse Dictionary and People Mentioned Within Entries

Following the alphabetical listings of terms and their related definitions, all headwords are listed again by subject matter. These listings are broken up according to the six discipline icons and then further broken down into categories. This allows readers to narrow down their search when they know what category a word belongs to but are unaware of its exact expression. Some terms may be listed within multiple categories, as applicable. (Definitions are not included in this section.)

Persons mentioned within entries are referenced by their last name. A brief biographical entry for each person mentioned can be found in Appendix A.

Positions Within the Industry

Included with this work is a listing of commonly used titles within the video game industry. Because these titles are often used inconsistently, the reader is cautioned against accepting the definitions here as authoritative; instead, the listing should be treated as a survey of titles and their descriptions as used throughout the industry. The listing follows the same guidelines as those for the dictionary portion of this work.

ALPHABETICAL LISTING OF WORDS AND TERMINOLOGY

80/20 rule

A mathematical generalization, named after Pareto and publicized by Juran, that 80% of benefits come from just 20% of the resources. Also known as the **Pareto Principle**. ♪

80% stereotype rule

An ideal, proposed by Bethke, that a game's writing should break expectations 20% of the time; breaking it more often will result in confusion on the player's part, less often will result in a loss of dramatic tension. ♪

2D

1. A classification of digital objects that are created with only height and width. ♪

2. A classification of video games in which the gameplay environment exists primarily on a single plane and thereby limiting actions to only two directions. ▣ ♪

2.5D

1. An art style that gives the impression that objects are three dimensional despite being displayed inside a 2D environment. Also known as **Pseudo-3D**. ♪

2. A 3D scene created by a series of flat (2D) images. ♪

3. A classification of video games in which the gameplay environment exists as multiple 2D layers stacked upon each other, giving the appearance of a third dimension. ▣ ♪

3D

1. A classification of digital objects that are created with height, width, and depth. 🖥
2. A classification of video games in which the gameplay environment exists as three perpendicular planes and thereby allowing actions within all directions. 🎲 🖥
3. A genre of video games that utilizes technologies that give objects within the game the illusion of depth when displayed. 🎲 🖥

4X

A subgenre of strategy games that focus on empire building through means of exploring, expanding, exploiting, and exterminating as coined by Emrich. ♪

A*

(*A-star*) A variety of similar pathing algorithms that are known for their efficiency. ▰

A-life

Artificial life. Software that attempts to simulate living systems and their evolution. ▰

AAA

(*Triple A*) A game of the highest quality. See also **Topshelf**. ♪

Abandoned

A game state in which at least one of the currently crucial players is no longer active in the game and thereby preventing the game from reaching its natural conclusion. 🎲

Abandonware

A nonlegal classification for software whose IP's ownership is believed to have been abandoned by its rights holders and whose state is therefore vague enough that unauthorized distribution is unlikely to meet legal challenges. ♪

Absolute superiority

A ranking in which a certain unit has complete domination over all other units. 🎲

Abstraction

1. A representation of an idea or object that does not attempt to match its literal or material qualities. See also **Simulation**. 🎲 🖥
2. The simplification of a real-world system into one that can be more easily manipulated by code. ▰

Acceleration

An increase in an object's speed over time. ■ ▮

Acceptance

An agreement to the contractual terms of an offer. ♪

Accessibility

1. How easily a product or feature can be used. ▣ ♪

2. An area of design focused on the usability of a product by those with limited physical or cognative abilities. ▣ ♪

Achievement

An award given to a player as an acknowledgement for in-game accomplishments but which do not have any impact on gameplay. ♪ ▣

ACID

Atomicity, Consistency, Isolation, Durability. A mnemonic used in database creation to ensure that all operations on the data are performed correctly. ■

Act structure

A method of dividing a narrative into separate, recognizable units. ✦

Actants layer

The actions and reactions of the characters to the events within a story. Also known as the **Performance Level**. ✦

Action

1. A genre of video games that focuses on eye-hand coordination challenges. ♪

2. The events and movement within a story or game. ▣

Action-adventure

A genre of video games that combines the elements of traditional adventure games with combat challenges. ♪

Action-response mechanic

A game mechanic in which players are provided an opportunity to counter another player's activity when that activity occurs, instead of having to wait until their turn. ▣

Action safe area

The area of a broadcast image that objects can appear in without risk of intersecting the monitor's or television's frame. See also **Title Safe Area**.

Active ability

A power that needs to be triggered by the player.

Active optical marker

A small blinking light that is mounted to an object during motion capture so a camera can track its movements when filming.

Activity diagram

An illustration, used within UML, of the logical flow of data through a program's states from start to end. See also **Flowchart**.

Actor

1. A virtual entity that performs an action within a game. Also known as a **Non-Player Character**.

2. A person who performs a role in an audio or video recording.

3. An object that exerts a force upon another object within a dynamic motion simulation.

Ad copy

The text used in an advertising message, either as print or speech.

Ad hoc testing

An evaluation method in which the tester's focus is not specifically assigned.

Ad shots

High-quality images intended for use during advertising.

Adapt stage

The phase in Agile Software Development in which the project's state is analyzed and elements that need to be refined are identified.

Adaptive AI

A feature in which the artificial intelligence considers the player's strategy and attempts to alter its own strategy to compensate.

Adaptive difficulty adjustment

A feature that allows a game to adjust its difficulty based on a player's performance. Also known as **Dynamic Difficulty Adjustment**. 🎮

Adaptive music

A sound track methodology in which the background music changes depending on the activity currently occurring within the game. Also known as **Dynamic Sound** and **Interactive Music**. ♟

Advance

Money paid for services that have yet to be performed. ♪

Advancement

The movement of a player further into a game's structure, which is usually expressed in terms of levels. 🎮

Advantage

A condition in which a player has a more beneficial position over her or his opponent. 🎮

Adventure

1. A genre of video games in which puzzle solving and narrative flow is emphasized over combat and resource management. ♪

2. The journey a hero undertakes. ⚔

Adversary search

An AI pattern that considers an opponent's potential responses when evaluating the strength of each move. ▦

Aesthetics

1. The subjective judgment of how enjoyable a game is. 🎮

2. The subjective judgment of how beautiful, valid, or pleasing a piece of art is. 🖌 ♟

3. The emotional response the designer intends to provoke in a player. 🎮

4. One of the three principle components of the MDA framework proposed by Hunicke, LeBlanc, and Zubek. In this framework, aesthetics are the player's emotional response to the game and are directly influenced by the game's dynamics. See also **MDA**. 🎮

AF

Anisotropic texture Filter. A method for improving the visual quality of textures when viewed at extreme angles by performing real-time calculations based on the camera's viewing angle.

Affiliate label deal

An agreement in which the developer shares some of the production and marketing costs thereby making their project more attractive to the publisher.

Affordance

The predictable functionality that an interface's component implies, such as a button's implication that it only functions when pushed, thereby leading the user to only attempt interactions that are supported by the interface.

AFK

Away From Keyboard. The status of a player who is not actively playing but whose character is currently in the game world.

Aftermarket

A phase following a product's release in which further products may also be released to expand upon the original.

AFTRA

American Federation of Television and Radio Artists. A labor union representing broadcast performers, journalists, and artists.

Agency

The capability of an entity to act inside and effect change within a system.

Agent

A person who represents one party during negotiations with another.

Agile software development

A rapid iteration design methodology in which the emphasis is on small tasks that can be easily adjusted and refined as opposed to plans that are long term and precisely defined.

Aggregation relationship

A class reliance in which an object is created from several different classes. Also known as an **"Owns a" Relationship**.

Aggro

Aggravate. A triggered condition within an artificial opponent so that it becomes hostile and which is usually determined by the distance between the player's character and the opponent. See also **Kiting** and **Leashing**.

Agon

Contest (Greek). Games of competition. Listed by Caillois as one of his four types of play.

AI

1. *Artificial Intelligence.* A field of study relating to computers' utilization of strategies as effectively as or more effectively than humans.

2. *Artificial Intelligence.* A game's ability to replicate the way a human uses strategy.

3. *Artificial Intelligence.* An NPC functioning as an opponent.

AI cheat

A technique of providing the AI with more benefits and resources than the player has in order to make up for a weakness in the AI's strategy or skill.

AI companion

An NPC that accompanies the player but acts semi-independently.

Alea

Dice (Greek). Games of chance. Listed by Caillois as one of his four types of play.

Algorithm

A finite sequence of instructions or calculations used to perform a task.

Algorithmic music

A method of composing a soundtrack based on mathematical calculations or code, often used to allow the game's action and music to interact with each other. See also **Adaptive Music**.

Aliasing

The pixilation of an image when it is displayed.

All-pay auction

A bidding structure, often seen in gambling games, in which all bids, including the losing ones, are collected.

Allusion

An indirect reference to something outside the story that the reader is expected to recognize. ♟

Alpha

The first phase of software development in which, traditionally, all of the basic functionality of the game has been implemented and the emphasis is on the implementation and correction of features and assets. ♪

Alpha-beta pruning

An AI routine that evaluates a potential move only as long as that move's possible consequences are no worse than any other previously considered move. ▬

Alpha channel

An additional channel, beyond the three color channels, used by graphics software to store the transparency information of an image. ▜

Alt

Alternative. A player's secondary or less frequently played character. ♪ ▣

Alternate ending

A resolution to a game that varies from other endings depending on the earlier choices made by the player. ♟ ▣

Alternating game

A game in which each side makes their moves in a consecutive, prearranged order. ▣

Ambiance

The mood created by the visual or auditory elements in a scene. ▜ ♣ ♟

Ambient light

A light source that fills the environment equally in all directions. ▜

Ambient music

In-game music played in the background during the game. ♣

Analysis model

The representation of the software's structure from the point of view of the developer. ▬

Anchor point

The beginning or ending point of a Bézier curve. ▜

Ancillary revenues

A source of income for a company that is not the company's primary or typical means of generating income. ♪

Ancillary rights

The rights to profit off of merchandise and other products that are derived from the original product. ♪

Animatic

An early animated test of a scene used to evaluate potential camera positioning and action. ▮

Animation

1. The illusion of an object's movement within a game or film created by rapidly adjusting their relative positions and poses within a scene. ▮

2. The process of creating a model's range of motions. ▮

Animation baking

The permanent conversion of a dynamic animation process into rendered frames. Also known as **Baking**. ▮

Animation blending

An animation technique, used primarily for facial animation, that alters the model based on different, adjustable attributes as values are assigned to them thereby creating a unique pose. Also known as **Blending**. ▮

Animation conversion

The process of preparing an existing model's animation data to be compatible with the game engine. Also known as **Conversion**. ▮

Animation cycle

A looping of images designed to create the impression of a repeating action, such as walking. See also **Walk Cycle**. ♪ ▮

Animation set

A collection of nonlooping actions designed to create the impression of a specific action, such as dying. ♪ ▮

Animator

A person tasked with rigging and animating objects in a game or film. ♪ ▮

Anisotropic texture filter (AF)

A method for improving the visual quality of textures when viewed at extreme angles by performing real-time calculations based on the camera's viewing angle. ▪

Antagonist

The character in a story that has the greatest amount of conflict with the protagonist. ▪

Antialiasing

A process of fading the sharp edges of a pixilated image to make them appear visually smoother. ▪

Anticipation of decision

The tension created by the player's expectation of having to make an important decision in the future. ▪

AoE

1. *Area of Effect.* A type of ability or power that can be targeted to a vicinity instead of at a unit. ▪

2. *Area of Effect.* The vicinity within the game's environment that is affected by an ability or power. ▪

API

Application Programming Interface. A standardized interface, hidden from the end-user, that allows software to access the resources of an operating system. ▪

App

1. *Application.* A computer program that performs a specific task or series of tasks for the end-user. ▪

2. *Application.* A small, downloadable program often designed specifically for mobile devices. ▪

Application (App)

1. A computer program that performs a specific task or series of tasks for the end-user. ▪

2. A small, downloadable program often designed specifically for mobile devices. ▪

Application Programming Interface (API)

A standardized interface, hidden from the end-user, that allows software to access the resources of an operating system. ▦

Application-Specific Integrated Circuit (ASIC)

A nonversatile chip designed for a specific task. ▦

Arc

1. The logical progression of a story. Also known as a **Story Arc**. ✏

2. The internal progression of a character throughout a story. Also known as a **Character Arc**. ✏

3. A path that curves in one direction. ▮

Arcade perfect

A port from an arcade version that retains all elements just as they existed in the original version. ♪

Arcade-style game

A genre of video games that replicates the type of gameplay found in video arcades, most notably gameplay with intuitive interfaces, rapidly escalating action, and simplified physics and object interactions. ♪

Archetype

A simplification of characters that perform similar roles within stories into a standardized model. ✏

Architecture document

A written description of a software's structure and components and the means by which they will be designed and implemented. ▦

Area light

A light source that emits from a plane in one direction with its strength along the plane's surface. ▮

Area of Effect (AoE)

1. A type of ability or power that can be targeted to a vicinity instead of at a unit. ▣

2. The vicinity within the game's environment that is affected by an ability or power. ▣

Armature

The underlying skeletal structure that supports a model. ▮

Array

An unalterable indexed list of elements within the code that the program can reference. See also **Vector**. ▮

Artifact

1. A piece of geometry that is displayed unintentionally. ♪ ▮
2. Any visual or auditory anomaly within a game. ▮ ♣
3. Any incidentally developed tangibles, such as documents and tools, generated during the creation of software. ▮

Artificial life (A-life)

Software that attempts to simulate living systems and their evolution. ▮

Artificial Intelligence (AI)

1. A field of study relating to computers' utilization of strategies as effectively as or more effectively than humans. ▮
2. A game's ability to replicate the way a human uses strategy. ▣ ▮
3. An NPC functioning as an opponent. ▣

ASIC

Application-Specific Integrated Circuit. A nonversatile chip designed for a specific task. ▮

Aspect ratio

The proportions of an image when described as a ratio of its width to its height. ▮

Assembly

Any one of several hardware-specific languages that approximates the natural language of the computer so that the software's instructions can be executed more quickly. ▮

Asset

Any piece of data, including sounds, models, and images, that is presented to the player during a game. ▮ ♣ ♪

Assigning

1. The storing of a value into a variable. ■

2. The delegating of responsibility to a team member. ♪

Assignment

The act of transferring some or all of a party's contractual rights or obligations to another party. ♪

Association

A relationship between two classes within a UML model. ■

Assurance game

A game in which the optimal strategy is for players to choose to cooperate. Originally posed as a scenario in which two hunters team up to collect bigger prey. Also known as a **Stag Hunt**. ▨

Asymmetric game

A game in which each player's starting state, either in terms of positioning, objectives, rule sets, abilities, or any combination of these elements. is varied from the others. ▨

Asymmetrical map

A level or map in which each player's starting position provides differing advantages and disadvantages. ▨

Asymmetrical objectives

Winning conditions assigned to each player that do not mirror each other's. ▨

Atomic challenge

A task a player must complete that cannot be further broken down into subtasks. The basic, indivisible building blocks of a game's challenges. ▨

Atomicity

A principle that each operation within a data manipulation process must perform correctly in order for the process to complete; a failure at any point in the process should reset any altered data to its previous state. ■

ATSC

Advanced Television System Committee. The standards set for digital televisions in North America and South Korea. ♪

Attack resources

The elements available to a player that can be used to initiate a threat.

Attenuation

A measure of how gradually an intensity decreases with zero attenuation resulting in a consistent level of intensity.

Attract mode

A demo mode used primarily by arcade games that is specifically designed to catch the attention of patrons and entice them to play.

Attribute

A trait of an object as specified by the data assigned to it.

Attribute balancing

The evaluation and adjustment of the inherent values of dissimilar advantages and their effect on gameplay.

Auction

A bidding system in which a player can seek to purchase additional resources by specifying an amount of resources she or he is willing to offer in exchange to other players.

Audio capture

The recording of a sound or series of sounds. Also known as **Capture**.

Authentication

The process of authorizing access based on an identification code or password.

Auto aim

A feature that automatically focuses on targets for the player.

Auto follow

A feature that allows the player's character to move through the environment by reproducing the path another character has recently run.

Auto-patcher

A software component that evaluates the current version of the program being used and, if a newer version is available, updates it to the newest version.

Auto run

A feature that allows the player's character to run through the environment with minimal input from the player. ▢

Autoattack

An attack that the player does not have to trigger; instead it is triggered by a game state, such as proximity to a hostile target. ▢

Autocast

An ability or power that the player does not have to trigger; instead it is triggered by a game state, such as proximity to a hostile target. ▢

Autoloot

A system that assigns discovered rewards to specific players' characters automatically, most often used in multiplayer games. ▢

Automap

A feature that automatically fills in the map as the player encounters new areas. ▢

Automated testing

A testing methodology in which player interaction is replaced by computer-driven instructions. Also known as **Scripted Testing**. ♪ ▣

Automatic mode cancellation

A feature that detects improper or abnormal inputs and, if found, shuts down a pending operation thereby freeing the player from having to cancel the operation manually. ▢ ▣

Autosave

A saving scheme that records the current game state when triggered by an event within the game. ▢

Avatar

The in-game representation of the player. ▢ ▮

Avoidance reward

A provided benefit that delays or prevents a negative consequence that otherwise would have occurred. ▢

B storyline

A secondary series of events that complicate the story and which often reinforces or contrasts the theme of the main plot. Also known as a **Subplot**. ✦

B2B

Business to Business. The marketing and supplying of materials, goods, or services between two business entities, such as wholesalers, manufacturers, or retailers. ♪

B2C

Business to Customer. The marketing and supplying of materials, goods, or services between a business and the general public. ♪

Back loaded

A type of contract in which payment occurs at the end of a project. ♪ ▣

Back matter

The ancillary elements placed at the end of a book or a report, such as an appendix or bibliography. ✒

Backdoor

1. An attack strategy of assaulting a defense or resource while the defender is preoccupied by a large, diversionary force. ▣

2. An unauthorized feature placed within a software program by its original programmers to allow them to have access to portions of the program or the hardware the program is installed on after they have left the project. ▰

Backface culling

A rendering technique in which polygons of an object that do not face the camera are not drawn. ▚

Background (b.g.)

1. A description of the elements and actions occurring behind the focus of the camera. ✒

2. The events that have occurred within a setting before the story begins. See also **Backstory.** ✒

Backlight

A light source that hits the back of an object thereby separating it from the background. Also known as a **Hair Light, Kicker Light,** or **Rim Light.** ▚

Backstory

The events that take place in the game's world before the player joins and which can be expressed with a flashback, in a prologue, implied with visual clues, addressed in supplemental material, or left unrevealed. ✒ ▣

Backtracking

1. A characteristic of some level designs in which the player is required to play through an area of the game world that has already been explored.

2. The returning to a section of the game already played through in order for the player to determine if he or she missed an item, event, or path.

Backwards induction

The creation of a strategy by starting from its desired end point and working backward through all the choices up to the current dilemma to determine the best action to take.

Baking

1. The solidifying of the results of a process to more efficiently use the results at the cost of being no longer able to make changes to the process.

2. A texturing technique for creating a new, more efficient texture by first rendering the surface of an object with the existing texture and lighting and then converting the resulting render into its own texture. Also known as **Rendering-to-Texture** or **Texture Baking**.

3. The permanent conversion of a dynamic animation process into rendered frames. Also known as **Animation Baking**.

4. The solidifying of the results of a simulation process thereby no longer requiring the system to perform calculations and, in doing so, increases its performance. Also known as **Simulation Baking**.

Balance

1. The measurement of effectiveness between differing strategies of gameplay. If two strategies offer the same level of effectiveness, assuming perfect execution, they are said to be balanced; strategies that yield widely different levels of effectiveness when compared to each other are considered poorly balanced.

2. The adjustment of the skills and abilities of the game's characters and units so that no player has an inherent advantage over another.

3. The adjustment of the challenges within a game so that they are appropriate for the skills required of the player at the point in which they are introduced.

4. An element of design that determines how much focal weight is given to any particular object within the scene in relation to all other objects.

Banding

An effect in which a color's gradation in an image has visual steps in it instead of a smooth, unnoticeable transition. ▮

Bandwidth

The available capacity that a connection has for the transmission of data, expressed as bits per second. ▰

Bang

The verbal expression of the *not* (!) symbol in some programming languages. ▰

Bargaining

A method by which a player may offer incentives to other players to encourage them to change an otherwise likely outcome. ▣

Bark

1. A random line of dialogue spoken by an NPC. ▮ ♟
2. A short, automatically triggered dialogue. ▮ ♟

Barn doors

Hinged panels on a spotlight used to obstruct its emission and thereby cropping the light's spill. ▮

Base

1. A central location in the game from which the player controls resources. ▣
2. The minimal number of users that can be assumed. ♪

Base stats

1. The initial stats at which a character begins. ▣
2. The stats of a character before they are modified. ▣

Bayesian learning methods

The input of a variety of data examples into an AI system which then infers a pattern or forms a hypothesis based on the probability and the uncertainty inherent in the sampled data. ▰

Beat 'em up

A genre of video games in which characters engage multiple opponents in martial arts–style combat, and often more than one at a time. Also known as a **Fighting Game**. ♪

Bechdel test

An evaluation of a film based on how strongly the female characters are developed; a character must pass all three to be considered minimally developed. Popularized by Bechdel, the criteria are: (1) the existence of two or more named female characters, (2) they converse with each other, and (3) their conversations are about something other than a man. Often applied to other medium using the same or similar criteria. ♟

Beer & pretzel game

A tabletop game, often with a humorous theme, that does not require a lot of concentration to play. ♪

Behavior

An activity that an object can perform as specified by the functions assigned to it. ▦

Behavior diagram

A UML chart that illustrates the changes that occur to the system's state during use. Also known as a **Dynamic Behavior Diagram**. ▦

Behavioral contrast

A response pattern in which the responder evaluates the potential reward in comparison to earlier rewards received. ▣

Behavioral game design

A game creation methodology that focuses on the player's physiological response to its rewards and punishments instead of on balance theory or designer's sensibilities. ▣

Benchmark

A quantifiable measurement of the performance of hardware or software determined by the use of a standardized criterion. ▦ ♪

Beta

1. The second phase of software development in which, traditionally, all of the features have been locked, all assets are in the game, and the emphasis shifts to testing and polishing. ♪

2. A release of the game to the public to evaluate its financial potential before determining if it will be further developed. ♪

Bevel

To alter a squared edge to a more sloped shape. 🖌

Bézier curve

A smooth, curving line whose shape is determined by points along its path thereby allowing it to be adjusted after its creation. By nature, these lines are infinitely scalable and are very efficient to store as data. See also **NURBS**. 🖌

BF

Bilinear texture filtering. A method of maintaining visual quality of a texel by having each pixel consider its surrounding texels whenever it is made larger or smaller. 🖌

B.g.

1. *Background.* A description of the elements and actions occurring behind the focus of the camera. ✎

2. *Background.* The events that have occurred within a setting before the story begins. See also **Backstory**. ✎

Bible

1. A reference document for a project that contains all of the continuity information, including any unpublished information considered a canon. ▣ ♪

2. The collection of all documents related to a project combined into one central document. ▣ ♪

Bid

The proposed terms of a contract. ♪

Bidding

A process of proposing an exchange of a specific amount of resources between players. ▣

Bidirectional Reflectance Distribution Function (BRDF)

A formulaic method of determining the reflection of an object considering its surface and the surface's angles to both the light and the viewer. 🖌

Big file system

The joining of multiple smaller files into one larger one to optimize the speed at which they can be accessed. ♪

Bilinear texture filtering (BF)

A method of maintaining visual quality of a texel by having each pixel consider its surrounding texels whenever it is made larger or smaller. ▌

Billboarding

A modeling technique of using a 2D plane that always faces the camera to simulate a 3D object. ▌

Binary space partitioning

A method of rendering 3D graphics by dividing objects' space into separate non-overlapping regions thus allowing the rendering engine, through referencing the divisional structure, to determine the most efficient order in which to draw the objects. ▌ ▓

Bind

1. To attach two objects together. ▌

2. To create an association between a key press or button press and an action. ▓

3. To associate a character with a specific location so that the location becomes that character's respawn point. ▣

Bind on Equip (BoE)

To affix an item to a character once the character places the item into a specific inventory slot. Once bound it cannot be traded, though it may be able to be sold or destroyed. ▣

Bind on Pickup (BoP)

To affix an item to a character once that character accepts the item into inventory. Once bound it cannot be traded, though it may be able to be sold or destroyed. ▣

Bind on Use (BoU)

To affix an item to a character the first time the character uses it. Once bound it cannot be traded, though it may be able to be sold or destroyed. ▣

Bio

Biography. A brief description of a character. ✦ ▣

Biography (Bio)

A brief description of a character. ⚒

Bit

1. An interactive component of a nondigital game such as a die, marker, or token. ▣

2. A component used as a proxy for a video game's asset during prototyping. ▣

3. A single element of data, expressed as a 1 or 0. ▣

Bit depth

A mathematical expression that defines, in bits, the number of colors that can be applied to a pixel. Also known as **Color Depth**. ▮

Bitmap

An image format in which the image is made up of pixels arranged in a grid. Also known as **Raster**. ▮

Biz Dev

Business Development executive. An employee charged with investigating and securing growth opportunities for the company and developing its sales and marketing strategies. ♪

Black Friday

The Friday after Thanksgiving, which traditionally starts the gift-buying season in the U.S. ♪

Blackbox testing

An evaluation process in which the tester is unaware of the product's intended functionality and outcomes. See also **Blind Testing**. ♪ ▮

Blending

1. An animation technique, used primarily for facial animation, that alters the model based on different, adjustable attributes as values are assigned to them thereby creating a unique pose. Also known as **Animation Blending**. ▮

2. An animation technique of adding additional frames between two cycles or sets so that the transition between the two appears seamless. ▮

3. A multitextural process of merging and overlapping textures to create a smooth transition between areas. ▮

Blind decision

A choice given to a player without providing enough information for him or her to make a meaningful decision. ▯

Blind testing

An evaluation process in which the person evaluating the product does not know exactly what they are evaluating. See also **Black Box Testing**. ♪

Blit (BLT)

Block Transfer. A rendering technique of storing large amounts of visual information in memory so that it can be quickly swapped in during a redraw. See also **BLT**. ▪ ▯

Block

A move that results in the collision of two objects with one object negating most or all of the negative effect that otherwise would be applied. ▯

Blocking

The placement of objects in and the directing of traffic through a scene. See also **Framing** and **Mise en Scene**. ▯ ▯

Bloom

A lighting technique in which a bright backlight spills over in front of an object thereby allowing it to replicate the effect light has on optical lens systems, such as cameras. ▯

Blow

An attack made with the hands. Also known as a **Punch**. ▯

BLT

Block Transfer. A rendering technique of storing large amounts of visual information in memory so that it can be quickly swapped in during a redraw. Also known as **Blit**.
 ▯

Blue screen

A method used to film certain elements against a blue background so they can be composited to a different background later. See also **Green Screen** and **Matte**. ▯

Blue Screen Of Death (BSOD)

A Windows error screen that informs the user that the operating system has become unstable. ♪ ▪

Bluff

A strategy in which a player attempts to convince an opponent that the player's game state is stronger than it really is. See also **Non-credible Threat**. ⊞

BoE

Bind on Equip. To affix an item to a character once the character places the item into a specific inventory slot. Once bound it cannot be traded, though it may be able to be sold or destroyed. ⊞

Boiler plate

1. Text that can be applied to multiple forms or in multiple contexts with little to no changes being made. ♪ ✎

2. A section of code whose structure is similar enough to other sections of code that it can be reproduced, often automatically within the program, and then modified as opposed to being written from scratch each time. ▬

3. Any section of code that is reused in multiple places with little or no changes made between their uses. ▬

4. The standard provisions within a contract. ♪

5. The standardized portion of a press release that provides information about the company or product. ♪

Bonus

An additional, optional compensation. ♪

Bonus stage

A level available only after completing an earlier series of levels with a high degree of proficiency thereby providing the player with an opportunity to receive additional rewards. ⊞

Book win

A strategy that, if played perfectly, will always lead to a win once the game state is set up to take advantage of it. ⊞

Boolean

1. A type of variable that has only two states. ▬

2. A search method that utilizes comparative operators to express a query. ▬

BoP

Bind on Pickup. To affix an item to a character once that character accepts the item into inventory. Once bound it cannot be traded, though it may be able to be sold or destroyed. 🖳

Boss

A unique AI opponent designed to be significantly more challenging than the other AI entities in that level. 🖳

Bot

A scripted program that performs actions for the player, often to give him or her an advantage over a live opponent. 🖳 ▦

Bottleneck

The location where the flow of instructions is at its slowest. ▦

Bottom-up AI

An artificial intelligence technique in which units are given individual goals while remaining unaware of an overall strategy. ▦

Bottom-up estimating

The creation of a schedule by dividing a project into its smallest components, projecting each individual component's time requirements for completion, then totaling all of the component projections together. ♪

Bottom-up planning

Scheduling of a project based on input from specialized lower-level team members. See also **Top-down Planning**. ♪

BoU

Bind on Use. To affix an item to a character the first time the character uses it. Once bound it cannot be traded, though it may be able to be sold or destroyed. ♪

Boundary testing

An evaluation process in which the focus is on the software's ability to handle inputs that are beyond the range asked for. ♪

Bounding box

A box, unseen by the player, that surrounds 3D objects in a game and is used to determine when a collision occurs. ▦ 🮲

Bow wash

An effect caused by some trilinear filtering optimization methods that constantly distort lines of displayed pixels as the camera moves through a scene. ▌

Box and docs

The printed material distributed with the game, such as the instruction manual and the display box. ♪ ▌

Box art

The images, text, and illustrations intended to be displayed on the product's packaging. Also known as **Cover Art**. ▌ ♪

Box modeling

A technique of polygonal modeling that creates basic 3D shapes and then sculpts them to match the intended subject. ▌

Box shots

Images, usually screen captures, that are intended to appear on the product's packaging. ▌ ♪

Braided plot structure

A division, described by Ryan, of the story into multiple, occasionally overlapping paths that the player can access by using multiple playthroughs or by switching between characters. ▟

Brainstorming

An early phase of decision making in which ideas are generated without restrictions. ♪ ▣ ▟ ▌ ♟ ▦

Branch predicting

A routine that speeds up system performance by anticipating a result and queuing up the relevant instructions so that, if and when the expected result is confirmed, the instructions are ready to be executed. ▦

Branching dialogue

A dialogue option that deviates the conversation to another subject or dialogue sequence. ▣ ▟

Branching narrative structure

The division of a story into sections that the player encounters in small chunks, each one accessed by a choice. ▟

Branching story

A storyline that splits into different paths allowing each player to experience different events based on his or her decisions. 🖺 ⚔

Brand

The identity of a product, service, or business as seen by its consumers. ♪

Brand manager

An employee tasked with ensuring all material related to an IP maintains certain standards and continuity. ♪

BRDF

Bidirectional Reflectance Distribution Function. A formulaic method of determining the reflection of an object considering its surface and the surface's angles to both the light and the viewer. ▓▌

Breach of contract

The failure of a party to meet the terms and conditions of an agreement. ♪

Bread-crumbing

1. The technique of placing rewards in specific locations so that the player collecting them will end up where the designer wants him or her. 🖺

2. The technique of dropping little bits of information over time so that the story unfolds slowly and requires players to explore the game's environment to uncover further information. 🖺 ⚔

Breadth-first search

An AI routine that evaluates the immediate results from each potential decision before moving on to evaluate the further ramifications of those initial decisions. ▰

Brightness

An element of design that determines an image's relative darkness. Also known as **Value.** ▓▌

Brooks' law

A general rule, proposed by Brooks, that "adding manpower to a late project makes it later." ♪ ▰

Browser-based

A classification of games that can be played through a standard Internet browser. ♪

BSOD

Blue Screen Of Death. A Windows error screen that informs the user that the operating system has become unstable. ♪ ▣

Budget

The projection of expenses and resources over a specified period of time. ♪

Buff

1. A skill or ability that temporarily increases a character's statistics. ▣

2. An increase in power to an existing character, item, skill, or ability due to an alteration to the mechanics of the game. ♪ ▣

Buffer

A temporary holding space for data that is often restricted to specific types of data. ▣

Bug

1. An error in the software's code. ▣

2. An unexpected result within a video game that detracts from gameplay. ♪

3. A quality assurance issue that could potentially result in fiscal losses for the game's publisher or developer. ♪

Bug tracking

The process of assigning responsibility and ownership to issues as they are discovered. ♪

Build

1. Any one of the many sequentially compiled and assembled versions of a specific piece of software, often used for testing and evaluation purposes. ♪

2. A game mechanic that allows a player to exchange resources to create or improve units. ▣

3. The allocation of resources during character creation and evolution to achieve a particular outcome in terms of strengths and abilities. ▣

Build notes

The information included with a specific version of the software, often to aid the user in their evaluation of the game's current state of development. See also **Regression List.** ♪ ▣

Build number

A sequentially numbered version of software used to track its development. ♪

Build time

The amount of time it takes the computer to compile a new version of the code. ▬

Bullet time

1. A visual effect created by rapidly revolving the camera around an object and shooting it in a rapid sequence, creating the impression of an extremely slow, fluidic motion of the object during playback. ▸❚

2. A trademarked name for specific methodologies of creating the bullet time effect. ♪

Bump mapping

A method of texturing in which the lighting on a surface is imitated, giving it an uneven, textured appearance. ▸❚

Bunny hopping

A method of moving by continuously using the jump button to gain some type of speed or evasion advantage. ▣

Burden of knowledge

The responsibility of the player to be aware of a mechanic in the game. ▣

Burning

The making of a permanent copy of data files by recording them to a CD or DVD. ♪

Burst damage

A large amount of damage that can be dealt quickly but not sustained for very long. ▣

Business Development executive (Biz Dev)

An employee charged with investigating and securing growth opportunities for the company and developing its sales and marketing strategies. ♪

Business to Business (B2B)

The marketing and supplying of materials, goods, or services between two business entities, such as wholesalers, manufacturers, or retailers. ♪

Business to Customer (B2C)

The marketing and supplying of materials, goods, or services between a business and the general public. ♪

Button

A user interface element that activates a feature when selected. ▣ ▪

Button mashing

Rapidly hitting random buttons or keys without knowing which attack or skill will be executed. See also **Spamming**. ▣

Buzz

The expressed anticipation for an unreleased project. ♪

C-K theory

A design theory that attempts to account for the uncertain nature of creativity by evaluating the interaction between concepts (the untested) and knowledge (the established). Also known as **Concept-Knowledge Theory**. ▣

Cabal development model

A decentralized iterative design process in which the role of game designer is filled by a team of members from different disciplines. Each member helps review and refine the current prototype for a short time before being replaced by another member of their discipline. Also known as **Valve Design Process**. ♪ ▣

Cache

A computer hardware component that serves as a temporary holding space for frequently requested data. ▪

Cake-cutting dilemma

An illustration of the fair division problem that is created when a resource is not divided evenly. The example given is of two pieces of cake being served with neither recipient believing the pieces to be equal. See also **Fair Division Problem**. ▣

Call

A request by the program for routines stored in memory or for services from hardware. ▪

Call stack

A dedicated structure for storing information related to currently active subroutines. Also known as a **Stack**. ▪

Camel casing

A programming technique of capitalizing certain letters of a variable's name, based on conventions, to improve its readability. ▪

Camera

1. A viewport through which the player sees the world while inside a game. 📷📱

2. The mechanism that determines the point of view and optical settings of a scene being rendered. 📷📱

Camera-ready artwork

Finished images whose quality is sufficient for reproduction during the printing process. 📷📱

Camera space

A 3D environment in which the objects' locations are given in relation to the camera. Also known as **Eye Space** or **View Space**. 📷📱

Camera system

The integration of cameras, their functionality, and their movements within a game. 📷📱 ◼ 🎲

Campaign

A series of gameplay segments separated by distinct goals through which the player must often progress in a predetermined sequence to meet a win condition. 🎲

Camping

A strategy, most often utilized in multiplayer games, of waiting at an enemy's spawn point to engage it before other players have an opportunity to. 🎲

Cancellation

The termination of a project before its completion. 🎵

Candidate move

An available play whose potential makes it worthy of further evaluation. Also known as a **Candidate Play**. 🎲 ◼

Candidate play

An available play whose potential makes it worthy of further evaluation. Also known as a **Candidate Move**. 🎲 ◼

Canon

The parts of a collection of works that are given credit for being core to the overall work's continuity and against which all other contributions are evaluated. 🎵 🎨 🎲

Cap

A limit to the maximum value that an ability, power, or skill can attain. See also **Level Cap**. 🖫

Capital costs

The one-time fixed expenses incurred during the establishment or redesign of a project. ♪

Capture

1. The collection of another player's resource that may or may not be eligible to be returned to that player. 🖫

2. The copying of an image as it appears on a monitor or other display device into a digital file. Also known as **Screen Capture**. 🖥

3. The recording of a sound or series of sounds. Also known as **Audio Capture**. ⛏

4. The process of recording the real-life movements of the parts of an actor's body within its 3D space and converting them so that they can be used as a template for an animated sequence within a virtual environment. Also known as **Motion Capture**. 🖥 ♪

Capture the Flag (CTF)

A mode of play that requires players to reach a certain location and often to return with a token (the flag) collected from that location. 🖫

Carebear

A player that prefers non-PvP versions of games; often used derogatorily. ♪ 🖫

Carmack's reverse

A technique in lighting in which the rendering process evaluates the surfaces lying outside of the shadow's volume to determine which pixels are affected. Promoted by *Carmack*. Also known as **Depth Fail** or **Z-Fail**. 🖥

Cartesian coordinates

A method of measuring 3D space by assigning positive and negative numerical values to each axis. Also known as **XYZ Coordinates**. 🖥 ▰

Cartridge

A media storage device that uses ROM chips encased in plastic. ♪

Cascade method

A design method such that once each stage is completed and deemed successful, it immediately continues on to the next stage without reexamining the earlier stages for any changes to their degree of success. Also known as the **Waterfall Method**. 🎲

Casting

1. The process of selecting actors to fill roles. 🎵 🖊 ♟

2. The process of applying the effects of a power or ability, particularly in a game set in a magical world. 🎲

Castoff

The approximate amount of space that the text and illustrations of a manuscript will occupy when typeset. 🖊

Casual game

A classification of games whose rules are relatively easy to learn and that require only a small amount of time for each play session. 🎵

Casual Multiplayer Online game (CMO game)

A genre of video games that supports a large number of players but does not require a large time commitment in each play session. Also known as a **Massively Multiplayer Online Social Game**. 🎵

Catch statement

A section of code that determines what happens when a specific exception is encountered, designed to allow a program to handle errors gracefully. ▦

CC

Crowd Control. An ability of the character that can be used to limit the number of units able to engage him or her at one time. 🎲

CCD

Cyclic Coordinate Descent. An iterative formula applied to an animation that optimizes each joint's angle via inverse kinematics, resulting in an efficient adjustment of complex bone chains. 🖌

CD key

An alphanumeric sequence included with authentic copies of the software that allows it to be installed or accessed. Also known as a **Key** or **Key Code**. 🎵

Cel shading

A rendering method that uses nonphotorealistic lighting to create a cartoon-style image.

Censorship

The requirement to remove material found objectionable by a government or social organization.

Centipede game

A competition in which players can increase the winning payoff by extending the game but at the risk that the other player may choose to end it and thereby collect the payoff for him or herself.

Central Processing Unit (CPU)

The microprocessor that performs the calculations required to execute a program's instructions.

CERO

Computer Entertainment Rating Organization. The organization that provides content and suggested age ratings for video games released in Japan. See also **ESRB** and **PEGI**.

CGI

Computer Generated Image. An image created by a computer graphics program.

Chain

A series of attacks that must be performed in succession to take advantage of their synergy. See also **Combo**.

Chain of responsibility pattern

A software design pattern in which each request passes through a sequence of objects so that when it reaches the terminal object it will have been properly handled.

Chamfer

A groove or angle cut into an edge of a surface.

Chance

A classification of any mechanic that relies on statistical probability instead of the player's judgment and ability. See also **Skill**.

Channel

1. A storage space for holding data related to a specific color within an image. 🖌
2. A pathway for sounds or data. ♣ ▦
3. A pathway for product distribution. ♪

Channeling

The steady expenditure of an in-game resource, such as manna, during which time no other actions can be taken and if interrupted results in receiving none of the benefits of having expended the resource. 🎲

Character arc

The internal progression of a character throughout a story. Also known as an **Arc**. ✍

Character brief

A description provided to the actor of the character she or he will be portraying. ✍

Character creation

A process that allows the player to configure and customize the character he or she will play in a game. Also known as **Character Generation**. 🎲

Character generation

A process that allows the player to configure and customize the character he or she will play in a game. Also known as **Character Creation**. 🎲

Character-level narrative structure

The embedding of preconceived attributes and behaviors into a character's object with the intent that a narrative will emerge naturally from those traits and behaviors. ✍

Chase algorithm

A formula used to determine the path of a predator object so that it reduces the distance between it and its prey. See also **Evasion Algorithm**. ▦

Chase music

In-game music designed to be played while the character is being pursued by enemies. ♣

Chat

The system used to allow in-game communication between players. 🎲

Chatterbot

An AI entity designed to replicate the conversation of a real person. �◼ ▣

Cheat code

A word, phrase, or numerical combination that unlocks a feature or ability that the end user is not expected to use during standard gameplay. ♪ ▣

Cheat sheet

A small card or piece of paper, often included with the manual, that provides a synopsis of the important elements of a game. Also known as a **Crib Sheet** or **Reference Sheet**. ▣ ♪

Cheating

1. A violation of a game's established rules to gain an advantage over an opponent. ▣

2. To compose a shot so that the elements appear differently when displayed than as they are arranged in reality. ▮

Check box

A user interface element that allows the user to select or deselect that option. ▣

Checkpoint

An intermediary location-based objective that is often required to be reached within a certain time limit. ▣

Checksum

A method for verifying that none of the data has been altered or corrupted by adding numerical values related to the data then performing a series of subtractions so that the result will then equal zero. Any copy of the data whose converted value does not equal zero signifies an alteration of the data. ▣

Chekhov's gun

A literary concept advanced by the Russian playwright Anton Chekhov that all objects introduced in a story should serve a dramatic purpose. Chekhov's example was a rifle that, if introduced at the beginning of the story, must be fired by the end. ◢ ▣

Chicken game

A game in which the players are all at risk of losing but in which the optimal strategy is to endure the risk the longest while still avoiding the critical point of loss. Also known as a **Hawk Dove Game**. ▣

Child

1. An object that receives some or all of its behaviors and attribute from another, superior object. See also **Parent**. ▦

2. A bone in an animated skeletal system that is influenced by the movements of a superior bone or joint. See also **Parent**. ʾ

3. A node that is influenced, at least partially, by a superior node. See also **Parent**. ▦ ʾ

Chip

1. A miniaturized electronic circuit. ♪ ♣

2. A microprocessor used in a computer. ▦

3. A piece used as a counter within a game. ▣

Chipped

A gaming system that has been modified to allow the playing of unauthorized copies of a game or to use its hardware in a way not supported by the manufacturer. See also **Jailbreaking** and **Modification**. ♪ ▦

Choice of law clauses

The portion within a contract that designates which jurisdiction's laws will be used for its interpretation. ♪

Chorus

An audio technique of sending the same sound through a channel several times with each instance slightly delayed so as to create an impression that multiple sources are creating the sound. ♣

Chrome

An element added to a game to improve on its theme but which has little effect on actual gameplay. See also **Window Dressing**. ▣

Chromo keying

The removal of select colors to make individual elements appear seamless when combined within a composite. Also known as **Color Keying** or **Keying**. ʾ

Cinematic

A non-interactive scripted event, often created outside of the game's engine, that provides further information about either the game's narrative or state. See also **Cutscene**. ʾ ▣ ✎

Clan

A community of MMO players who engage in in-game activities for the common benefit of their members. ♪ 🂠

Class

A blueprint object that contains all of the common attributes and behaviors of each member that will be created from it. ▰

Class diagram model

A structured representation of a system that illustrates the relationship between the classes used within the system. ▰

Clean

The removal of any remnants of older code or software from a system. See also **Wipe**. ▰ ♪

Clearcast

A triggered ability or power that does not consume resources. Also known as **Freecast**. 🂠

CLI

Command Line Interface. A text-based method for entering information into and displaying information on a system. See also **GUI**. ▰

Click-through agreement

A license presented in electronic format in which one party has the option to accept or decline it by selecting the desired option when it appears. Also known as a **Clickwrap Agreement**. ♪

Clickwrap agreement

A license presented in electronic format in which one party has the option to accept or decline it by selecting the desired option when it appears. Also known as a **Click-Through Agreement**. ♪

Client

1. A person who hires another to perform a specific task. ♪
2. A computer that receives instructions from a host system. ▰

Climax

The point in a story at which a conflict reaches its highest point of tension. ✍

Clip

1. An audio or video segment. 🎞 ♟

2. The placement of an object in a way that it intersects with another object's geometry resulting in an overlap of the two. 🎞

3. An in-game item that supplies additional ammo for the player, often used to replace rounds already spent. ▣

Clip space

A virtual 2D environment in which a 3D scene is projected in order for the rendering engine to determine what can be culled from the scene without affecting its appearance. Also known as **Homogeneous Clip Space**. 🎞

Clipping

1. The overlapping of surfaces. 🎞

2. A rendering technique in which geometry that is not within the camera's field of view is not drawn. 🎞

3. The cutting off of a sound's range due to its amplification beyond the allowed maximum output. ♟

Clipping plane

A division, parallel to the camera, within a 3D environment in which objects or portions of objects that are on one side are rendered and those on the other side are not, thereby reducing the amount of time required to render the scene. See also **Far Plane** and **Near Plane**. 🎞

Clone

A game designed to be as identical as possible to a previously released game. ♪

Clone and tweak

A process for designing a game by basing it heavily on a previously released game and then changing it just enough to avoid legal issues. ▣

Close combat

Combat between units or characters that takes place while they are adjacent to each other. Also known as **Melee**. ▣

Closed

The state of an issue that has been resolved. ♪

Closed architecture

A platform in which any modification of the hardware must be approved by the platform's manufacturer. See also **Open Architecture**. ▪ ♪

Closed beta

A stage in the development process, usually of a massively multiplayer game, when a limited number of the general public are invited to play as part of the evaluation process. See also **Open Beta**. ♪

Closed caption

The text display of sounds within recorded or live media to provide accessibility to audience members who are deaf or hard of hearing. See also **Subtitles**. ♟ ♣

Closure

The mental completion of a visual image when a portion of it is missing in its representation. ▪ ▣

CMO game

Casual Multiplayer Online game. A genre of video games that supports a large number of players but does not require a large time commitment in each play session. Also known as a **Massively Multiplayer Online Social Game**. ♪

CMYK

Cyan, Magenta, Yellow, Key. A color method utilizing the subtraction of Cyan, Magenta, Yellow, and Black from a base white color to make additional colors. Also known as **Four-Color Process**. ▪

Co-op mode

A game mode that allows multiple players to work together within the game. ▣

Code

1. The written instructions that make up a program that a computer executes. See also **Source Code**. ▪
2. An alphanumeric sequence that grants access to a program or unlocks additional content. ♪

Code-fix methodology

A rapid-prototyping software development methodology in which the focus is on rapid cycling through the coding and testing phases with features added on an as-needed basis. Also known as the **Extreme Programming Method**. ♪ ▪

Code release

The third phase of software development in which, traditionally, all the features and assets have been tested and the emphasis is on confirming the fixes. Also known as **Gamma** and **Release Candidate**. ♪

Code release candidate

A build that is being evaluated for distribution. Also known as a **Final Candidate** or **Release Candidate**. ♪

Code Release Checklist (CRC)

1. The listed criteria used for evaluating software during its final review before publication. ♪

2. A final formal review of the software to determine its suitability for commercial distribution. ♪

Code Release Group (CRG)

A specialized team that evaluates a release candidate to ensure that it meets the minimal release criteria before it is sent for duplication and distribution. ♪

Code review

An evaluation by the team members' peers of the program's code. ■

Codec

Coder/decoder. A program that compresses and decompresses audio or video into and from a specific format. ⬛ ♣ ⬛

COG

Cost of Goods. The total investment in materials and labor that were used in the manufacturing of a product over a defined time period. Often expressed on a per unit basis. ♪

Cognitive immersion

The capture of the player's focus by the mental challenges presented within a game, as described by Björk and Holopainen. Also known as **Strategic Immersion**. ▣

Collectable game

A game that allows players to continually expand their collection of game pieces to customize their starting game state. ▣

Collection play

An activity within a game that centers upon the accumulation of items, often organized into sets, by the player and which may or may not have an effect on game-play. 🎲

Collision

The intersecting of two objects' bounding boxes in the game world thereby representing an interaction. ▦

Collision detection

The section of code used to evaluate if two objects have collided. ▦

Collision reaction

The response of objects when their bounding boxes have intersected each other. ▦

Color

A design element that determines the viewer's perception of the reflection of a light wave off an object and is composed of three elements: hue, value, and saturation. 🖌

Color bleeding

The property of virtual light that allows it to carry with it the color of the surface it has bounced off of. Also known as **Radiosity**. 🖌

Color depth

A mathematical expression that defines, in bits, the number of colors that can be applied to a pixel. Also known as **Bit Depth**. 🖌

Color keying

The removal of select colors to make individual elements appear seamless when combined within a composite. Also known as **Chromo Keying** or **Keying**. 🖌

Color temperature

The measurement of heat as it relates to the color of light that the heat is producing. Some lighting and rendering systems allow the assignment of this attribute in order to create a more realistic looking environment. 🖌

Colored lighting

Illumination that has a hue applied to it. 🖌

Combat system

The mechanics and methods used to resolve unit versus unit conflict. 🎲

Combo

Combination. A string of consecutive actions performed in a particular sequence that allows the player to take advantage of the synergy between them. See also **Chain**.

Comes Out in the Wash (COW)

1. A colloquialism for a set of elements that neutralize each other.

2. A colloquialism for a minor, somewhat unintended effect that is neutralized by the other elements in the game and that, if removed, would require the remaining elements to be rebalanced.

3. A colloquialism for an unintended robustness within a section of code that enables it to handle more cases than for which it was designed.

Command Line Interface (CLI)

A text-based method for entering information into and displaying information on a system. See also **GUI**.

Command pattern

A software design pattern that stores requests as encapsulated objects thereby allowing the requests themselves to be manipulated and handled in the same manner as other objects.

Comment out

To designate a portion of code as a notation so that the compiler will ignore it.

Comment statement

A plain language notation, often an explanation, written inside the source code in a way that it will not affect the compiler.

Commons dilemma

An illustration of the conflict between short-term self-interest and the long-term common good when dealing with limited resources. The example is of a common plot of land owned by several people. If everyone tries to collect all of the resources at the same time, the land will become barren, whereas if they cooperate and take turns, the land can continue to renew its resources and feed everyone sufficiently. Also known as the **Tragedy of the Commons**.

Community pool

A collection of resources that are shared by all players.

Compatibility

1. The ability of two elements to work together without issues. ♪ ▣ ▣

2. A phase of testing in which the software is evaluated on various hardware configurations to ensure that it runs as expected regardless of which configuration is used. See also **Configuration Testing**. ♪ ▣

Compensating factor

A benefit given to a weaker element to better balance it against the stronger elements in a game. ▣

Compensative balancing

A method of balancing by implementing options or resources that have both benefits and disadvantages inherent in them. ▣

Competitive analysis

The evaluation of the strengths and weaknesses of existing businesses that offer similar goods and services. ♪

Compilation

A collection of previously released works bundled together for a rerelease. ♪ ♣

Completion achievements

A reward given to the player acknowledging her or his ability to finish an assigned task. See also **Measurement Achievements**. ▣

Completion date

The date by which a contracted activity must be finished. ♪

Compliance testing

An evaluation process that focuses on the software's capability to meet certification requirements. ♪

Component balancing

The evaluation of the inherent value of similar advantages and their affect on gameplay by reducing them to a common denominator. ▣

Component-based development

A design model in which the system is divided into separate interconnected blocks thereby allowing certain blocks to be altered or switched out without negatively affecting the whole system. ♪ ▣

Component diagram

1. A chart used in UML to illustrate the structural relationship between the parts of a system. ■

2. A component diagram in which the parts illustrated are limited to encapsulated and exchangeable modules. ■

Composite pattern

A software design pattern that allows all members of a group of objects, usually similar in nature, to be treated the same. ■

Compositing

The layering of multiple images into a common scene. ▮

Composition relationship

A class reliance in which one class is completely dependent on another class and cannot exist without it. See also **"Has a" Relationship**. ■

Compression

1. The reduction in the size of a data file by encoding it into a mathematical expression or algorithm. Also known as **Data Compression**. ■ ▮ ♦

2. The reduction of the player's area of control within an environment. ▣

Computer Entertainment Rating Organization (CERO)

The organization that provides content and suggested age ratings for video games released in Japan. See also **ESRB** and **PEGI**.

Computer game

A game designed to run on a personal computer. ♪

Computer-generated Image (CGI)

An image created by a computer graphics program. ▮

Con

1. *Convention.* A publicized gathering of people with similar interests. ♪

2. *Consider.* A function that allows a player to evaluate the threat an enemy unit represents. ▣

Concept

1. A premise on which a more complex idea is based. ▣ ♪

2. The space, as defined by C-K theory, in which proposals are evaluated based on desired outcomes. ▣

Concept art

A collection of traditional illustrations used to convey the intended style and content of a game's visual assets before they are created digitally. ▚▌

Concept doc

1. A description of the project, its expected budget, team composition, and company background that is often used as part of the pitch process. Also known as a **Proposal Doc** or **Vision Doc**. ♪

2. A description of the project at its earliest stages that is used in team communications. Also known as a **Proposal Doc** or **Vision Doc**. ♪ ▣

3. Any summary of the project that emphasizes its viability and is distributed to potential investors or publishers to increase their interest. Also known as a **Proposal Doc** or **Vision Doc**. ♪ ▣

Concept-knowledge theory

A design theory that attempts to account for the uncertain nature of creativity by evaluating the interaction between concepts (the untested) and knowledge (the established). Also known as **C-K Theory**. ▣

Conceptualization

The envisioning of an object, system, or idea in such a way that its form and function can be adequately described and evaluated. ▣

Conditional dialogue

Dialogue that is used only when a certain trigger has been activated. ▟ ▣

Conditions

1. The specific and measurable terms that must be met in order for a party to fulfill their contractual obligations. ♪

2. The requirements that must be met before the game, level, or mission can end. ▣

3. The requirements that must be met in order for an event to trigger. ▣ ▮

Cone of vision

The scope of a 3D landscape within which an AI entity can detect objects thereby simulating typical, human-like vision. ▣ ▮

Configuration testing

An evaluation process in which the focus is on how the software performs on different combinations of hardware and operating systems. See also **Compatibility**. ♪

Conflict

1. The tension between forces within a story that must be resolved in order for the story to reach its conclusion. ♟

2. The tension between the player and his or her opponent. ▣

Consider

A function that allows a player to evaluate the threat an enemy unit represents. ▣

Considerations

The inducing elements that are exchanged between the parties when they enter a contract. ♪

Consistency

A principle that all data must be validated before being written into the database. ▦

Console

The hardware that constitutes a stand-alone gaming device. ♪

Console game

A game designed to run on a stand-alone gaming device, often specifically a non-handheld console. ♪

Constant

A permanent placeholder for a value that does not change during gameplay, such as the point value of a specific object. See also **Variable**. ▦

Constitutive rules

1. Searle's description of rules that, by their nature, create the game. ▣

2. Salen's and Zimmerman's description for rules that creates a game's mathematical framework. ▣

Constraint

A limitation placed on a model's movements. ▮

Construction chart

A listing of resources needed by the player to build new units within a game. ▣

Consumer research

The evaluation of potential consumers based on their previous purchasing history, stated preferences, and observed behavior. ♪

Content design

The development and implementation of the assets and storyline of a game. ▣

Context menu

A menu whose current options are limited to those applicable to the current state of the software. Also known as a **Context-sensitive Menu.** ▣

Context-sensitive camera

A camera that is automatically controlled in such a way that it attempts to move into the best position in order to show the action occurring in a scene. ▮

Context-sensitive menu

A menu whose current options are limited to those applicable to the current state of the software. Also known as a **Context Menu.** ▣

Contingency

The rules set that determines when rewards are allocated. ▣

Contingency planning

The inclusion of a buffer to account for unpredictable events that might arise during a project's duration. ♪

Contingency reserve funds

An account in which resources are set aside for unexpected events or changes during a project's development. ♪

Continuity

1. The cohesiveness of the action and setting of a story as it progresses from moment to moment. ✎ ▣ ▮

2. The consistency of an element, such as a character or an object, as the game moves through time. ▣ ✎

3. The consistency the attributes of a model's sections have with each other. ▮

Continuous LOD

Continuous Level of Detail. A technique in which a 3D model's geometry is continually and subtly altered as the camera gets closer to it, allowing the highest detailed version of the model to appear when the camera is moved to its nearest allowed distance. See also **Discrete LOD**.

Contour

The line, shape, or outer casing of an object's body or figure.

Contract

A legally binding agreement between two or more parties.

Contrast

1. The difference between a light and dark area of an image that often creates a point of focus.

2. The differences between two characters that are often used to emphasize a story's theme.

Control point

1. A point that lies outside the NURBS and can be moved to alter its shape. Also known as a **Control Vertex**.

2. A location within the game world that the player's forces must occupy in order to meet a mission objective or win condition.

Control scheme

The physical methods, such as keystrokes and button presses, by which the player's intended actions are translated to the game environment.

Control vertex

A point that lies outside the NURBS and can be moved to alter its shape. Also known as a **Control Point**.

Controller

1. A handheld input device often used with gaming consoles.

2. A chip that is responsible for managing access to certain peripheral elements of the hardware.

Convention (Con)

A publicized gathering of people with similar interests.

Convergence

The merging of two separate technologies into a new form or application. ♪ 🄸

Conversion

1. The process of converting the code and assets designed for one platform over to another platform. Also known as a **Port**. ♪ ▪ ⅈ

2. The process of preparing an existing model's animation data to be compatible with the game engine. Also known as **Animation Conversion**. ⅈ

Cookie cutter

A character customization method in which the attribute points are assigned by the player in a way that attempts to follow a standard or recommended template. ♪ 🄸

Cooldown

A timing buffer built into a skill, attack, or ability to delay how often it can be used. 🄸

Copy protection

Any one of many methods used to discourage and prevent unauthorized reproduction of a product. ♪

Copyright

1. The legal tenet that the creator of a work that expresses an idea has ownership over that expression the moment it is fixed to a medium. ◣ 🄸 ♪ ⅈ ♣

2. The registered claim that a specific work belongs to the claimant. ◣ 🄸 ♪ ⅈ ♣

Core gameplay

The central elements of the game that constitute the basic experience a player has. 🄸 ♪

Core mechanic

1. The precise expression of a game's rules and systems. 🄸

2. The primary principle of the rules and interactions that provide the basis for gameplay. 🄸

3. The activity or activities the player is required to master in order to succeed within the game. 🄸

Corporate CD/DVD

A media file that describes a company, created for showing or distributing during an expo or convention. ♪

Corpse camping

A strategy of waiting near the location where another player's character has died in order to engage that player when they return to claim items that were left at that location, most often on their avatar's corpse. ▣

Corpse run

The travel by a character who has recently respawned to the place of their recent death to retrieve items that remained on his or her avatar's corpse. ▣

COS

Curve on Surface. The placement of a curved path along the surface of an object, usually with the intention of trimming the object. ▮

Cost

1. The fee or charge related to the purchase of goods or services. ♪

2. The expenditure of resources required to perform an action or pursue a strategy. ▣

Cost curve

The benefit of an asset or strategy compared to its expense. ▣

Cost of Goods (COG)

The total investment in materials and labor that were used in the manufacturing of a product over a defined time period. Often expressed on a per unit basis. ♪

Cost Per Unit (CPU)

The expense incurred in making each individual instance of a product. ♪

Cover art

The images, text, and illustrations intended to be displayed on the product's packaging. Also known as **Box Art**. ▮ ♪

Cover letter

A letter, accompanying a proposal, that focuses on the product's potential within the market. ♪

COW

1. *Comes Out in the Wash.* A colloquialism for a set of elements that neutralize each other.

2. *Comes Out in the Wash.* A colloquialism for a minor, somewhat unintended effect that is neutralized by the other elements in the game and that, if removed, would require the remaining elements to be rebalanced.

3. *Comes Out in the Wash.* A colloquialism for an unintended robustness within a section of code that enables it to handle more cases than for which it was designed.

Cowboy coding

An independent style of programming, commonly considered poor practice, in which no defined methods or conventions are used, thereby allowing each team member to follow his or her own individual preferences. Most often used derogatorily to describe such a style as reckless and counter-productive.

CPU

1. *Central Processing Unit.* The microprocessor that performs the calculations required to execute a program's instructions.

2. *Cost Per Unit.* The expense incurred in making each individual instance of a product.

Crack

A file, almost always illegal, that allows the user to bypasses the copy protection features of a software program.

Crafting

A system, designed to simulate the real-world construction of items, in which the player can create new assets from collected resources, often by means of combining components.

Crash

The abrupt, unintentional ending of a program.

Crawl

1. The uniform movement of text across the screen.

2. The movement through space while maintaining as low a posture as possible.

CRC

1. *Cyclic Redundancy Check.* A method of verifying that a transmission has not been altered or corrupted by applying an algorithm to the original data thereby creating a number against which the transmitted data can be compared. ■

2. *Code Release Checklist.* The listed criteria used for evaluating software during its final review before publication. ♪

3. *Code Release Checklist.* A final formal review of the software to determine its candidacy for commercial distribution. ♪

Creative Commons

1. Any of several licensing agreements, designed by the Creative Commons organization, that allow for the public distribution of work without releasing copyrights into the public domain. ♪

2. The organization responsible for the creation and promotion of the Creative Commons licenses. ♪

Creative design doc

A description of the artistic direction of a game. ▣ ▮ ♪

Creative design review

An evaluative stage in which an independent critique of the product, its assumption, and the processes in its development are made. ♪

Creative director

1. The person tasked with maintaining a brand and other IP-related issues within a company. ♪

2. The person in charge of the vision of a project and who may or may not be the same person as the lead designer. ♪

Credits list

The collection of the names of all contributors to a project as well as their role or position. ♪

Creep

1. A low-level AI entity that is automatically generated at a spawn point and follows (i.e., creeps along) an assigned path. See also **Minion.** ▣

2. The adding of unplanned features into a video game thereby potentially delaying its release. Also known as **Feature Creep**. ▣ ♪

CRG

Code Release Group. A specialized team that evaluates a release candidate to ensure that it meets the minimal release criteria before it is sent for duplication and distribution. ♪

Crib sheet

A small card or piece of paper, often included with the manual, that provides a synopsis of the important elements of a game. Also known as a **Cheat Sheet** or **Reference Sheet**. ▣ ♪

Crippleware

Software that is distributed in a limited functionality version to encourage the end user to purchase a fully functional version of the software. ♪

Crit

Critical hit. An attack's randomly triggered effect that yields more benefits than it otherwise normally would. ▣

Critical hit (Crit)

An attack's randomly triggered effect that yields more benefits than it otherwise normally would. ▣

Critical objective

A criterion that must be met to achieve a win condition. ▣

Critical patch

A postrelease section of code that is considered a high priority by the developer and often leaves the software unstable or unsecured until it is applied. ♪ ▮

Critical path

1. The only correct solution to a game. ▣

2. The sequence of tasks within a project's schedule that must be completed in order for the project to reach a successful conclusion. ♪

Critical path methodology

A process for calculating the length of a project by determining the earliest and latest period at which tasks can begin without causing delays to the project. ♪

Critical point of loss

The point within the game at which a loss has become inevitable, even if not immediate. ▣

Crop

To remove an outer section of an image. ▓▌

Cross-collateralization

An accounting practice of combining the royalties earned and advance payments made for multiple products or versions of the product so that the success of one product can be used to offset the expenses of a less successful product before payments are made. This is in contrast to allowing such royalties and advances to be determined separately for each individual product. ♪

Cross-genre

A game that contains enough features that are staples of multiple genres so that it does not solidly fit into any one genre. ♪

Crossover

1. An appearance of a character from one title in another character's publication. ♪

2. The negotiated and legal appearance of one company's IP in another company's product. ♪

Crowd Control (CC)

An ability of the character that can be used to limit the number of units able to engage him or her at one time. ▣

CRPG

1. *Computer Role-Playing Game.* A role-playing game subgenre, commonly designed for the PC, that often focuses on player-controlled character progression and nonlinear gameplay. ♪

2. *Console Role-Playing Game.* A role-playing game subgenre, commonly designed for consoles, that often focuses on scripted character progression and linear gameplay. ♪

Crunch time

A phase during the development cycle in which a team must significantly increase its productivity to meet a deadline, often by increasing man-hours. ♪ ▣ ▓ ▓▌ ♣

CTF

Capture the Flag. A mode of play that requires players to reach a certain location and often to return with a token (the flag) collected from that location. ▯

Cubic environmental map

A technique for creating the impression of a distant environment by placing the camera within a large cube and attaching a texture representing the environment onto each of the cube's inner faces. ▮

Culling

The removal of unseen geometry from a 3D environment so that the engine does not spend time rendering it. ▮

Curvature

The degree to which a line bends. ▮

Curvature continuity

The connection of two curves or surfaces in such a way that they share a common angle or arc. Also known as **G2 Continuity**. ▮

Curve on Surface (COS)

The placement of a curved path along the surface of an object, usually with the intention of trimming the object. ▮

Customer support

The personnel assigned as a point of contact for the public and intended to increase customer satisfaction by providing them with solutions to issues related to the product. ♪

Cut-scene

A scripted event that is separate from standard gameplay and which is often indicated by a change in camera view or perspective. See also **Cinematic**. ⚔ ▯ ▮

CYA

Cover Your Arse. A philosophy that each team member should, at a minimum, be able to defend his/her own actions and decisions. ♪ ▯

Cyclic Coordinate Descent (CCD)

An iterative formula applied to an animation that optimizes each joint's angle via inverse kinematics resulting in an efficient adjustment of complex bone chains. ▮

Cyclic Redundancy Check (CRC)

A method of verifying that a transmission has not been altered or corrupted by applying an algorithm to the original data thereby creating a number against which the transmitted data can be compared. ■

d

Die or *Dice* (notation). An object that, when rolled, generates a random outcome. Often designated by a "d" between two numbers; the number that follows it represents the number of potential outcomes that the die can provide and the number that precedes it represents the number of times it should be rolled to form a total. 2d6, for example, would signify rolling two six-sided dice. ▨

D-pad

Directional pad. A set of integrated buttons on a controller that is often used to indicate the desired direction of movement. ♪ ■

Daily Active Users (DAU)

The number of unique end users that accesses a site or application within 24 hours, particularly in reference to social media. ♪ ▨

Daily delta report

A listing from each member of the team that specifies what tasks were completed by the end of the day. ♪

Damage

1. The currently accumulated reduction of a character's or object's health. ▨

2. The amount of negative health applied to a character or object from a source. ▨

3. The repercussion suffered by one party when another party to an agreement fails to meet their obligations. ▨

Damage avoidance

Any reduction of damage dealt before it is assigned to a target. This is often an all-or-nothing damage reduction used to simulate the effects of dodging or escaping. ▨

Damage mitigation

Any reduction of damage assigned before it is applied to the target. This is often a percentage or fixed amount reduction used to simulate armor or toughness. ▨

Damage Over Time (DOT)

An effect that causes a character's health to drop gradually over a period of time. ▨

Damage Per Second (DPS)

The amount of damage to an opponent that a particular attack or strategy yields within one second.

DAT

Digital Audio Tape. A magnetic medium used to store recorded sound in a digital format.

Data

A collection of measurable information. See also **Datum**.

Data compression

The reduction in the size of a data file by encoding it into a mathematical expression or algorithm. Also known as **Compression**.

Database Manager Report (DMR)

An abbreviated listing of the current state of all reported issues in QA and the rate at which new issues are being found. Exists in a daily and weekly version.

Datum

1. A reference item added to a 3D model's file but is not part of the model itself.

2. A single piece of measurable information. See also **Data**.

DAU

Daily Active Users. The number of unique end users that accesses a site or application within 24 hours, particularly in reference to social media.

Day and date

A release date that is concurrent with a release of another product. See also **Simultaneous Release**.

Dead

The state of a player whose avatar has been removed from the game; may be permanent or temporary. See also **Permadeath**.

Dead draw

A situation in which gameplay can continue but without a realistic chance that any player will be able to reach a win condition.

Dead room

A recording studio that has an absence of echo.

Deadlock

1. A condition in which multiple processing tasks are queued but cannot continue because each is waiting until the other performs a specific function. ▩

2. A condition within a game in which a player can make no further progress due to an event that can no longer be triggered. Also known as a **Lock**. ▣

Deadlock game

A game in which the strategy that is in the player's best self-interests is also the best strategy for the players' mutual interests. ▣

Deathmatch

A mode of play in which the object is to kill opponents as often as possible within a predetermined time period. ▣

Debuff

1. A skill or ability that removes a buff from an opponent. ▣

2. A skill or ability that temporarily reduces an opponent's statistics. ▣

Debug

The identification and correction of code errors. ▩

Decal

A two-dimensional image overlaid across a 3D object's existing texture. ▩

Deceleration

A decrease in an object's speed over time. ▩ ▩

Decorator pattern

A software design pattern in which objects can be given new independent behaviors during runtime. ▩

Dedicated server

A system, within a network, whose sole function is to host the game as opposed to simultaneously hosting and playing. ▩ ♪

Defect pooling

A quality assurance methodology in which two separate QA teams test the software independently. The degree of overlap in the bugs reported by the two teams can be used to predict the likelihood of the existence of unreported bugs; a high overlap indicates a low likelihood of unreported issues, and vice versa. ♪

Defect seeding

The intentional inclusion of bugs into software to track the completeness of the QA testing. When all included bugs are discovered, the likelihood of the majority of all unintended bugs having been discovered is high. ♪

Deferred rendering

A shading method in which the results of a shader's calculation is stored in a buffer so that it only needs to be drawn once. ▮

Degenerate strategy

1. A strategy that is easy to carry out. ▣

2. A strategy that is simplified from its more complex form. ▣

3. A strategy that becomes viable only because of a flaw in the game's design. ▣

Delay

1. An option a player can use to avoid taking an action until later in the turn. ▣

2. An effect in which an auditory signal is played back shortly after it is created. ♣

Delimited

Text that has been separated, most commonly by means of punctuation, into individual sections of data. ▦

Deliverable

The materials that are due as specified under an agreement and which often represent the end of one phase of development and the beginning of another. ♪

Delivery method

The means by which a product is distributed to customers. ♪

Demo

1. *Demonstration.* An incomplete version of the game distributed with the intention of creating consumer interest in it. ♪

2. *Demographic.* A potential market's subsection that is defined by the similar traits of the individuals making up that subsection. ♪

Demo mode

A mode in which a game simulates gameplay either to attract the attention of a potential player or to provide playing instructions. ♪ ▣

Demo reel

A sampling of one's best work presented in a video format. 🔦 🎵

Demo script

The prepared statements and planned activities for presenting a product to outside parties, such as the media. 🎵 🖌

Demographic

A potential market's subsection that is defined by the similar traits of the individuals making up that subsection. 🎵

Denouement

The resolution of a story in which all of the loose ends are tied up. Also known as the **Falling Action**. 🖌

Departmental budget

The projection of expenses and resources over a specified period of time for an individual section of an organization. 🎵

Dependency

An element that another element within a structure relies upon. 🎵 ▦

Deployment design

The plan for distributing software components. May refer to in-house deployment or deployment to consumers. 🎵

Depth buffer

A data storage area that holds information on each pixel's depth within a scene. Also known as a **Z-buffer**. 🔦 ▦

Depth complexity

The number of times, on average, that each pixel in a scene or portion of a scene is calculated during rendering. 🔦

Depth cueing

A blending process in which the distance of objects determines how much they blend visually with the background. 🔦

Depth fail

A technique in lighting in which the rendering process evaluates the surfaces lying outside of the shadow's volume to determine which pixels are affected. Also known as **Carmack's Reverse** or **Z-Fail**. 🔦

Depth-first search

An AI routine that evaluates all possible outcomes from a potential decision before moving on to evaluate a different potential move. ▪

Depth map

A texture that allows diffuse light to shine through parts of the model it is applied to based on the model's thickness at various coordinates. Also known as **Translucent Map** and **Translucent Shadow Map**. ▪

Depth pass

A technique in lighting in which the rendering process evaluates the surfaces lying inside of the shadow's volume to determine which pixels are affected. Also known as **Z-Pass**. ▪

Derivative work

A work that is based on an earlier, preexisting work. ♪

Design document

1. A detailed blueprint describing how a game will work. ▥ ♪

2. A brief document describing the key elements of a game. Also known as a **Concept Doc** or **Treatment**. ▥ ♪

3. A detailed document that describes all elements of a game and often includes concept art, backstory, and style guides. Also known as a **Game Bible**. ▥ ▪ ♪

Design for cause

A philosophy of game design that the simulation aspect of a mechanic must be preserved even at the expense of a mechanic's performance or effect. See also **Design for Effect**. ▥

Design for effect

A philosophy of game design that the performance and result of a mechanic is more important than its realism. See also **Design for Cause**. ▥

Design pattern

Any one of the limited number of software engineering templates that exist for solving commonly encountered problems. ▪

Design requirements

The listing of features that a game will support. ▥ ♪

Design risk

The inherent risk that a product will not achieve its intended design goal. ♪

Design scalability

The ability of a system to gracefully handle an increase in the number of users. ▨ ▦

Design spec

The technical specifications that a product is intended to meet. ♪

Despawn

The abrupt removal of an object or character from the game world by means other than direct player interaction. ▨

Destructible terrain

A feature that allows for the deterioration of environmental objects and landscapes due to damage. ▨ ▮

Deterministic algorithm

An AI formula used by an object so that it can reach a predetermined state in as consistant a method as possible. ▦

Deus ex machina

God in the Machine (Latin). A literary technique in which the resolution is reached by an unpredictable and improbable turn of events, such as the last-minute appearance of a powerful character that had not been previously introduced within the story. Named from the practice in Greek plays of having a god appear on stage to resolve the hero's problem. ▰

Dev kit

Development Kit. A set of tools necessary for the development of products on a specific platform, provided to developers. ▦

Developer

A company tasked with the creation of a game. ♪

Development testing

The evaluation of a small, often recently implemented, section of the software. ▦ ♪

Dialogue

The words spoken by a character. ▰ ▲

Dictator

A player that can, without the cooperation of any other players, determine the specific outcome of a game's event. 🎲

Die (d)

An object that, when rolled, generates a random outcome. Often designated by a "d" between two numbers; the number that follows it represents the number of potential outcomes that the die can provide and the number that precedes it represents the number of times it should be rolled to form a total. 2d6, for example, would signify rolling two six-sided dice. 🎲

Difficulty curve

The game's ability to challenge players throughout its progression as demonstrated on a graph. 🎲

Difficulty independence

The ability of a game to maintain its identity across all levels of difficulty. 🎲

Difficulty level

A setting that allows the player to choose how challenging the game is. 🎲

Diffuse light mapping

The simulation of realistic lighting by applying a texture that defines how much light is absorbed into or reflected off of a 3D model. 🖌

Diffuse lighting

Light that is spread out so that it does not create a highlight effect. 🖌

Digital Audio Tape (DAT)

A magnetic medium used to store recorded sound in a digital format. ♟

Digital dailies

The collected set of in-progress CGI works assembled every 24 hours for evaluation. ♪

Digital Rights Management (DRM)

The systems, often technological in nature, used to combat illegal copying and transferring of digital content. ♪

Dilemma

A choice between two negative outcomes. Also known as **Morton's Fork.** 🎲

Dir

Directory. A virtual location in which data files are indexed, organized, and stored. ▪

Direct damage

Damage that is targeted and applied immediately when it hits. See also **Direct Heal**. ▣

Direct heal

Healing that is targeted and applied immediately when it hits. See also **Direct Damage**. ▣

Directed network narrative structure

A division, described by Ryan, of the story into paths that the player can diverge onto but which, at certain points, converge back to a central storyline. ⚔

Directional light

A light source that emits across the environment equally from one direction. ⚑

Directional pad (D-pad)

A set of integrated buttons on a controller that is often used to indicate the desired direction of movement. ♪ ▣

Directness of conflict

The degree to which opponents can explicitly affect each other's game state as described by Crawford. ▣

Directory (Dir)

A virtual location in which data files are indexed, organized, and stored. ▪

DirectX

Microsoft's standardized APIs designed for multimedia and games. ▪

Disband

The dissolution of a group or party. See also **Kick**. ▣

Discourse level

The logical sequence of events within a story. Also known as the **Event Layer**. ⚔

Discrete LOD

Discrete Level of Detail. A technique in which multiple versions of a 3D model are displayed based on their nearness to the camera, with the highest detailed version loading only when the camera is moved to the closest of several predefined distances. See also **Continuous LOD.**

Displacement mapping

A method of texturing in which a 3D model's geometry is adjusted in accordance to the data provided by a height map.

Disruption

Any negative, nondestructive effect applied to a unit within a game.

Distracter

A potential response designed to create the impression that the list of choices being presented to the player offers more strategies than there really are. Sometimes used to provide flavor or mood and not intended to be evaluated as a real strategy decision.

Distributor

A company tasked with transferring a game from the publisher to either the retailer or directly to the consumer. Includes both physical and downloadable versions of a game, though the distributor may or may not be the same for both versions.

Divide and choose

A fairness mechanic in which one player selects an option and the other player determines which one of them follows that option. Named after the premise of having one person cut two pieces from a pie and the other person choosing who gets which piece.

DLC

Downloadable Content. Digital media, often an expansion or add-on to existing content, that an end user can access and retrieve from a network.

DLOD

Dynamic Level of Detail. A technique in which a formula is used to smoothly adjust a model's quality at runtime thereby allowing the game engine to render only the details the player is likely to be able to notice at any given distance.

DMR

Database Manager Report. An abbreviated listing of the current state of all reported issues in QA and the rate at which new issues are being found. Exists in a daily and weekly version.

Dominant strategy

A strategy that is the most likely path to victory thereby rendering all other strategies weak choices. ⌨

Doppler effect

A phenomenon of sound in which its frequency increases as its source gets nearer and decreases as the source moves farther away. ♟

DOT

Damage Over Time. An effect that causes a character's health to drop gradually over a period of time. ⌨

Downloadable Content (DLC)

Digital media, often an expansion or add-on to existing content, that an end user can access and retrieve from a network. ♪

Downtime

1. A lull in development when portions of the team have little project-related work to do. ♪

2. A portion of the game when a player has little active involvement. ⌨

3. The time period when a system is not available to the public, either due to a failure or scheduled maintenance. ▪

DPS

Damage Per Second. The amount of damage to an opponent that a particular attack or strategy yields within one second. ⌨

Draft

1. A version of a document that is subject to revision. ✎

2. A process of dividing resources between players in a turn-based sequence. ⌨

Drain

A game mechanic whose purpose is to remove resources from players. Also known as a **Sink**. ⌨

Dramatic tension

The emotional response by the audience to a conflict between two opposing forces that builds over the course of a narrative. ✎

Draw

1. A command or function within a program for displaying an image on screen.

2. A situation in which the game ends without either player achieving a victory condition. Also known as a **Push**.

3. To take from a pool of resources.

Draw distance

The maximum distance from the camera within which a game engine will draw objects. See also **Clipping Plane, Far Plane,** and **Near Plane**.

DRC

Dynamic Range Compression. A method of achieving consistent sound levels by adjusting the highest and lowest volumes of a sound clip to fit within a determined span.

Driver

Software that allows a specific piece of hardware to interact with the operating system and its applications. Most often used in reference to PCs. See also **Socket** and **Firmware**.

DRM

Digital Rights Management. The systems, often technological in nature, used to combat illegal copying and transferring of digital content.

Drop down list

A user interface element that contains a list of predefined options that appear when accessed from a menu.

Dry audio

Sounds that remain unaltered both during and after their recording session.

DTMB

Digital Terrestrial Multimedia Broadcast. The standards set for digital televisions in China.

Dubbing

The adding of voices to a sound track.

Dummy

A player whose actions have no real effect on the game but is necessary for the game to be played. 🔲

Dump

The transfer of a large collection of data into one container, such as a file or hardware device. See also **Frame Dump**. ▦ ⚑

Dungeon crawl

An RPG game that predominantly takes place in a maze environment. ♪

Dupe

1. *Duplication*. The erroneous reproduction of an in-game object. ♪

2. *Duplication*. An indication that an issue listed has already been reported. ♪

Durability

A principle that modified data should have the intended level of permanency and be capable of surviving system failures. ▦

Duration

The length of time an ability or power remains in effect. 🔲

Dutch auction

A bidding structure in which the seller continues to lower his price until it is agreed to by a buyer. 🔲

DVB

Digital Video Broadcast. The standards set for digital televisions in Europe, Australia, and parts of Africa. ♪

Dynamic behavior diagram

A UML chart that illustrates the changes that occur to the system's state during use. Also known as a **Behavior Diagram**. ▦

Dynamic bot

An AI entity that is programmed to create its own pathing as it moves throughout a level. ▦

Dynamic difficulty adjustment

A feature that allows a game to adjust its difficulty based on a player's performance. Also known as **Adaptive Difficulty Adjustment**. 🔲

Dynamic labyrinth narrative structure

The division of a story into separate, self-contained sections each of which is only accessible when the preceding module has been completed. Also known as **Modular Narrative Structure** and **Modulated Narrative Structure**. ♟

Dynamic Level of Detail (DLOD)

A technique in which a formula is used to smoothly adjust a model's quality at run-time thereby allowing the game engine to render only the details the player is likely to be able to notice at any given distance. ♟

Dynamic lighting

Real-time lighting that can be affected by the elements inside a scene. ♟

Dynamic modeling

The expression in UML of a system's components that change over time. ■

Dynamic motion synthesis

An animation method in which the behaviors and attributes assigned to a model are used to calculate an appropriate series of movements. ♟

Dynamic play

The fluid alteration of a player's strategy in response to an opponent's strategy. ▣

Dynamic plot

A plot that is alterable by the player's actions within a game. Also known as an **Interactive Plot**. ♟

Dynamic Range Compression (DRC)

A method of achieving consistent sound levels by adjusting the highest and lowest volumes of a sound clip to fit within a determined span. ♣

Dynamic scalability

The ability of a game to remain playable regardless of the number of players involved. ▣

Dynamic sound

A sound track methodology in which the background music changes depending on the activity currently occurring within the game. Also known as **Adaptive Music** and **Interactive Music**. ♣

Dynamics

1. How separate elements in a game can and do affect each other. ⌨

2. One of the three principle components of the MDA framework proposed by Hunicke, LeBlanc, and Zubek. In this framework, dynamics are player-induced effects and are directly influenced by the game's mechanics and exert their affect on the aesthetics of the game. See also **MDA**. ⌨

3. The mechanics of movement of a mass by a force. Also known as **Kinetics**. ▲ ▣

Earn out

The point at which a product's sales have allowed its publisher to recoup any and all of the advanced payments they have made. ♪

Easing equation

A formula applied to an animation to adjust its speed, particularly when starting, stopping, or changing direction, often used to give an animated object's movement a more natural appearance. ▲ ▣

Easter egg

Something hidden within a game by its developers, usually related to an inside joke or reference, that is not expected to be encountered or recognized by the typical player. ♪ ⌨

ECC

Error Checking and Correcting or *Error Correcting Code*. A feature in hardware or software that makes a second, coded version of the data so that it can be verified for accuracy after being transmitted or transferred, resulting in a larger file being sent but not requiring any additional information or verification. ▣

Economy

The system of resource creation, management, and trade within a game. ⌨

Edge

The portion of a polygon that terminates its surface and where polygons can attach to each other. ▲

Edge modeling

A method of modeling in which the edges of a polygon or patch are extruded thereby creating the overall shape as segments are modified. ▲

Edit Decision List (EDL)

A list of recordings with time codes that provides editors with information on when each segment begins and ends. ♣

Edit point

A point that lies inside the NURBS and can be moved to alter its shape. ᵇ▮

Editors' day

A day set aside during the production cycle to allow the outside press access to the project. ♪

EDL

Edit Decision List. A list of recordings with time codes that provides editors with information on when each segment begins and ends. ♣

Edutainment

A category of entertainment software that emphasizes its educational elements. ♪

Effects (F/X)

The elements in a scene that are simulated, either while the action is recorded or added in afterward. Also known as a **Special Effect**. ᵇ▮

Elastic equation

1. A formula used to derive the energy transferred when objects rebound off of a surface. ▰

2. A formula applied to an animation that adjusts its speed and direction when it collides with another object. ᵇ▮

Electronic game

A stand-alone game manufactured using electronic components. ♪

Elo

1. A rating system, created by Elo, that measures the skill level of players based on a statistical evaluation of not only the result of the contest but on the strength of the opponent faced. ▣

2. Any rating system that uses a strength-of-opponent-faced algorithm to determine the ranking of players. ▣

EMA

Entertainment Merchants Association. An international trade association that represents home entertainment–based retailers, distributers, studios, and publishers. ♪

Emboss

To raise a shape out of an existing surface.

Emergence

The evolution of dynamics beyond that inherent to a system.

Emergent behavior

An AI's conduct that is derived from its interaction with either the environment or another entity, making its exact reactions difficult to predict.

Emergent gameplay

The intentional or unintentional evolution of game dynamics beyond those directly designed into a game and whose effects on overall gameplay may be either beneficial or harmful.

Emergent storytelling

The story that evolves from the player's imagination during gameplay and may be in addition to or in lieu of a scripted story.

Emissive lighting

A light attached to an object's surface so that the object appears to be emitting light in all directions.

Emote

An animation a player's avatar can perform to convey an emotion.

Emotional immersion

The capture of the player's focus by the game's use of compelling story and character developments, as described by Björk and Holopainen. Also known as **Narrative Immersion**.

Emulation

The ability of one system to mimic the functionality of another.

Encapsulation

1. The technique of hiding the internal mechanisms of a process from the user thereby giving the user access only to requisite inputs and outputs.

2. Combining game elements so that they function and are viewed by a player as a single element.

Encounter

A confrontation between two opposing forces within a game.

Encryption

The conversion of data into a coded sequence, usually for security reasons.

End game

The period of gameplay when an outcome is inevitable or nearly inevitable if the optimal strategy is applied.

End sequence

The final sequence of a game, including its ending cinematics.

End user

The intended user of a product once it has been released commercially.

End User License Agreement (EULA)

A contract between the consumer and the publisher of a game detailing each party's rights in regard to ownership and use of the software.

Engine

1. A software toolset whose purpose is to provide some or all of a video game's core functionality.

2. A classification of real-time software programs and routines that provide a specific continuous function within a larger software environment, such as a graphics rendering or physics calculations.

3. A collection of software toolsets working in conjunction to create a video game's overall framework.

Engine proof

Work designed to show that the selected engine is capable of supporting the game's features.

Engrave

To carve a shape into an existing surface.

Enrage

A triggered effect in which a character's stats increase, either until defeated or for a limited time. Often utilized in the design of bosses.

Entertainment Merchants Association (EMA)

An international trade association that represents home entertainment–based retailers, distributers, studios, and publishers. ♪

Entertainment Software Rating Board (ESRB)

A private, self-regulatory body that assigns ratings to the content of and provides advisory guidelines related to specific video games sold in the U.S. and Canada. See also **CERO** and **PEGI**. ♪

Entity

1. Any player or virtual being within a game. ▣

2. Any object in a game that interacts with another object. ▣

Environment

1. The area in which actions take place in a video game. ▣

2. The replication of a world's natural or man-made geometry that serve as a background for the game's action. ▮ ▣

3. The visual representation of a location within the game world. ▮ ▣

Envision stage

The phase of Agile Software Development in which the creation and refining of a project's ambitions, scope, and methodologies are done. ♪

Episodic game

A game that is released in small sequential sections. ♪

Ergonomics

The study of how humans can comfortably and optimally interact with other systems, particularly ones that are mechanical and technological in nature. ♪ ▣

Error Checking and Correcting (ECC)

A feature in hardware or software that makes a second, coded version of the data so that it can be verified for accuracy after being transmitted or transferred. Also known as **Error Correcting Code**. ▪

Error Code

A numerical indicator, sometimes accompanied with text, that provides a reference to a fault that has occurred in the software. ▪

Error Correcting Code (ECC)

A feature in hardware or software that makes a second, coded version of the data so that it can be verified for accuracy after being transmitted or transferred. Also known as **Error Checking and Correcting**. ▣

ESRB

Entertainment Software Rating Board. An independent regulatory body that assigns ratings to the content of and provides advisory guidelines related to specific video games sold in the U.S. and Canada. See also **CERO** and **PEGI**. ♪

Essence statement

A one-sentence summary that defines a product. ♟ ♪

Establishing shot

Footage that is designed to provide crucial information about the location of a scene before the action starts. ♟ ▮

EULA

End User License Agreement. A contract between the consumer and the publisher of a game detailing each party's rights in regard to ownership and use of the software. ♪

Euler angles

A series of three-dimensional parameters for orientating and rotating rigid bodies in 3D graphics but which is susceptible to gimbal-lock. See also **Quaternion**. ▣ ▮

Eurogame

A classification of board games, named for their popularity in Europe, known for their quick setup and relatively short play sessions. ♪

Eustress

A positive physiological response, such as fulfillment or enjoyment, that comes from participating in a challenging activity. ▣

Evasion algorithm

A formula used to determine the pathing of a prey object so that it increases the distance between it and its predator. See also **Chase Algorithm**. ▣

Event

1. An action that is triggered from outside the code. ▣
2. A series of triggered actions performed by a script or section of code. ▣

Event diagram

A chart used in UML to illustrate the order in which the processes interact with one another. Also known as an **Event Scenario,** a **Sequence Diagram**, and a **Timing Diagram**. ▪

Event layer

The logical sequence of events within a story. Also known as the **Discourse Layer**. ♪

Event scenarios

A chart used in UML to illustrate the order in which the processes interact with one another. Also known as an **Event Diagram**, a **Sequence Diagram**, and a **Timing Diagram**. ▪

Evolutionary prototyping

A development process in which a working, nearly featureless version of the game is created and experimented with first and then new features are implemented on an as-needed basis. Also known as the **Sandbox Design Method** or **Testbed Design Method**. ▣

Exception

An error in a code's execution that causes the program or routine to stop abruptly. ▪

Exception handling

The methods used to allow a program to handle errors gracefully instead of causing it to abruptly end. ▪

EXE

Executable. A file that contains an application's core instructions and can often be used to launch a program. ▪

Executable (EXE)

A file that contains an application's core instructions and can often be used to launch a program. ▪

Executive summary

A concise and simple description of a game's concept, unique selling points, and sales potential. ♪

Exercise

The optional acceptance of an offer that has been extended by a previously agreed-upon contract. ♪

Exhaustion rule

The right of a consumer to resell products they have legally purchased without requiring the permission of or paying reimbursement to the original copyright holder. Also known as the **First-Sale Doctrine** and **Right of First Sale**. ♪

Expansion

A sequel to a game, often limited in scope, that requires the installation of the original game to function. ♪

Experience

A system that controls character progression by rewarding points that, when accumulated, unlock additional benefits. ▣

Experience Points (XP)

The points awarded a player that measure her or his progression in developing their character and which are used to determine when additional benefits are unlocked. ▣

Experiential density

The amount of activity that a player experiences in a specific unit of time or area, as described by Birdwell. ▣

Explicit animation

A classification of animation in which the vertices of a model's geometry at each step in the cycle are stored and played back in order thereby creating smooth but memory-intensive animation. See also **Implicit Animation**. 🖌

Exploit

The use of an emergent strategy that is allowable by the game but is considered unfair by the majority of its players. ▣

Exploration music

In-game music designed to be played while the character is transitioning from place to place, as opposed to while performing specific activities. ⛏

Exploratorium structure

The placement of the story into nonessential areas of the game, requiring a player to voluntarily explore the environment to fully access its narrative elements. Also known as an **Exploratory Narrative Structure**. ✎

Exploratory narrative structure

The placement of the story into nonessential areas of the game, requiring a player to voluntarily explore the environment to fully access its narrative elements. Also known as an **Exploratorium Structure**. ♪

Explore stage

The phase of agile software development in which a project's features are experimented with and developed. ♪

Exposition

Information crucial to a story's logical sense that is delivered through dialogue instead of the characters' actions. ♪

Extensible Markup Language (XML)

An open standard for documentation encoding that allows stored text to be parsed by a program yet edited separately from the program's code. ▦

Extinction

The termination of a reward's availability. ▨

Extreme Game Development (XGD)

An agile design process, proposed by Demachy, in which regularly interspersed milestones serve as iterative cycles and the design team adjusts its project after each milestone based on the producer's feedback. ▦ ♪

Extreme Programming method (XP method)

A rapid-prototyping software development methodology in which the focus is on rapid cycling through the coding and testing phases with features added on an as-needed basis. Also known as **Code-fix Methodology**. ▦ ♪

Extremely flexible project planning formula

A variation of the PERT formula, adapted by Irish, that predicts the amount of time needed to finish a project based on weights given to best- and worst-case scenarios. Defined as Time = (2xBest) + (3xWorst) + (Likely)/6. ♪

Extrusion

Pulling out a portion of a model to create a new shape. ▪

Extrusion modeling

A polygonal modeling technique that lays down a 2D outline of a model and then extrudes the edges to create its third dimension. ▪

Eye candy

Art whose primary purpose is to capture the viewer's attention.

Eye space

A 3D environment in which the objects' locations are given in relation to the camera. Also known as **Camera Space** or **View Space**.

F/X

Effects. The elements in a scene that are simulated, either while the action is recorded or added in afterward. Also known as a **Special Effect**.

F2P

Free to Play. A distribution method in which the player is not charged to gain access to the game.

Façade pattern

A software design pattern in which an object functions as a streamlined interface to simplify interactions with a complex body of code.

Face

The portion of a polygon that is enclosed by its edges.

Face-to-Face (FTF)

A mode of play in which the players are in the same location, allowing them to interact in person. See also **Over the Board**.

Faceted

The composition of a model through uniform or nearly uniform shapes.

Facial capture

The recording of the movements that make up an actor's facial expressions to reproduce them digitally. See also **Performance Capture**.

Faction

1. An alliance between NPCs in which the favor of its member's toward a player can be increased through certain actions, often at the expense of earning the disfavor of another coalition's members. See also **Subfaction**.

2. A numerical measure of how favored a player's actions are by a certain alliance of NPCs. Also known as **Faction Points**.

Faction points

A numerical measure of how favored a player's actions are by a certain alliance of NPCs. Also known as a **Faction**. ⬚

Factory method pattern

A software design pattern in which a centralized routine defines the general features of an object but its exact features are determined by separate routines thereby allowing greater flexibility in an application's design. ▰

Fade in

1. The gradual increase in an image's brightness from black. ▰ ▮

2. The gradual increase in a sound's volume from silence. ▰ ♟

Fade out

1. The gradual decrease in an image's brightness to black. ▰ ▮

2. The gradual decrease in a sound's volume to silence. ▰ ♟

Fail

The designation of a submission that is not satisfactory. See also **Pass**. ♪

Failover

The capability of a system to transfer all loads, functions, operations, and requests from a failed component to a backup or redundant component without an interruption of service. ▰

Fair division problem

An inherent problem of resource management in which the asymmetrical allocation of resources is often viewed as unfair based on the bias of the recipients. Also known as the **Cake-cutting Dilemma**. ⬚

Falling action

The resolution of a story in which all of the loose ends are tied up. Also known as the **Denouement**. ▰

False dilemma

A choice in which the player is given fewer options than the situation would normally allow and therefore may conflict with her or his desired course of action. ⬚

Fanservice

1. Nudity or near-nudity that is unnecessary for a scene but added to titillate the audience. ♪

2. Anything unnecessary to the scene but added to entertain a show's or game's core fans. ♪

Far plane

A division of the 3D environment that determine the greatest distance from the camera in which objects will still be rendered. See also **Clipping Plane, Draw Distance, and Near Plane.** ♪

Farming

The act of repetitively collecting resources. ▣

Fast tracking

Attempting to shorten the overall length of a project by adjusting the resources devoted to a task or series of tasks within that project. ♪

Fatality

A specialized attack performed against an incapacitated character that results in a spectacular and, most often, gruesome death. ♪ ▣

Feasibility

The likelihood that a product will satisfy its intended goal. ♪

Feature

An element within a game that is intended to enrich the player's experience. ▣

Feature creep

The adding of unplanned features into a video game thereby potentially delaying its release. Also known as **Creep.** ▣ ♪

Feature list

A description of all of the abilities and aspects of a product, often used to pitch a product or as a contractual requirement. ♪ ▣

Fed-Ex quest

A mission requiring a character to travel to pick up or deliver an item. ▣

Feedback

1. Information given to players so they understand the consequences of their decisions. ▨

2. A sound that has been infinitely looped through a series of input and output devices, resulting in excessive amplification. ♣

3. Output generated by a system that serves as input for another process by that system, often for the purpose of modifying or controlling that system. ▪

4. Opinions and comments about a product collected from evaluation sessions or similar sources during or after development. ♪

5. Information related to an activity that is gathered from the participants in that activity. ♪

Feelie

A trinket included in the game's packaging, often used to help with player immersion. ♪

FFA

Free For All. A mode of gameplay in which all players are in competition against each other, as opposed to being divided into teams. ▨

Fidget

An animation cycle for a character that is played when the character is otherwise motionless. Also known as **Idle Animation**. ▮

Field

A user-interface element that allows text and numbers to be entered into a predefined area. Also known as a **Text Box**. ▨ ▪

Field of view

The area and distance that can be seen through a game's camera. ▮

Fighting game

A genre of video games in which characters engage each other, most often one-on-one, in martial arts–style combat often with attacks that rely on extreme elements such as weapons or superpowers. See also **Beat 'em Up**. ♪

Fill light

A soft light focused on an object used to illuminate its shape and to separate it from the shadows. ▮

Filleting

Adding to a surface's material to make the transition between components smoother. ◗▮

Final candidate

A build that is being evaluated for distribution. Also known as a **Code Release Candidate** or **Release Candidate**. ♪

Finalize stage

The phase of Agile Software Development in which the project is concluded and production documentation is complete. ♪

Financial modeling

The representation of the project from a budgetary view. ♪

Finishing move

An attack option, usually in fighting games, that is only available when an opponent is near defeat. ▣

Finite game

A game with a limited number of players, each of whom have a limited number of strategies from which to choose. ▣

Finite state machine

An abstraction of a behavioral system, often used as an AI technique, in which each condition, or state, has a limited number of options, consequently allowing the entire system to be simplified into a flowchart. ▰ ▣

Firmware

Low-level programmed instructions designed to control the functionality of an electronic device. See also **Driver** and **Socket**. ▰

First-person camera (FP camera)

A camera that provides a view of the scene from a character's perspective. ◗▮ ▣

First-person shooter (FPS)

A genre of video games in which the player's primary activity is shooting enemies and in which the camera is positioned so that the player sees the events as if looking through the character's eyes. ♪

First Playable Prototype (FPP)

1. The first demo of a game that can be played independent of its developmental tools. ♪

2. A stage of development, defined by the investors or publisher, when the current version of the game is considered a rough but accurate example of the envisioned product. ♪

First-sale doctrine

The right of a consumer to resell products they have legally purchased without requiring the permission of or paying reimbursement to the original copyright holder. Also known as the **Exhaustion Rule** and **Right of First Sale**. ♪

Fixed budget

A firm limitation on the amount of financial resources that a project can spend. Also known as a **Static Budget**. ♪

Fixed costs

An expense that is not dependent on the volume of business done. ♪

Fixed deadline

A firm limitation on the amount of time the project has before it must be finished. ♪

Fixed device

An in-game object that a player can interact with but which cannot be moved or relocated. Also known as a **Fixed Object**. ▣

Fixed interval reward

A benefit that is available only after a set period of time, which the participant is aware of or can deduce. See also **Variable Interval Reward**. ▣

Fixed object

An in-game object that a player can interact with but which cannot be moved or relocated. Also known as a **Fixed Device**. ▣

Fixed ratio reward

A benefit that is available only after successfully repeating an action a set number of times, which the participant is aware of or can deduce. See also **Variable Ratio Reward**. ▣

FK

Forward Kinematics. An animation technique in which, whenever the core of an object is moved, the peripheral elements, such as arms and legs, adjust accordingly. See also **Inverse Kinematics**.

Flash

1. Adobe's web-based platform for transferring multimedia content.

2. A data storage chip that allows for rapid rewriting and is often used in portable devices due to its durability and small physical size.

3. The process of erasing data from a ROM chip.

Flashback

A jump in the narrative to an event that has occurred earlier in the story's chronology.

Flashforward

A jump in the narrative to an event that will occur later in the story's chronology.

Flat shading

A simple lighting method in which the entire face of each polygon is lit uniformly based on its angle to the light source.

Flavor text

Written descriptions designed to create immersion into the game's setting as opposed to providing information that is relevant to gameplay.

Flexible budget

A modifiable limitation on the financial resources that a project can use, with the adjustments usually based on changes in costs. Also known as a **Variable Budget**.

Flexible deadline

A modifiable limitation on the amount of time the project has before it must be finished.

Flicker fusion threshold

The point at which the rate of an intermittent light's flickering begins to appear as a constant and steady light source.

Flight path

A predetermined path that the character travels on while moving from one location in the world to another, particularly when the simulated mode of travel is flying. See also **Ride Path**. 🖰 🖳

Flow

1. The movement of tasks through a work environment. ♪

2. The variation in pacing throughout a story. ✎

3. The immersion into an activity by means of an energizing focus as described by Csíkszentmihályi. 🖰

Flow model

A methodology devised by Csíkszentmihályi to encourage a state of immersion in the participants and which requires skills, goals, feedback, and uncertain, but influence-able, outcomes. 🖰

Flowchart

A graphical illustration of a process using shapes and symbols to represent steps and actions. See also **Activity Diagram**. 🖳 🖰 ♪

Fly through

1. A demonstration of the game in which the camera moves independently across the level to show different elements. ♪ 🖋

2. The movement of the camera through a scene as if it were flying. ✎

Flyweight pattern

A software design pattern that minimizes the amount of memory used by creating one object to represent a variety of objects with similar characteristics and then adding additional unique attributes only as needed. 🖳

FMV

1. *Full Motion Video*. A live-action or animated prerecorded clip played within a game but through a separate media player. 🖋

2. *Full Motion Video game*. A genre of video games in which a significant portion of the action is composed of prerecorded video clips. ♪

Focus

1. The primary object to which a camera draws the viewer's attention. ✎ 🖋

2. The drawing of the player's attention to only currently valid options thereby aiding in information reduction. 🖻 ▪ ⍟

3. The clarity of an object's image. ⍟

4. The adjustment of a camera's lens to allow a specific object to be seen clearly without blur. ⍟

5. The concentration of attacks onto a specific enemy unit to reduce the overall strength of the engaged opponents before moving onto another target. 🖻

6. The concentration of resources onto a central point. ⍟ 🖻 ♪

Focus group

A testing group made up of potential consumers and often fitting a specific demographic that is given exposure to a product in order to gauge their reaction to it. ♪

Fog of war

A method of hiding information from a player by revealing only certain sections of the playing field, such as those occupied by or adjacent to the player's units. 🖻

Foley

The manufacturing, recording, and placement of sounds that are designed to substitute for the original, natural sounds in a scene. ♣

Font

A complete set of typographical characters designed with a common style and categorized by size, weight, and typeface. ✉ ⍟

Force multiplier

An element that when combined with other existing factors yields a greater benefit than other comparable elements. 🖻

Foreshadowing

1. A subtle drawing of the reader's attention to a detail that will play a crucial point later in the story. ✉

2. A symbolic element within a story which serves as an analogy to some later, central event. ✉

Fork

1. An action a player makes that forces an opponent to choose between two negative outcomes. 🖻

2. A section of code that creates a duplicate of a thread or process. ▧

Form follows function

The design premise that the finished product's appearance or aesthetics should evolve from the function it is intended to serve. ▣

Formal budget

The projection of expenses and resources over a specified period of time for the entirety of an organization. ♪

Forum

An online site in which visitors can hold discussions by posting messages that are then archived so that others can respond. ♪

Forward engineering

The design method of first creating generalized and abstract concepts then designing specific practical elements for the implementation of those concepts into a system or product. See also **Reverse Engineering.** ▣ ♪

Forward Kinematics (FK)

An animation technique in which, whenever the core of an object is moved, the peripheral elements, such as arms and legs, adjust accordingly. See also **Inverse Kinematics.** ▮

Forward rendering

A shading method in which each surface is drawn multiple times, once for each light hitting it, with cumulative results. ▮

Forward shadow mapping

The application of a hazy distortion to an existing shadow map based on information stored in the eye space, thereby creating a softer shadow. ▮

Four-color process

A color method utilizing the subtraction of Cyan, Magenta, Yellow, and Black from a base white color to make additional colors. Also known as **CMYK.** ▮

Fourth wall

The barrier between the real world of the audience and the fictional world of the performers. ◢

FP camera

First-person camera. A camera that provides a view of the scene from the character's perspective. ▟ ▦ ▱

FPP

1. *First Playable Prototype.* The first demo of a game that can be played independent of its developmental tools. ♪

2. *First Playable Prototype.* A stage of development, defined by the investors or publisher, when the current version of the game is considered a rough but accurate example of the envisioned product. ♪

FPS

1. *Frames Per Second.* A standard measurement of how often a scene can be redrawn. A low frames per second rate results in choppy animation. See also **Frame Rate**. ▟ ▦

2. *First-Person Shooter.* A genre of video games in which the player's primary activity is shooting enemies and in which the camera is positioned so that the player sees the events as if looking through the character's eyes. ♪

Fractal structure

A form of narrative, described by Ryan and largely theoretical, in which the story is presented early in the narrative and does not substantially change over time but expands instead. ✦

Frag

Fragment. To kill another player's character, particularly in a first-person shooter. ▱ ♪

Frame animation

An animation method that replaces a model with the next version in a sequence each time a frame is redrawn. ▟

Frame dump

The placement of multiple, usually consecutive, images into one compilation. See also **Dump**. ▦ ▟

Frame rate

How quickly a displayed image can be redrawn. See also **Frames Per Second**. ▟ ▦

Frame rate locking

The automatic altering of the quality of a game's rendering to maintain the frame rate at the threshold level if the frames displayed per second threaten to drop below a selected threshold. ■ ᵇ↑ ♪

Frames Per Second (FPS)

A standard measurement of how often a scene can be redrawn. A low frames per second rate results in choppy animation. See also **Frame Rate**. ᵇ↑ ■

Framing

1. The positioning of the elements in a scene to achieve the greatest aesthetic value when viewed by the audience. See also **Blocking** and **Mise en Scene**. ᵇ↑

2. The use of the same or similar elements at the beginning and end of a scene or story to provide reference, continuity, or perspective. ⚒

Framing narrative

The placing of non-interactive sequences at the beginning and end of a scene or series of scenes within a game to serve as a prologue and epilogue to the story. ⚒ ▣

Free For All (FFA)

A mode of gameplay in which all players are in competition against each other, as opposed to being divided into teams. ▣

Free rider

A player who receives the benefit of another player's strategy without incurring any of its risk. ▣

Free to Play (F2P)

A distribution method in which the player is not charged to gain access to the game. ♪

Freecast

A triggered ability or power that does not consume resources. Also known as **Clearcast**. ▣

Freeform surface

A form created without rigid mathematical relationships. See also **Parametric Surface**. ᵇ↑

Freemium

A game in which the core is free to play, but is designed to strongly encourage the purchase of premium content by withholding significant portions of the game until purchased. ♪

Freerunning

A form of personal movement through an obstacle-filled environment that emphasizes stylized and acrobatic actions such as flipping, somersaulting, and spinning. See also **Parkour**. ▱

Freeware

A freely distributed version of software that often allows the consumer to send in a voluntary contribution if they believe the quality of the program justifies it. ♪

Freeze

1. An error in which the display no longer updates either because the rendering process no longer functions properly or due to the lack of new data being transmitted. Also known as a **Lock Up**. ▪ ♪

2. To no longer allow a set of elements, such as art assets or features, to be altered during the development process. Also known as a **Lock**. ♪ ▮ ♣ ▪ ▱

Frequency of decision

How often a player needs to make an active choice. ▱

Fresnel effect

The principle of physics that the amount of light a surface reflects is based on the observer's viewing angle. ▮

Fringe gamer

A player who is familiar with the game or game genre in question but does not play regularly. ♪ ▱

Front loaded

1. A type of contract in which payment occurs at the beginning of the project. ♪

2. A type of resource that provides its greatest benefit to the player at the start of the game. ▱

Front-loaded development model

A production method in which the investigation into new concepts and technologies are heavily skewed toward the early development phase thereby allowing high-risk options to be explored before preproduction ends. ♪

Front matter

The elements placed at the beginning of a book or report that are ancillary to it, such as a title page or table of contents. ♪

Frustum

A shape that is intersected by two planes, one which forms its proximal boundary and the other which forms its distal boundaries. Often used in reference to the viewing area in a virtual environment where the two planes are the near and far clipping planes. ♪

Frustum culling

The removal of objects or portions of objects from the rendering process that occupy positions outside the viewing frustum. ♪

FTF

Face-to-Face. A mode of play in which the players are in the same location, allowing them to interact in person. ▣

Full Motion Video (FMV)

A live-action or animated prerecorded clip played within a game but through a separate media player. ♪ ♣

Full Motion Video game (FMV)

A genre of video games in which a significant portion of the action is composed of prerecorded video clips. ♪

Fumble

An attack's randomly triggered effect that yields a negative result beyond simply missing the target. ▣

Fun

1. A sense of enjoyment, relaxation, or accomplishment derived from an activity. ▣

2. A nonserious activity that stimulates its participants. ▣

Fun button

An imaginary button used to represent the features of a game that the players will enjoy. ⊞ ♪

Fun factor

The facets of a game that create a sense of enjoyment for the players. ⊞

Function

1. The purpose of an element. ⊞

2. An ability of an element within a game. ⊞

3. An individual section of code designed to do one task, often written in a way so that it can be easily reused either in the same or other projects. ▆

Functional budget

The projection of expenses and resources over a specified period of time for a specific project or task within an organization. ♪

Functional fixedness

The resistance of users to interact with an object or concept in unfamiliar ways. ⊞

Funneling

A narrowing in the environment that restricts the movement and flow of objects through it and is often used to limit the paths available to the player and control the pacing of the action. ⊞

Future compatible

The continual viability of a product after its release, particularly in regard to potential future products. ♪ ⊞

Fuzzy logic

An AI technique that incorporates a variety of values instead of just true and false when evaluating a problem. ▆

Fuzzy milestone

A milestone whose completion criteria are subject to different interpretations. ♪

G0 continuity

The connection of two curves or surfaces in such a way that they meet at a common point or edge without gaps. Also known as **Positional Continuity**. ▮

G1 continuity

The connection of two curves or surfaces in such a way that they share a common direction at the point of connection. Also known as **Tangency Continuity**.

G2 continuity

The connection of two curves or surfaces in such a way that they share a common angle or arc. Also known as **Curvature Continuity**.

Gambit

An action that sacrifices some of a player's immediate strength to provide an advantage to that player's overall position.

Gambling games

A classification of games in which the player risks and may receive real resources, such as money. Games of this type often focus more on luck than skill.

Game

1. A structured play activity in which goals are pursued while following rules.
2. A challenge with nonpermanent consequences.
3. An environment, often a board, in which play occurs.
4. A professional activity based on the challenges derived from a similar play activity.
5. An activity of make-believe.

Game bible

1. A reference document for a game that contains all of the continuity information, including any unpublished information considered canon.
2. The collection of all other documents related to a game combined into one central document.

Game card

A ROM device that houses a distributable copy of a game, most often used for portable console systems.

Game configuration system

The means and methods of control over a game's technical and practical performance that is provided to the user.

Game design

The creation and balance of the concept, theme, rules, and assets of a game. ⌨

Game proposal

1. A detailed submission of a game concept for potential development. ♪

2. The document used to detail a potential game's concept. ♪

Game state

The properties of all elements of a game and the condition those elements are in at any particular time. ⌨

Game theory

1. The study, primarily by mathematicians and economists, of competitive systems such as games to describe and predict dynamic movement within a real-world system. ⌨

2. The descriptions, principles, elements, and goals of game design. ⌨

Game time

Passage of time as it occurs within a game world. ⌨

Game tree

A real or hypothetical graph representing all possible states within a game by means of a branching hierchy. Primarily used in the development of an AI as a means for it to determine the best possible solution. ▧ ⌨

Game view

The portion of a game's state that is viewable to any one player at a specific time. ⌨

Gamemaster

A person charged with running a game and serving as a referee for any disputes. ♪ ⌨

Gameplay

The experiences of the players that result from their participation in a game. ⌨

Gamma

1. The brightness of a pixel after it is affected by the voltage of the device on which it is displayed and is often adjusted to ensure the variations within the image's details are detectable by the human eye. ▌

2. The third phase of software development in which, traditionally, all of the features and assets have been tested and the emphasis is on confirming the fixes. Also known as **Code Release** and **Release Candidate**. ♪

Ganking

The killing of another player's character, usually with some element of surprise. ♪ 🗔

Gantt chart

A chart, named after Gantt, designed to illustrate a project's schedule by using bars to convey the length of time required for each of the project's components. ♪

Garbage in, garbage out

A programming principle in which the quality of the results is directly tied to the quality of the code that generated them. ▨

Garbage matte

A mask, often crudely made, that is used to exclude large sections of an image. ▨

Gate

The direct transportation of a character from one spot in the game world to another. Also known as **Teleport**. 🗔

Gating

Restricting a character's travel within the game world until a certain condition is met. 🗔

Gedanken experiment

Thought experiment (German). An experimentation process in which a theory, particularly one that would be difficult to test physically, is tested mentally. 🗔

Generalization relationship

A class reliance in which one class exists as a subset of the other class. See also **"Is a" Relationship** or **"Is a Kind of" Relationship**. ▨

Generative substrate

The rules and constraints of the game itself that affect the story. Proposed by Lindley as a variant of the traditional narrative's structural substrate. ▨

Genetic programming

A machine learning technique in which the AI attempts to achieve a goal by creating mutations of its algorithm. ▨

Genre

A way of categorizing games by user expectations.

Geometric

Having the characteristics of precisely measured lines and shapes.

Geometry

The polygons that make up a 3D model's physical structure.

Ghost

1. A setting that shows the player a semitransparent image to guide them through a level and which may represent the optimal path, the most recent path taken by the player, an opponent's path, or the currently most successful path taken.

2. The object used to represent a pathing when the ghost setting is on.

3. A feint duplicate image imposed over a rendered or printed image.

Gibs

Giblets. Fragmented body parts that are independent of their model.

Gimbal-lock

The loss in functionality of one of the rotational axes used to manipulate a 3D object.

Glass master

The highly polished glass reproduction made from a gold master and from which all other copies of a CD or DVD are manufactured.

Gloss mapping

A texturing method in which the shininess across a 3D object can be varied by directing specific texels to reflect specular light more strongly than others.

Goal

1. The objective that must be met before the player can progress to the next section of a game.

2. The victory condition of a game.

Goal-Oriented Action Planning (GOAP)

A top-down AI method in which an actor is not given a specific action to reach its goal but rather a series of choices from which it must determine the most efficient strategy.

GOAP

Goal-Oriented Action Planning. A top-down AI method in which an actor is not given a specific action to reach its goal but rather a series of choices from which it must determine the most efficient strategy. ▪

God-game

A genre of video games in which the player assumes an omnipotent perspective and interacts with the environment in a managerial or constructional role. ♪

Gold

1. The master version of a game that is shipped to the manufacturer for reproduction. There generally is more than one gold master made for backup purposes. Also known as a **Gold Master** and a **Master**. ♪

2. The phase of development between when the game has been submitted for duplication and when it arrives at retail locations. Also known as having **Gone Gold**. ♪

3. A type of monetary resource popularly used as a baseline for valuation in RPGs and many other games. ▱

Gold master

The master version of a game that is shipped to the manufacturer for reproduction. There generally is more than one gold master made for backup purposes. Also known as **Gold**. ♪

Golden rule of balance

A tenet stated by Rollings and Morris that, "A player should never be put in an unwinnable situation through no fault of their own." ▱

Gone gold

The phase of development between when the game has been submitted for duplication and when it arrives at retail locations. ♪

Gouraud shading

A lighting technique in which color intensity is based on an estimation of the needs of the entire surface instead of calculated on a polygon-by-polygon basis, allowing the lighting to have a more gradual effect on the model and, as a result, give it a smoother appearance. ▪

GPU

Graphical Processing Unit. A microprocessor dedicated to performing the necessary calculations to aid in efficient image rendering. ▤

Grand coalition

A working together of all otherwise competing players to achieve a common goal. ▣

Grand strategic scale

A high-level, army-by-army scope that simulates not only the militaristic elements within a war but also other elements such as economic, political, and diplomatic systems, particularly used in reference to wargames. See also **Operational Scale, Strategic Scale,** and **Tactical Scale.** ▣

Granularity

The degree to which a system can be broken down into its smallest elements. ▣ ▤

Graphical User Interface (GUI)

An icon-based method for entering information into and displaying information on a system. See also **Command Line Interface.** ▤ ▮ ▣

Graphical Processing Unit (GPU)

A microprocessor dedicated to performing the necessary calculations to aid in efficient image rendering. ▤

Gray market

A semi-legal means of distribution often discouraged by the manufacturer. Commonly seen in regions in which a product has not been authorized for sale. ♪

Green disc

A molded disk that has not yet been stamped. ♪

Green light

The approval of a project for development. ♪

Green screen

A special effects method in which certain elements are filmed against a green background so that they can be composited onto a different background later. See also **Blue Screen** and **Matte.** ▮

Grid

A 2D layout of equally spaced horizontal and vertical lines. ▮ ▤

Griefing

An action or series of actions by a player intended solely to spoil another player's enjoyment of a game. See also **Nuclear**. ▣

Grinding

A strategy of progressing through a game by repetitively performing similar actions after the skills associated with those actions have been mastered thereby making such a means of advancement tedious. See also **Treadmill**. ▣

Group gaming

A genre of games that focuses on local multiplayer interaction. See also **Party Game**. ♪

Guardian

An obstacle designed to test a hero's worth before allowing him to continue his quest, as described by Campbell. In video games this role is usually filled by a mini-boss. ♠ ▣

GUI

Graphic User Interface. An icon-based method for entering information into and displaying information on a system. See also **Command Line Interface**. ▣ ▮ ▣

Gutted

A retail box that has had the product removed for display purposes, with the intent of returning the removed content at the time of purchase. ♪

Hack and slash

A subgenre of RPGs that focuses nearly entirely on fast-paced combat. ♪

Hair light

A light source that hits the back of an object thereby separating it from the background. Also known as a **Backlight**, **Kicker Light**, or **Rim Light**. ▮

Hall of mirrors

A graphical error in which a texture infinitely repeats, usually as a result of an error in the redraw instructions. ♪ ▮

Handicapping system

A reward system that provides a player with increased advantages the worse he or she does in order to balance the game. ▣

Handle

The node attached to an anchor on a Bézier curve that allows adjustments to the line's curvature.

Haptic

A method of providing user feedback through the sense of touch by various means, such as force, vibration, and resistance.

Hard architecture

A project structure that is rigid and difficult to adjust.

Hard cap

A limit that is fixed and cannot be expanded by any means.

Hard copy

A printed version of text or code.

Hard room

A recording studio with a notable amount of echo thereby creating the impression of a larger but empty room.

Hardware

The physical components of a computing system.

Hardware abstraction

The writing of platform-independent code so that it can be ported more easily.

Hardware acceleration

The use of hardware to perform some of the functions of the software in order to speed up performance.

Hardware T & L

Hardware Transform and Lighting. The use of a noncentral processor, such as those found on a video card, to perform the transformation and lighting steps of rendering.

Hardware Transform and Lighting (Hardware T & L)

The use of a noncentral processor, such as those found on a video card, to perform the transformation and lighting steps of rendering.

"Has a" relationship

A class reliance in which one class is made up, in whole or in part, from other classes. See also **Composition Relationship**.

Hate list

A record, based on events during combat, that prioritizes the combatants on which an AI entity will focus. Also known as a **Threat List**.

Hawk dove game

A game in which the players are all at risk of losing but in which the optimal strategy is to endure the risk the longest while still avoiding the critical point of loss. Also known as a **Chicken Game**.

HDR

High Dynamic Range. An imaging technique that provides a greater range of luminescence than normal photography and thereby creates more realistic images.

Header file

A section of code included at the top of its sequence that lists what libraries the program can access.

Heads-Up Display (HUD)

1. *Heads-Up Display.* The tactical overlay in air combat or weapon sim games.

2. *Heads-Up Display.* Any visual user interface.

Heal over time

An effect that restores hit points to a target slowly over a period of time.

Health points

A numerical way of measuring the quantity of a character's health, with zero representing death. Also known as **Hit Points**.

Height map

An image of an object's texture that uses one of its stored values, such as luminescence, to generate the displacement of that object's geometry.

Hero

1. The protagonist of a story or game.

2. A character showing positive moral qualities as determined by his or her culture.

Hero's journey

1. Campbell's analysis of mythology that proposes the existence of central, universal elements in nearly all folklore. It has been adapted at times as a template for story structure. ⚎

2. The narrative adventure of a protagonist as it relates to Campbell's work. ⚎

Heuristic

1. A formulaic guideline used in problem solving. ▦

2. A limiting criteria applied to the search space accessible to the AI so that only the conditions that are likely to yield a positive result are considered. ▦

Hex

A six-sided space or tile most commonly used in tabletop wargames. ▣

Hidden object game

A subgenre of puzzle games that requires locating specific items within a scene. ♪

Hidden story structure

A form of narrative, described by Ryan, in which the story is divided into sections that the player can uncover in any order but which ultimately can be reassembled into a linear storyline. ⚎

Hidden surface removal

Any of the numerous processes used for determining which faces of a 3D object are occluded and therefore do not need to be rendered. Also known as **Visible Surface Determination**. ▮

High availability

The continuous and predictable accessibility of certain functions within a system. ▦

High concept

The embodiment of a project by focusing on its unique premise, often expressed in a concise statement. See also **Theme**. ▣ ⚎

High Dynamic Range (HDR)

An imaging technique that provides a greater range of luminescence than normal photography and thereby creates more realistic images. ▮

High-level software design

The creation of an outline of the components and layers of a software project that occurs early in the development process. Also known as **Software Architecture**. ▰

High-Order Surface (HOS)

The process of storing a model's geometry by defining it as a mathematical expression with a limited number of control points instead of as a large array of vertices. ▮

Highlight

1. The changing of the color and/or brightness of an element to show that it is the current selection. ▮

2. A bright reflection off of a reflective surface. Also known as a **Specular Light**. ▮

3. An area of an image that is brighter than its surrounding areas. ▮

Historical simulation

A subgenre of wargames in which an historical military conflict is presented to the players to be reenacted, though allowing for different actions and results. See also **Military Simulation** or **Wargame**. ♪

Hit

1. A move that results in the collision of two objects with one object inflicting a negative effect on the other. ▣

2. A product that has achieved a high level of a success. ♪

Hit points

A numerical way of measuring the quantity of a character's health, with zero representing death. Also known as **Health Points**. ▣

Hobson's choice

A single option presented to the player whose only decision is to take it or not. ▣

Homebrewed

An independently developed game that lacks the required licensing to be produced and distributed, and therefore not officially recognized by the game's publisher. ♪

Homogeneous clip space

A virtual 2D environment in which a 3D scene is projected in order for the rendering engine to determine what can be culled from the scene without affecting its appearance. Also known as **Clip Space**. ▮

Honor system

1. A system of play that relies on the player obeying rules that are not directly enforced by the game. See also **Play Nice Rules**. ⊞

2. A points system used to reward players for success while participating in an activity of the game, particularly used in reference to *World of Warcraft*. ⊞

3. A system used to gauge the behavior of the player's character, often with repercussions to the character's abilities or the game's story. ⊞

Hook

The unique element of a story or game that captures the audience's imagination and interest. ⚔ ⊞ ♪

Horde mode

A mode of play in which a player must fight off a series of attacks that comes in waves with each wave increasing in difficulty. ⊞

HOS

High-Order Surface. The process of storing a model's geometry by defining it as a mathematical expression with a limited number of control points instead of as a large array of vertices. ▮

Host

A computer that provides client systems with instructions. ▬

Hot seat

A mode of play in which players take turns on the same computer thereby requiring players to switch seats whenever their turn is done. ⊞

Hot spot

1. The centering point of a frame in traditional animation. ▮

2. A location in which a user can connect wirelessly to a network. ♪

3. An area on the screen that is designed to initiate a particular activity when clicked on or moused over. ▬

Hotkey

A keystroke, often designed as an alternative to selecting an icon, that initiates an action or series of actions. ⊞

Hotpatch

An unscheduled release of an update, often due to the urgency of the issue that it is intended to fix. ♪

Housekeeping

The period in gameplay when nonstrategic actions such as shuffling cards, updating scores, etc., are undertaken to clarify the game state and streamline play. ▣ ▪

House rules

1. A variation to the rules upon which a group of players have agreed. ▣

2. A collection of variant rules that a group of players have created for themselves. ▣

Hub and spoke narrative structure

A division of a story into easy-to-navigate modules that radiate out from one central location. See also **Modular Narrative Structure.** ✍

HUD

1. *Heads-Up Display.* The tactical overlay in air combat or weapon sim games. ▣ ▪

2. *Heads-Up Display.* Any visual user interface. ▣ ▪

Hue

The chromatic element of color. ▪

Hull

The shape constructed from a NURBS. ▪

Human motion engine

A middleware program designed to replicate the kinetics of human movement. ▪ ♪

Hybrid game

A game that has elements of more than one genre. ▣

Hyperstory

A narrative created from linking several individual stories or fragments of stories together allowing the audience to move from point to point, and often from character to character, within the narrative. ✍

"I win" button

An imaginary button that represents a feature that, if used, would make winning too trivial. ▣

Icon

A simplified visual representation of another object or action that is used to communicate quickly and efficiently. ✦ ▮

Idle animation

An animation cycle for a character that is played when the character is otherwise motionless. Also known as a **Fidget**. ▮

IK

Inverse Kinematics. An animation technique in which the peripheral elements of an object are moved and the core body adjusts accordingly. See also **Forward Kinematics**. ▮

Ilinx

Games of sensory alteration. In Caillois' list of four types of play, the examples given relate to those with physiological elements, such as vertigo. ▣

Image Quality (IQ)

1. The measurable, technical quality of an illustration or picture. ▮
2. The overall aesthetics of a scene. ▮

Immersive gameplay

1. Gameplay that is so engaging the player's awareness of her or his physical environment is diminished. ▣ ♪
2. A particularly engrossing section of a game. ▣ ♪

Imperfect information

Knowledge about the game state that has been hidden from some or all of the players. See also **Perfect Information**. ▣

Implementation requirements

The standards and policies used during software coding. ▰ ♪

Implementation risk

The inherent risk to investors that a product cannot feasibly be manufactured. ♪

Implicit animation

A classification of 3D animation in which the movements themselves are stored in memory and applied to a model when needed. See also **Explicit Animation**.

Implied contract

A statement that constitutes an agreement, even in the absence of a signed contract.

Implied line

A suggested, nonphysical connection between two points, such as the angle between a character's eyes and the object she or he is looking at.

Implied rules

Salen and Zimmerman's description of rules that are not expressly listed and therefore rely on the players' interpretation.

In-house

A department within a company whose duties might otherwise be handled by a third party.

Inbetweens (Tweens)

Animation frames created to smooth the transition between keyframes.

Inciting incident

The event that puts a story into motion.

Incremental accretive design

A design practice, described by Crawford, of taking an existing design and producing a new product by adding or improving one or more features.

Independent contractor

A contributor to a project that provides a service without entering into an employee-employer relationship with the contractee.

Individual objectives

Assigned win conditions that vary for each player.

Infinite loop

A logic error that results in the same section of code repeating continually and therefore never reaching a normal conclusion.

Inflection

The point at which a curve changes from concave to convex or vice versa.

Information hiding

The principle that a system should be broken down into individual modules with very limited accessibility so that they are protected from unwanted manipulation while still being conducive to design changes. ■

Information reduction

The process of separating out the essential information from a larger collection of information.

Information transmission

The means by which data or other forms of information are communicated. ■

Infotainment

A product created to provide information while entertaining. ♪

Ingredient

An object in the game that can be combined with other objects to permanently craft a separate object. See also **Recipe**.

Inheritance

The assigning of a relationship between two classes or objects in which one of them passes some or all of its attributes and behaviors to the other. See also **Parent** and **Child**. ■

Initial concept

The first stage of the design process in which core ideas about the game are explored.

Inset map

A small version of the play field that shows the immediate area, the orientation of the player's avatar, and its current position. Also known as a **Mini-Map** or **Strategic Map**.

Install base

The number of units of a product that are currently in use by consumers. ♪

Installer

An independent program, sometimes created by a third party, that automates the installation of the software on an end user's system. ♪ ■

Instance

1. An object that is modeled after a base class object but exists independently of it. ▰ ▨

2. A specific version of a location created for and available to a small number of players in an MMO, allowing them to interact with that environment without interference from other players. Once created, the instance lasts for only a limited time before being removed from the game, though additional instances of that location can be created as needed. ▨

Insurmountable obstacle

A challenge that the player may encounter without having the means to overcome it, thereby bringing play to a halt. ▨

Integration testing

An evaluation of code and its performance once the individual modules have been combined. ▰

Intellectual Property (IP)

The exclusive ownership of the nonphysical elements of a creation such as its concept, expression, design, and representation. ♪

Intensity

1. How strongly a game element affects the game state. ▨

2. The emotional impact of a visual or auditory element. ▜▮

3. The brightness of a color. ▜▮

4. The strength of a sound. ♣

5. The strength of a light. ▜▮

Interactive cut-scene

A scripted cinematic event, separate from standard gameplay, that allows the player to continue to interact with the environment or characters. See also **Quick Time Event**. ▜▮ ▨ ⚒

Interactive music

A sound track methodology in which the background music changes depending on the activity currently occurring within the game. Also known as **Adaptive Music** and **Dynamic Sound**. ♣

Interactive plot

A plot that is alterable by the player's actions within a game. Also known as a **Dynamic Plot**. ✟

Interactive prototype

A version of a game, often quickly and crudely made, that allows a team to experiment in a test bed environment. ♪ ▣ ▨

Interface

An abstracted control scheme that simplifies and regulates how two elements interact with each other. ▨ ▣

Interface requirements

The listing of APIs and protocols that will be used by a game. ▣ ♪

Interlaced scan

A method of displaying an image on a monitor by drawing alternating lines in two separate passes. See also **Progressive Scan**. ▮ ♪

Internship

A training position, often for college or university students, in which the employee can receive practical experience in exchange for working at a reduced rate of pay. ♪

Interpolation

The use of sampling data at specific points to predict the existence and value of uncalculated or uncollected data. ▣ ▮

Interrupt

1. An ability, power, skill, or attack that prevents an opponent from concluding an action they started. ▨

2. The disruption of an action while it is being performed. ▨

Intransitive interrelationship

A comparative value system in which the superiority of one element over another does not confer superiority or inferiority between any other set of elements. In rock-paper-scissors, for example, a rock's superiority over scissors does not confer rock's superiority over paper, even though scissors is superior to paper. Superiority and inferiority do not follow a linear hierarchy but instead are set irrespective of the relationship those other elements have with each other. ▨

Inventory

1. The collection, storage, and arrangement of items a character possesses. ▱

2. The stock of product on hand. ♪

Inverse Kinematics (IK)

An animation technique in which the peripheral elements of an object are moved and the core body adjusts accordingly. See also **Forward Kinematics**. ▮

IP

Intellectual Property. The exclusive ownership of the nonphysical elements of a creation, such as its concept, expression, design, and representation. ♪

IQ

1. *Image Quality.* The measurable, technical quality of an illustration or picture. ▮

2. *Image Quality.* The overall aesthetics of a scene. ▮

"Is a kind of" relationship

A class reliance in which one class exists as a subset of the other class. See also **Generalization Relationship**. ▰

"Is a" relationship

A class reliance that states one class is also a member of another class. See also **Generalization Relationship**. ▰

ISDB

Integrated Services Digital Broadcast. The standards set for digital televisions in Japan and South America. ♪

Isolation

A principle that data should only be accessible when there are no modifications from other functions pending. ▰

Isoline

A curve in which the location of its points, when expressed as numerical coordinates, share a common value. ▮

Isometric view

An illustration of a 3D object showing its height, length, and depth but without utilizing the natural distortion caused by perspective. ▮

Isoparm

Isoparametric curve. A curve that is imbedded into a NURBS's surface. ⚲▮

Item decay

The gradual deterioration of an asset's benefits that can occur over time or as a result of being used. ▣

Item level

A value assigned to an item that limits its use or effective use to only characters of that level or higher. ▣

Item mall

A location in a game in which the player may purchase upgrades by means of micro transactions. ♪ ▣

Iteration

1. The act of repeating a function or process. ▰
2. The repetition in an algorithm with the result of one calculation being used as the input for the next pass. ▰
3. A version of the product created from an iterative process, often expressed numerically. ♪

Iterative depth

A timed AI search method in which the search depth increases with each pass as long as time remains. ▰

Iterative design

A design process that features repetitive redesigning, retesting, and reevaluation of the product with the aim of incrementally improving it with each cycle. ▣ ♪

Jaggies

The appearance of stair-step artifacts in a curved or diagonal line, often due to poor resolution or aliasing. ⚲▮

Jailbreaking

The unauthorized removal of restrictions on a technological product, such as a mobile phone or console. See also **Chipped**. ♪ ▰

Job requirements

A listing of tasks and skills necessary to perform adequately in a certain position. ♪

Judder

A stutter in a video image, often caused by the conversion process. 📷

Juggle

The use of a combination of attacks that, once started, does not give an opponent an opportunity to counter. 🎮

Kamikaze

A high-risk, high-reward strategy of sending units into combat from which they have little chance of surviving, with the expectation that they will do significant damage before being defeated. 🎮

Kernel

The core component of an operating system. 💻

Key

1. An item that a character must possess to advance to another location in the game. 🎮

2. An entry in Window's registry of settings and options. 💻

3. An alphanumeric sequence included with authentic copies of the software that allows it to be installed or accessed. Also known as a **CD Key** or **Key Code**. ♪

4. An element that a character must possess to unlock a puzzle. 🎮

5. To place a desired pose or other element at a specific point during an animation's timeline. 📷

Key code

An alphanumeric sequence included with authentic copies of the software that allows it to be installed or accessed. Also known as a **CD Key** or **Key**. ♪

Key light

The principal light source affecting an object that has been placed so that the light hits the front of an object. 📷

Key promise

An essential element of a product that is guaranteed to the consumer. ♪

Keyframe animation

An animation method in which specific poses are established first and the intervening poses are generated later to smooth out the transition between those specific poses. 📷

Keygen

Key Generator. A program that attempts to generate the security code needed to install or gain access to a program. ♪

Keying

1. The act of coordinating a pose within an animation's timeline. 🖍

2. The removal of select colors to make individual elements appear seamless within a composite. Also known as **Chromo Keying** or **Color Keying**. 🖍

Keylogging

The use of a device or software to record the activity of a user, often for the purpose of obtaining private information, such as logins and passwords. ♪

Kick

1. An attack made via the legs. 🎮

2. To forcibly remove an individual from a group or party. 🎮

3. To forcibly remove a player from the game. 🎮

Kicker light

A light source that hits the back of an object thereby separating it from the background. Also known as a **Backlight**, **Hair Light**, or **Rim Light**. 🖍

Kill fee

A negotiated payment that becomes due if the project is cancelled by the contracting party before work is finished. ♪

Kill on Sight (KOS)

A designation that a certain character should be immediately attacked if seen. 🎮

Kill Stealing (KS)

The act of finishing off an opponent that has already been heavily damaged by another player with the intent of gaining credit for the kill. 🎮

Killer app

Software that is so in demand that it alone guarantees the commercial success of the platform for which it was designed. ♪

Killing blow

An attack that brings a target to its defeated state. Some games give bonuses to the player who is credited with the killing blow. 🖳

Kinetics

The mechanics of movement of a mass by a force. Also known as **Dynamics**. 🖊️🖳

King of the hill

A mode of play that requires a player or team of players to remain within a specific location for a certain amount of time while the opponents try to take that position from them. 🖳

Kingmaker

1. A mechanic that allows one player to award another player the win. 🖳
2. A player whose actions intentionally allow another player to win. 🖳

KISS

Keep It Simple, Stupid. A design principle that the most effective designs are the ones easiest to understand and implement. 🖳🖳

Kiting

A strategy in which a player avoids direct combat from a pursuing opponent by intermittently dealing damage while retreating. See also **Aggro** and **Leashing**. 🖳

Knots

Points that divide a spline into sections. 🖊️

Knowledge

The space, as defined by C-K theory, in which proposals are evaluated based on known truths. 🖳

KOS

Kill On Sight. A designation that a certain character should be immediately attacked if seen. 🖳

Kriegsspiel

Wargame (German). Any one of several early 19th-century military simulations that used miniatures and which is the forerunner to today's strategy games. Initially created by Georg von Resiswitz to train Prussian officers. See also **Wargame**.♪

KS

Kill Stealing. The act of finishing off an opponent that has already been heavily damaged by another player with the intent of gaining credit for the kill. ▣

Lag

1. A delay in transferring information through a network. Also known as **Latency**. ▄

2. Any slowdown in performance by the hardware. ♪

Laser Beam Recorder (LBR)

The machine that burns the gold master's data onto the glass master in preparation for mass reproduction. ♪

Laser game

A classification of video games based on their use of laser disks as a medium and that often combine animated sprites over a pre-recorded video background. ♪

Latency

A delay in transferring data through a network. Also known as **Lag**. ▄ ▣

Lathe

The creation of a surface by rotating a NURBS around a fixed axis. ▮

Lattice

A container that, when manipulated, applies similar manipulations to any object placed inside it. ▮

Launch

1. The initial distribution process of a product. ♪
2. The release of a product to consumers. ♪

Launch title

Software released at the same time as the platform it was designed for. ♪

Layer

An overlay that allows additions or adjustments to an image. ▮

LBE

Location-Based Entertainment. A form of computer-generated media that is intended to be viewed at a certain geographical location, such as an amusement park. ♪

LBR

Laser Beam Recorder. The machine that burns the gold master's data onto the glass master in preparation for mass reproduction. ♪

LD

Link Dead. The state of a player who has lost connection to a game but whose avatar remains in the game world. ♪

Lead

An employee tasked with the management of a team. ♪

Lead architect

A person tasked with breaking down the game's technical requirements into programming elements. ♪

Lead time

The amount of time needed by the publisher in order for a print run to be completed by its due date. ♪

Learning curve

1. The time and effort it takes a player before she or he is proficient at playing a game. ▣

2. The time and effort it takes a team member to achieve a level in which they can contribute at the required level. ♪

Leashing

1. Triggering an AI entity to follow one player while another player attacks it. See also **Aggro** and **Kiting**. ▣

2. The returning of an AI entity to its spawn point after it has been lead away. ▣

Leaver

A player with a reputation of quitting games before they are finished. ♪ ▣

Leeching

A strategy of gaining rewards shared by a group while not assuming the risks that the other members within the group do. ▣

Lens flare

The internal reflection of light off the physical lens of a camera as recorded by the camera. ▮

Letter of Intent (LOI)

A brief description of a potential agreement that a party has interest in pursuing. ♪

Letterbox

A mask with heavy black borders placed around an image to maintain a certain aspect ratio while still filling the display area. 🖳

Level

1. An environment in a game world that a player is expected to successfully navigate through in order to progress in the game. 🎮

2. An overall challenge that a player is expected to successfully solve to progress to the next challenge. 🎮

3. A ranking of how far a character has progressed, often tied to an increase in abilities and attributes. 🎮

4. A position along a hierarchy that indicates a strength relative to all other positions and which can often be improved upon. 🎮

Level cap

A limit on how far the player can advance in terms of experience throughout the game. See also **Cap**. 🎮

Level design

A combination of environment, NPCs, props, lighting, and other assets in a cohesive way to provide context and create challenges within a game. 🎮 🖳

Level editor

Software used to create new versions of the game-world's environment or its subsections. ♪ 🖳

Level of Detail (LOD)

1. How detailed a model is compared to other versions of itself. 🖳

2. A technique of creating several different versions of a model, each with different levels of detail, and swapping the models in and out based on the distance the camera is from the model. This allows the game engine to render only the details the player is likely to be able to notice at any given distance. 🖳

Library

1. A collection of generated assets within a studio. ♪

2. A collection of widely distributed and standardized functions and other programming-related modules so that they do not have to be created from scratch. ▓

License

The permission granted to one party allowing them the use of another party's property. ♪ ⁿ▮ ♣ ✄

Licensee

The party that has been granted permission to use another party's property. ♪ ⁿ▮ ♣ ✄

Licensing

The legal temporary acquisition of an intellectual property by a second party to include it in their own work or product. ♪

Licensor

The party that grants permission to another allowing the use of their property. ♪ ⁿ▮ ♣ ✄

Lieutenant

A unique AI opponent that is designed to be more challenging than typical enemies but not as difficult as a boss. Also known as a **Mini-boss**. ▤

Light space

A 3D environment in which object locations are given in relation to the light source. ⁿ▮

Light spill

The overflow of light beyond the surface area it is designed to illuminate. ⁿ▮

Light trespass

The existence of light on a surface it is not intended to hit. ⁿ▮

Limb slicing

The ability to have a game object's peripheral elements, such as arms or tentacles, separated from its core in real time. ⁿ▮ ▤

Limited-decision animated stories

A subgenre of animated video games in which the gameplay is briefly paused to allow the player to make a selection from a limited list of options and, once the choice is made, the game plays out the consequences of that choice, allowing further input only when another decision is needed. ♪

Line

1. A section of dialogue to be spoken by an actor. ⚔ ⛫

2. A unit of written instructions within the code. ▣

3. The placement of units in a military simulation so that their control of an area is contiguous. ▣

4. A design element that consists of a mark used to separate space and create form. ▚

5. A collection of similar products often tied together by a common branding or IP. ♪

Line of Sight (LOS)

1. A defined field of vision extending outward from a character to determine which objects are obstructed from its view. ▣

2. The unobstructed view of a target. ▣

Linear

1. Progression that occurs in only one direction. ⚔ ▣

2. A calculation whose results can be plotted as a straight line. ▚ ▣

Linear design

A philosophy of game creation in which the focus is on limiting the players' options during gameplay to only efficient strategies thereby reducing the difficulty of the game particularly for new players. See also **Modular Design**. ▣

Linear level design

A level design method in which the player is expected to progress through the map in a predetermined order. ▣

Linear texture filter

A technique for smoothing the transition between pixels in which a texture is scaled by averaging the values of the texels surrounding the sample point. ▚

Link Dead (LD)

The state of a player who has lost connection to an online game but whose avatar remains in the game world. ♪ ▣

Link editor

A compiling tool that combines multiple related files. Also known as a **Linker**. ▨

Linker

A compiling tool that combines multiple related files. Also known as a **Link Editor**. ▨

List box

A user interface element that contains a listing of predefined options arranged in a defined area. ▨

Load screen

An image, usually full-screen size, that is displayed while the hardware loads a portion of a game. Also known as a **Loading Screen**. ▨ ▮

Load time

The amount of time it takes the hardware to transition from one section of a game to another. ▨ ♪

Loader

An operating system component that reads the content of a launched program into memory so that it will run. ▨

Loading bar

A bar, usually animated, used to show that the loading process is under way. ▨ ▮

Loading screen

An image, usually full-screen size, that is displayed while the hardware loads a portion of a game. Also known as a **Load Screen**. ▨ ▮

Lobby

A virtual room in which users can join and talk with each other. Multiplayer games often require all players to join the same lobby before their game can begin. ♪ ▨

Localization

The process of preparing a product for introduction into a foreign market, including any needed translations and ensuring adherence to local law, ratings, and cultural standards. ♪ ✐ ♟

Location-Based Entertainment (LBE)

A form of computer-generated media that is intended to be viewed at a certain geographical location, such as an amusement park. ♪

Lock

1. A type of puzzle that needs a specific item, often referred to as a key, to complete. ▣

2. A state in the game in which there are no longer any valid strategies for a player to improve her or his position. Also known as a **Deadlock**. ▣

3. To no longer allow a set of elements, such as assets or features, to be altered during a project's development. Also known as **Freeze**. ♪ ⫶ ▲ ■ ▣

Lock-on victory

A point in a game when a winning outcome is inevitable. ▣

Lock up

An error in which the display no longer updates either because the rendering process no longer functions properly or due to the lack of new data being transmitted. Also known as a **Freeze**. ■ ♪ ⫶

LOD

1. *Level of Detail*. How detailed a model is compared to other versions of itself. ⫶

2. *Level of Detail*. A technique of creating several different versions of a model, each with different levels of detail, and swapping the models in and out based on the distance the camera is from the model. This allows the game engine to render only the details the player is likely to be able to notice at any given distance. ⫶

Loft

The creation of a surface between two or more NURBSs from the shapes of those NURBSs. See also **Skinning**. ⫶

Log

A file that records a chronology of events. ■

Logic error

An unintended consequence in a software program that results from it having followed instructions that are inconsistent with the user's desired outcome. ■

Logline

A one-sentence description of a project that is used to generate interest in it. ⬯ ▣

Logo

A symbol used to represent a company or brand. ⫶

LOI

Letter of Intent. A brief description of a potential agreement that a party has interest in pursuing. ♪

Loose coupling

A programming technique of using an indirect reference between classes by means of an interface. ■

Loot

Reward objects in a game that are usually transferable from character to character. ▣

LOS

1. *Line of Sight.* A defined field of vision extending outward from a character in order to determine which objects are obstructed from its view. ▣

2. *Line of Sight.* The unobstructed view of a target. ▣

Lose condition

A game state in which the player reaching it is removed from the game. Also known as a **Loss Condition**. ▣

Loss condition

A game state in which the player reaching it is removed from the game. Also known as a **Lose Condition**. ▣

Loss leader

A product that sells for a loss but is intended to encourage further purchases that eventually will make up for that loss. ♪

Lossless

A compression method that retains all data thereby maintaining quality. See also **Lossy**. ⬆ ■

Lossy

A compression method that discards data to conserve space and which thereby results in a loss of quality. See also **Lossless**. ⬆ ■

Lotcheck

Nintendo's list of technical guidelines for third-party publications on their console. ♪

Lottery-based decision making

A strategy in which choices are made fairly but with no weight given to the more logical or reasonable options, such as drawing straws to see who gets into a lifeboat, for example. 🎲

Low budget

A project in which little resources have been allocated for its completion. ♪

Ludology

The study of games, including their history, sociological impact, and design theories. 🎲

Ludus

1. *To play* (Latin). Relating to games, fun, play, school, or sports. 🎲

2. *To play* (Latin). On Caillois' scale, games with an affinity for a formal rule structure. 🎲

MacGuffin

An object that is central to a story only because of the importance placed on it by characters in the story. Also known as a **McGuffin**. ✒

Magnetism

A UI feature in which specific attempted actions are automatically attracted to a certain object or type of object thereby requiring less precision by a player to associate the two. Mouse click magnetism, for example, requires less precision by the user when clicking on an object. 🎲 ▪

Main

The most common or preferred character that a player plays as during a game. ♪ 🎲

Main menu

The screen in which players can make their initial choice to play the game or exit. 🎲

Maintainability

The ease at which code can be modified. ▪

Man-hours

A budgetary element that accounts for the total number of hours worked by all employees and can be altered by either changing the number of hours each employee works or the total number of employees. ♪

Manual

A printed or electronic document for the player that includes instructions for playing the game and occasional flavor and background information. ♪ ✍

Manufacturer testing

The testing of software by the manufacturer of the console the game was designed for to ensure it meets their standards. ♪

Manufacturer's Suggested Retail Price (MSRP)

The market price that the manufacturer states its product can be sold for under current market conditions. Also known as the **Suggested Retail Price**. ♪

Map

1. An in-game visual representation of the environment the character travels through. ▣ ▮

2. The materials or textures to be applied to a model. ▮

3. The placement of materials or textures onto a model. ▮

4. To create a relationship between a hardware user interface element, such as a button, and the action executed in-game, such as a jump. ▰

5. A level, particularly one that is capable of being loaded independently of other levels. ▣

6. A representation of the playing surface or environment a game takes place in and often used to simplify level editing. ▣ ▮

Marginal superiority

A minor advantage that one unit has over another. ▣

Market research

An evaluation of potential consumers and competitors within the current environment, particularly in regard to supply and demand. ♪

Market risk

The inherent risk that a product will not sell sufficiently. ♪

Market share

1. The percentage of intended consumers who have purchased the product. ♪

2. The percentage of units sold that are manufactured by the company versus the total amount of units sold by all companies. ♪

Marketing Development Funds (MDF)

Money set aside for promoting and advertising a product. ♪

Mask

An overlay used to protect portions of an image while other sections are being altered. ▚

Massively Multiplayer Online (MMO)

A classification of online games that allows for large numbers of players, usually in the hundreds or thousands, to be online in the same game world at the same time. ♪

Massively Multiplayer Online Role-Playing Game (MMORPG)

A subgenre of RPG games in which a large number of players interact while developing their characters in a persistent or semi-persistent world. ♪

Massively Multiplayer Online Social Game (MMOSG)

A genre of video games that supports a large number of players but does not require a large time commitment in each play session. Also known as a **Casual Multiplayer Online Game**. ♪

Master

An original or first-generation copy of digital media from which all other copies are made. There are often several identical copies designated as masters for backup and security purposes. See also **Gold.** ♪

Master use license

Permission to reproduce a recording given by the rights holder. ♣

Master verification

The process of examining and evaluating the quality of a proposed disk for use as an original master from which to make copies. ♪

Matchmaking

A process by which a multiplayer game assigns players as either team members or combatants. ♪ ▣

Material system

1. The process for organizing, ordering, and combining, textures. ▚

2. A data storage structure that contains not only the mapping information about a texture but the physical properties as well, providing the game engine with the ability to assign those properties to any object using that texture. ▚ ♪

MATs

Milestone Acceptance Tests. The criteria used to determine if a submission fulfills the requirements of a milestone. ♪

Matte

An area of an image that has been masked out in order for another image to be inserted in its place. See also **Blue Screen** and **Green Screen**. ▓▌

MAU

Monthly Active Users. The number of unique end users that accesses a site or application within 30 continuous days, particularly in reference to social media. ♪

Maxed out

A player character that has advanced all skills and attributes to their maximum level thereby preventing them from increasing any further. ▣

Mayamatic

A traditional animatic combined with imported 3D models. ▓▌

McGuffin

An object that is central to a story only because of the importance placed on it by characters in the story. Also known as a **MacGuffin**. ✉

MDA

Mechanics, Dynamics, and Aesthetics. A game design framework developed by Hunicke, LeBlanc, and Zubek that focuses on the design counterparts to the distinct components of a game: rules, systems, and fun. ▣

MDF

Marketing Development Funds. Money set aside for promoting and advertising a product. ♪

Meaningless decision

A choice offered to a player in which none of the outcomes have an effect or all outcomes have the same effect. ▣

Measurement achievements

A reward given to the player acknowledging the degree of success (i.e., performance level) he or she has had in completing a task. See also **Completion Achievements**. ▣

Mechanics

1. Rules or interactions of a game that stimulate further gameplay. ▨

2. One of the three principle components of the MDA framework proposed by Hunicke, LeBlanc, and Zubek. In this framework, mechanics are the allowable actions of the players and exert their affect on the dynamics of the game. See also **MDA**. ▨

Mediator pattern

A software design pattern that simplifies the communication process and increases code reusability by having the communication between objects handled by an intermediary object. ▪

Meier's maxim

A rule which dictates that a game should be composed of "a series of interesting choices." Based on Meier's definition of games. ▨

Melee

Combat between units or characters that takes place while they are adjacent to each other. Also known as **Close Combat**. ▨

Memory card

A slot-based storage device popular on consoles. ♪ ▪

Memory consumption

The accumulation of stored data that, if unchecked, could overrun a system's resources. ▪

Memory leak

The failure of a program to release data from memory when no longer needed eventually leading to total memory consumption. ▪

Menu

A user-interface option that allows a user to select from several predefined options that may or may not display further options. ▨ ▪

Menu bar

A user-interface element that contains a list of options consolidated into a row or column. ▨ ▪

Menu system

The collection of elements that allows a user to navigate through a software's various options. 🖳 ▣

Merge

To join two elements together. 🖌

Mesh

1. A group of polygons connected by their shared vertices in order to represent an object. 🖌

2. A method of visualizing solid 3D objects in a see-through manner by using lines and perspective to illustrate the size and shape of the object. Also known as a **Wireframe**. 🖌

Metagame

1. The basic mechanics and dynamics of a game when all aesthetics are stripped. 🖳

2. The currently best-suited strategies and play styles for a game, particularly for one that changes over time, such as an MMO or CCG. 🖳

Metagaming

An approach to gaming that focuses on the system in its abstract form rather than through the intended emersion. 🖳

Metal family

The master collection of the metal father, mother, and sons for a product. ♪

Metal father

The metal surface removed from the glass master after it has undergone electroplating during the manufacturing process for CDs and DVDs. It is designated as a master image and one or more mother images are then created from this surface. ♪

Metal mother

A reverse image made from the metal father from which metal sons can be made. ♪

Metal son

An identical image of the father, from which all copies of a disk are stamped out. See also **Stamper**. ♪

Metallization

The placement of an aluminum layer onto a CD or DVD during its manufacturing in order for the laser to be reflected. ♪

Method level testing

An examination of the functionality of a subroutine by testing it in isolation from other subroutines. ■

Micro transactions

A payment method in which a player can choose to pay a small fee to access certain elements of a game. ♪

Micromanagement

A focus on small, commonplace decisions by someone better suited to be making more large-scale decisions. ▣ ♪

Middleware

Software created by a third party that aids in game development. ♪

Milestone

An agreed upon-criteria that marks a point in a game's development process. In contracts, milestone completions often determine when payments are made. ♪

Milestone Acceptance Tests (MATs)

The criteria used to determine if a submission fulfills the requirements of a milestone. ♪

Military simulation

A subgenre of strategy games in which historical or potential military conflicts are presented in a way that encourages the use of realistic military strategies and tactics that correlate closely to those used in militaristic encounters. Also known as a **Wargame**. ♪

Mimicry

Games of make-believe. Listed by Caillois as one of his four types of play. ▣

Min-maxing

A strategy, often used in character creation, in which a player places the maximum amount of resources into one attribute or other game element, leaving all others at their minimum. ▣

Mind mapping

A method of classification used in brainstorming sessions that allows a free-form association of objects without prioritizing. 🖻 ✍

Mini

Miniature. A detailed game piece that represents a character or unit in a tabletop strategy game, often crafted to scale. 🖻

Mini-boss

A unique AI opponent that is designed to be more challenging than typical enemies but not as difficult as a boss. Also known as a **Lieutenant**. 🖻

Mini-map

A small version of the play field that shows the immediate area, the orientation of the player's avatar, and its current position. Also known as an **Inset Map** or a **Strategic Map**. 🖻 🔺

Miniature (Mini)

A detailed game piece that represents a character or unit in a tabletop strategy game, often crafted to scale. 🖻

Miniature game

A tabletop game in which the physical representations of units are small-scale models and their placement and orientation on the play area is important to the mechanics of the game. ♪

Minimax

1. A strategy in which a player maximizes his or her potential reward in a zero-sum game by minimizing the potential reward granted by an opponent's strategy. Also known as **Minmax**. 🖻

2. An AI algorithm that uses the minimax strategy. Also known as **Minmax**. ▪

Minimax matrix

A grid that demonstrates the cost-to-benefit ratio of various options. ♪ 🖻 ▪

Minion

A low-level AI entity that is often designed to assist either the player or a higher-level AI entity. See also **Creep**. 🖻

Minmax

1. A strategy in which a player maximizes his or her potential reward in a zero sum game by minimizing the potential reward granted by an opponent's strategy. Also known as **Minimax**.

2. An AI algorithm that uses the minimax strategy. Also known as **Minimax**.

MIP mapping

Multum In Parvo mapping. "*Many in a small place*" (Latin). A technique in which multiple versions of a texture, each of a different size, are stored in a map to reduce the time it takes to rescale a texture.

Mirror match

A challenge, often limited to combat games, in which a player must compete against an AI that has identical skills.

Mise en scene

Placing on stage (French). The entirety of the arrangement and composition of a presented scene. See also **Blocking** and **Framing**.

Mission

An objective or series of objectives, usually military in nature, that must be completed to progress through the game.

Mission statement

A declaration of an organization's intention and standards with a focus on its current state.

MIT approach

A design approach, described by Gabriel, that ranks correctness, consistency, and completeness higher than simplicity. Also known as **The Right Thing**.

Mixed strategy

A strategy formed from the alteration of a pure strategy or the combination of several pure strategies used to confuse or mislead an opponent.

MMO

Massively Multiplayer Online. A classification of online games that allows for large numbers of players, usually in the hundreds or thousands, to be online in the same game world at the same time.

MMORPG

Massively Multiplayer Online Role-Playing Game. A subgenre of RPG games in which a large number of players interact while developing their characters in a persistent or semipersistent world. ♪

MMOSG

Massively Multiplayer Online Social Game. A genre of video games that supports a large number of players but does not require a large time commitment in each play session. Also known as a **Casual Multiplayer Online Game**. ♪

Mo-cap

Motion capture. The process of recording the real-life movements of the parts of an actor's body within its 3D space and converting them so that they can be used as a template for an animated sequence within a virtual environment. Also known as **Capture**. 👆 ♪

MOB

Mobile Object. A generic, artificial opponent, often in reference to an MMORPG. ▣

MOBA

Multiplayer Online Battle Arena. A video game genre that combines elements of real-time strategy with PVP team battles. ♪

Mobile games

A classification of games played on portable, traditionally nongaming devices, such as cell phones. ♪

Mock-up

A version of an asset or product made to demonstrate what the final version will look like. 👆 ♪ ▣

Mod

1. *Modification.* An alteration, usually unofficial and unsupported, made to a game that changes it from its original design. ♪ ▣

2. *Modification.* An alteration to a gaming system that allows it to play unauthorized copies of a game or to be used in a way not supported by the manufacturer. See also **Chipped**. ♪

3. *Moderator.* A person tasked with supervising discussions in a forum, organizing the threads, and ensuring the posts meet the standards of the site. Often expected to respond to common questions posted by forum visitors. ♪

Modchip

Modification chip. An electronic circuit added to a gaming system to bypass or alter the limitations and restrictions of the system. See also **Chipped**. ♪

Mode

A setting that determines the manner in which a game will be played. ♪ ▣

Model

A computer-generated 3D graphical representation of an object or entity crafted for a game or film. ▌

Model sheet

1. The illustration of a character or object from different orthographic views, designed so that the modeler can use it as a reference within a 3D modeling program. ▌

2. The illustration of a character in different stances crafted to convey to the animators the character's range of poses, gestures, and facial expressions. ▌

Modeler

A person tasked with creating the 3D objects for a game. ♪ ▌

Moderator (Mod)

A person tasked with supervising discussions in a forum, organizing the threads, and ensuring the posts meet the standards of the site. Often expected to respond to common questions posted by forum visitors. ♪

Modification (Mod)

1. An alteration, usually unofficial and unsupported, made to a game that changes it from its original design. ♪ ▣

2. An alteration to a gaming system that allows it to play unauthorized copies of a game or to be used in a way not supported by the manufacturer. See also **Chipped**. ♪

Modifier

An instruction or operator that alters the value of a variable. ▟

Modular design

A philosophy of game creation in which the focus is on expanding the players' options during gameplay to allow for dynamic strategies which can vary greatly from game session to game session. See also **Linear Design**. ▣

Modular narrative structure

The division of a story into separate, self-contained sections, each of which is only accessible when the preceding module has been completed. Also known as **Dynamic Labyrinth Narrative Structure** and **Modulated Narrative Structure**. ✗

Modularity

How easily a system can be dissected and recombined thereby allowing parts of it to be modified without having to address the whole system. ▦ ▣

Modulated narrative structure

The division of a story into separate, self-contained sections, each of which is only accessible when the preceding module has been completed. Also known as **Dynamic Labyrinth Narrative Structure** and **Modular Narrative Structure**. ✗

Module documentation

A notation that summarizes a section of code so that its purpose can easily be identified. ▦

Mograph

1. *Motion graphics*. Illustrations, shapes, and text that appear to move or change while being displayed or broadcast. ▮

2. *Motion graphics*. A field of graphic design concerned with the creation of motion graphics. ▮

Moiré pattern

The strobe effect created by changing the viewing angle of repeating unaligned patterns that overlap one another. ▮

Monaural (Mono)

An audio signal that travels only through one channel. See also **Stereo**. ♣

Mono

Monaural. An audio signal that travels only through one channel. See also **Stereo**. ♣

Montage

A series of clips assembled in a way that compresses the chronology of the events shown into a short sequence. ✗ ▮

Monthly Active Users (MAU)

The number of unique end users that accesses a site or application within 30 continuous days, particularly in reference to social media. ♪ ▣

Mood

The emotional tone of a scene. 🖋 ♣ 🖌

Moral

The ethical point or message of a story. See also **Theme**. 🖋

Moral decision

A choice presented to the player that requires him or her to make an ethical evaluation of the situation. 🖋 🎲

Morphing

The gradual altering of one image into a second image. 🖌

Morton's Fork

A choice between two negative outcomes. Also known as a **Dilemma**. 🎲

Motif

An element, often symbolic, that reoccurs within a story. 🖋

Motion blur

The visual distortion in an image caused by its movement. 🖌

Motion capture (mo-cap)

The process of recording the real-life movements of the parts of an actor's body within its 3D space and converting them so that they can be used as a template for an animated sequence within a virtual environment. Also known as **Capture**. 🖌 ♪

Motion graphics (mograph)

1. Illustrations, shapes, and text that appear to move or change while being displayed or broadcast. 🖌
2. A field of graphic design concerned with the creation of motion graphics. 🖌

Move

The specific action a player performs during her or his turn. Also known as a **Play**. 🎲

Movement

A design element that infers an object's speed and direction of travel within a stationary scene. 🖌

MSRP

Manufacturer's Suggested Retail Price. The market price that the manufacturer states its product can be sold for under current market conditions. Also known as **SRP.** ♪

MUD

Multiple-User Dungeon. A text-based game world that simultaneously accommodates multiple players. ♪

Multiple-User Domain. A text-based virtual world that simultaneously accommodates multiple users who gather together for a specific purpose. ♪

Multiboxing

The playing of a video game on multiple systems at the same time by a player. ♪ ▣

Multipass

A process in which the scene is composited by means of multiple renderings. ▒❚

Multiplayer

1. A mode of gameplay that allows more than one player to compete at the same time in either a cooperative or competitive style. ▣

2. A classification of video games in which the chief mode of play is either cooperative or competitive with other human players. ♪

Multiplayer Online Battle Arena (MOBA)

A genre of video games that combines elements of real-time strategy with PVP team battles. ♪

Multiple-User Domain (MUD)

A text-based virtual world that simultaneously accommodates multiple users who gather together for a specific purpose. ♪

Multiple-User Dungeon (MUD)

A text-based game world that simultaneously accommodates multiple players. ♪

Multiplicity

An attribute in UML that determines how many objects from one class can be owned by an object from another class. ▪

Multisampling

A variation of supersampling in which only some components in the scene, such as polygon edges, are rendered using the supersampling technique. See also **Supersampling.** ▒❚

Multitexturing

The simultaneous use of more than one texture on a polygon.

Murder sim

Games that involve the violent killing of human or human-like characters; used derogatorily.

Musical sting

A short, musical phrase used to emphasize a mood or tension at a certain point in a scene.

N-gon

A polygon that has more than four sides thereby preventing it from being reliably rendered within a game engine.

N-patching

A technique for rendering high-quality curved surfaces from a low-poly model by using information stored in the polygons' normal and tessellation data.

NAB

Not a Bug. A designation that a reported issue is working as intended.

Naked edge

An edge of a poly or surface that does not join with the edge of another poly or surface.

Naked mage syndrome

A strategy in which a character carries none of her or his primary equipment into battle to prevent the loss of or damage to that equipment.

Naming convention

A specific policy on the identity given to files so that indexing remains consistent.

Naming policy

The standards, often employed in MMOs, that dictate what names are acceptable for players to assign to their characters and provides guidelines as to what is considered objectionable.

Narrative

The events of a story, the effect they have on the characters, and the order in which they occur.

Narrative design

A design approach that emphasizes storytelling and its cohesiveness with the other elements of game design. ▣ ✦

Narrative immersion

The capture of the player's focus by the game's use of compelling story and character developments, as described by Adams. Also known as **Emotional Immersion**. ▣

Narrative layer

The audiovisual elements that convey the story to the audience. ✦

Nash equilibrium

The concept in game theory, proposed by Nash, that a state can be reached in which there is no benefit to any player in altering his or her strategy based on the awareness that the other players would receive no benefit in altering their strategies. ▣

Natural language interface

An interface that allows users to communicate with a system in a manner similar to how they normally would with other people. ▣

Natural mapping

Arranging interfaces and controls in an intuitive manner. ▣

Navigability

The allowed direction of flow through a modeled system. ▪

NDA

Non-Disclosure Agreement. A legal contract designed to prevent public disclosure of a company's methods, practices, and projects. ♪

Near dominant strategy

A strategy that, while not always successful, has the greatest chance for success and therefore is the most logical strategy to employ. ▣

Near plane

A division of the 3D environment that determines the nearest distance from the camera in which objects will begin to be rendered. See also **Clipping Plane, Draw Distance,** and **Far Plane.** ▪

Nearest neighbor method

A texture filtering technique in which the color value assigned to new pixels that are created when scaling are based on the pixels nearest them, thereby resulting in extremely efficient computation but also introducing aliasing errors. Also known as **Point Sampling**. 🕯

Need before greed

A principle that loot should go to players based on how useful it is to them instead of based on how badly they want it. 🎲

Negative feedback loop

A control mechanism that grants a beneficial or punitive effect that serves to preserve the status quo, such as granting an AI opponent greater speed during a race while it is behind. See also **Positive Feedback Loop** and **Rubber Banding**. 🎲

Negative space

The empty area around an object in an image. 🕯

Negative testing

A QA philosophy in which the focus is on evaluating the software's ability to perform correctly when encountering unexpected situations. Also known as **Testing to Fail**. ♪

Negotiable consequence

A negative outcome that a participant of an activity can change or avoid either by mutual agreement or by declining involvement. Sometimes listed as a requirement in order for an activity to meet the definition of a game. 🎲

Nerf

A decrease in power to an existing character, item, skill, or ability due to an alteration in the mechanics of the game. ♪ 🎲

Network

1. An interconnected group of computers. ▓
2. The connecting of computer systems to each other for the purpose of sharing or transmitting information. ▓

Network Operating Center (NOC)

The location from which a network is controlled. ▓ ♪

Neural network

An AI system made up of separate units that collectively function to recognize data patterns and adapt to them. ▓

New game plus

A mode in which the game starts from the beginning but the character has all of the items and advancements from an earlier finished playthrough. 🄳 ♪

New Jersey style

A design approach, described by Gabriel, that ranks simplicity higher than correctness, consistency, and completeness. Also known as **Worse is Better**. 🖳 ♪

New Product Development (NPD)

The means and methods by which newly created goods are brought to market for the first time. ♪

Newbie

A player that lacks experience; often used derogatorily. Also known as a **Noob**. ♪

Next gen

The name given to the current generation of consoles, which are often considered the seventh generation. Includes the X-Box 360, PS3, and Wii. ♪ 🖳

Ninja looting

The rapid collecting of loot by a player before other players realize it is available. 🄳

NOC

Network Operating Center. The location from which a network is controlled. 🖳 ♪

Nodal narrative structure

The division of a story into paths that the player can follow from point to point and which may create multiple variations or endings to the storyline. �

Nodal pathing

A pathfinding system in which specific waypoints have been included throughout the level for the AI to follow. 🖳

Node

A point of intersection on a graph or structure. 🖳 ♈ 🄳

Node tree

An advancement structure for the capabilities that a character or player can earn in which progression is in one direction but often branches. Furthermore, before players can choose a particular advancement, they must have access to any underlying nodes. Also known as a **Skill Tree** or **Tech Tree**. 🄳

Node web

An advancement structure for the capabilities that a character or player can earn in which progression can come from several different directions. Furthermore, before players can choose a particular advancement, they must have access to any or all of the connecting nodes. Also known as a **Skill Web** or **Tech Web**. 🖱

Non-compete agreement

A contractual agreement that a party will not engage in a venture that is similar to the business ventures of the other party. ♪

Non-credible threat

A strategy that relies on an opponent reacting to an action made by a player who cannot actually afford to take advantage of it. See also **Bluff**. 🖱

Non-Disclosure Agreement (NDA)

A legal contract designed to prevent public disclosure of a company's methods, practices, and projects. ♪

Non-parametric decision

A choice in which the chance of success must be calculated by evaluating the potential of unknown and inconsistent factors. See also **Parametric Decision.** 🖱

Non-Player Character (NPC)

1. Any character in the game that is not controlled by a player. 🖱 🖉
2. An AI character that has noncombat interaction with a player. 🖱 🖉
3. A virtual entity that performs an action within a game. Also known as an **Actor.** ■ 🖱

Non-Uniform Rational B-Spline (NURBS)

A precisely defined surface that is used as a basic unit for NURBS modeling and, when combined with other NURBSs, gives them their 3D appearance. 🖋

Nonlinear

1. A type of level design in which a player is allowed to choose from multiple pathways to progress through a map. 🖱
2. A type of story progression in which the events do not occur in chronological order. 🖉
3. A classification of video games in which there is more than one way for the player to progress through its events. 🖱

Noob

A player that lacks experience; often used derogatorily. Also known as a **Newbie**. ♪

Normal

1. The direction in which the front side of a polygon faces. 🔧

2. An indicator that displays which direction the front side of a 3D model's polygons are facing. 🔧

Normal mapping

A technique for creating the illusion of depth within a texture by storing information in an RGB-formatted version of the map that can be used to alter the way light reacts to it. 🔧

Normalization

1. The adjustment of a sound's volume so that it is consistent with other sounds used in the game. ♣

2. The categorization and organization of data in a manner that makes data storage and retrieval more efficient. ▪

Normalized device space

A 2D environment in which object locations are given in relation to a window on the display. 🔧

Note

1. Feedback, verbal or written, given by someone in authority, primarily relating to the creative process. ♪

2. A sound used in music that has a specific pitch. ♣

Notional camera

A virtual or theoretical camera, particularly one used to view a scene within a virtual environment. 🔧

NPC

1. *Non-Player Character.* Any character in the game that is not controlled by a player. ▣ ✎

2. *Non-Player Character.* An AI character that has noncombat interaction with a player. ▣ ✎

3. *Non-Player Character.* A virtual entity that performs an action within a game. Also known as an **Actor**. ▪ ▨

NPD

New Product Development. The means and methods by which newly created goods are brought to market for the first time. ♪

NTSC

National Television System Committee. The standards set for analog video signals in North America, Japan, South Korea, and others. Among other things it determines the display ratio of a television. ♪

Nuclear

A retaliatory strategy that has little chance of improving a player's position and is instead employed to reduce another player's chances as well. See also **Griefing** and **Poison Pill**. ▨

Number crunching

1. The process of evaluating a proposal by making a mathematical comparison between it and an alternative. ♪

2. A code sequence that performs complex mathematical calculations. ▪

3. A player's skill at handling mathematical calculations to determine the effectiveness of a potential strategy. ▨

Numerical reasoning

The ability of a player to perform mathematical functions. ▨

NURBS

Non-Uniform Rational B-Spline. A precisely defined surface that is used as a basic unit for NURBS modeling and, when combined with other NURBSs, gives objects their 3D appearance. ▸

NURBS modeling

Non-Uniform Rational B-Spline modeling. A modeling method that allows the creation of highly detailed shapes and precise curves with little stored data but, due to slow rendering times, is not preferred when real-time rendering is needed. See also **Polygonal Modeling**. ▸

Object

1. A visual asset. ▸

2. The object-oriented method of programming. See also **Object Oriented**. ▪

3. Any virtual entity created by code. ▪

Object code

The compiled instructions that constitute a computer program and which is made from the source code. ▪

Object diagram

An illustration used in UML that focuses on a particular set of instanced objects, their attributes, and their correlation to each other. ▪

Object level testing

An examination of an object's functionality by testing how it interacts with different sections of code. ▪

Object manager

A programmed subsystem that allows the manipulation of multiple objects through one centralized section of code. ▪

Object oriented

A programming method that focuses on creating the individual ingredients of a program as modular components, each containing their own data sets and functions, which can be independently manipulated and controlled. ▪

Object-oriented narrative structure

The embedding of a game's story elements into blocks from which a plot can be constructed. ▪

Object space

A 3D environment in which an object's location is given in relation to itself. ▪

Object tracking

The ability of the AI to maintain an awareness of an object's location. ▪

Objective

1. A task whose completion is required for a player to progress through a game. ▪

2. A win condition. ▪

Obstacle

1. Anything that impedes a player's progress. ▪

2. A challenge the hero must overcome thereby revealing his or her character. ▪

Obstacle avoidance

A pathfinding technique in which the AI is told to circumvent any barriers between it and its target. ■

Obvious decision

A choice presented to a player in which only one option is advantageous to him or her. ▣

Occluder

An object within a virtual environment that prevents the player from seeing another section of the environment. ▣

Occlusion

1. The visual blocking of one surface by another. ▮

2. The blocking of light from reaching an object thereby creating a shadow. ▮

3. The complete blocking of sound by an object in its path. ▲

Occlusion culling

A rendering technique in which polygons that are blocked by another surface are not drawn. See also **Hidden Surface Removal**. ▮

OEM

Original Equipment Manufacturer. A type of product that is sold or otherwise released to another company to be rebranded and bundled with one of their products. Primarily used within the video game industry, as its definition and usage varies greatly in other industries. ♪

Offer

A proposal that outlines the contractual terms of an agreement. ♪

Offset mapping

A mapping technique that creates a greater sense of depth within the texture by altering the texture based on the angle at which it is viewed. Also known as **Parallax Mapping** and **Virtual Displacement Mapping**. ▮

Ogee

A shape created from the joining of a convex and a concave curve thereby resulting in a shape similar to an elongated "s." ▮

OGSS

Ordered Grid Super Sampling. A supersampling method in which the samples are taken from aligned areas. See also **Supersampling**. ⬛

On rails

Progression in a game that is so linear that the player feels a loss of meaningful control over the events of the game. ⬛ ⬛

On rails shooter

A subgenre of shooters in which the player follows a predefined path from which he or she is unable to veer. Also known as a **Rail Shooter**. ♪

On the nose

Dialogue with little to no subtext thereby resulting in it having an unnatural feel. ⬛

One off

A production run, usually for evaluation or approval purposes, in which only one copy is made. ⬛ ⬛ ♪

OOC

1. *Out of Character.* A designation that the player is speaking as the player and not as the character. ♪

2. *Out of Character.* A channel designated for chat that is unrelated to the game's events. ♪

Opacity

An attribute of an object that determines how much light passes through it. ⬛

Open

The state of an issue that has not yet been resolved. ♪

Open architecture

A platform in which modifications to the hardware are allowed without requiring approval by the platform's manufacturer. See also **Closed Architecture**. ⬛ ♪

Open beta

A stage in the development process, usually of a massively multiplayer game, when the general public as a whole is invited to play in order to test the game. See also **Closed Beta**. ♪

Open/closed

A programming principle that code should be open to expansion but closed to modification. ▰

Open narrative structure

The absence of any true structural division of the narrative, so that the character can encounter (or avoid) fragments of the story in any order. ✊

Open source

Software whose code has been made available to the end user by its rights holder, though it may have restrictions on its commercial use. ♪

Open world

A nonlinear form of progression in which the player has access to most of the gameworld's environments at all times. ▣

Operant conditioning

The psychological concept, introduced by Skinner, that willingness by an entity, such as a player, to perform an action is based on its evaluation of the likelihood of receiving a reward or avoiding a punishment. ▣

Operation

A function that an object of a class can perform. ▰

Operational rules

Salen's and Zimmerman's description of rules that provides instruction to the player on how to interact with the game thereby effectively distinguishing it from other games with similar constitutive rules. ▣

Operational scale

A militaristic, mid-level, company-by-company scope that simulates a specific series of battles or conflicts within a war, particularly used in reference to wargames. See also **Grand Strategic Scale, Strategic Scale,** and **Tactical Scale.** ▣

Operator

A symbol used to signify a mathematical process, such as addition or multiplication. ▰

Optical markers

Any surface-mounted device used in motion capture that provides a means for the camera to visually locate the position of the object it is tracking. ▮

Optimal strategy

The strategy that yields the best possible outcome. ▣

Option

1. A choice the player can make during gameplay. ▣

2. A contractually available offer that one party can elect to accept at a time later than that of the originating contract. ♪

Order of execution

1. The sequence in which a program executes its instructions. ▪

2. The rules that dictate the sequence in which the player can perform his or her actions. Also known as **Play Sequence, Sequence of Play, Turn Order,** or **Turn Sequence.** ▣

Ordered Grid Super Sampling (OGSS)

A supersampling method in which the samples are taken from aligned areas. ▮

Ordering

The process of arranging items in a sequence. ▪ ▣

Organic

Having the characteristics of something that is or was alive. ▮

Original Equipment Manufacturer (OEM)

A marketing practice in which a product is sold to another company so that it can be bundled with one of their products. ♪

Original music

Musical content produced expressly for the game. ♣

Originating document

A central marketing document that lists all key information regarding a product. ♪

Orthographic

A planar view of an object showing only one of its sides. ▮

OTB

Over the Board. A mode of play in which players sit opposite each other with the playing surface between them. See also **Face-to-Face.** ▣

OTS camera

Over-the-Shoulder Camera. A viewpoint established behind a character that frames his or her upper body and which follows him or her around. 🎥

Out of Character (OOC)

1. A designation that the player is speaking as the player and not as the character. 🎵

2. A channel designated for chat that is unrelated to the game's events. 🎵

Outsourcing

The subcontracting of part or all of a project to a third party. 🎵

Over the Board (OTB)

A mode of play in which the players sit opposite each other with the playing surface between them. 🎲

Over-the-Shoulder camera (OTS camera)

A viewpoint established behind a character that frames his or her upper body and which follows him or her around. 🎥

Overbuilding

A design principle of exceeding standards so that additional and unexpected additions can be made in the future without affecting the base design. 🎲

Overdraw

The rendering of an occluded surface. 🎥

Overengineered

The refinement and/or expansion of an idea or product to the point that its primary functionality is diminished. 🎲

Overhead

1. The amount of resources consumed by an essential process. ▪️

2. The amount of resources consumed by all processes. ▪️

3. The inherent cost of running a project disregarding any variables that directly contribute to profits. 🎵

Overscan

The area of a video image beyond what is ultimately intended to be seen by the viewer. 🎥

Ovoid

Egg shaped; an oval with one side made of a sharper curve than the other.

"Owns a" relationship

A class reliance in which an object is created from several different classes. Also known as an **Aggregation Relationship**.

P & L statement

Profit and Loss statement. A financial disclosure that summarizes a company's expenses, costs, and earnings.

Pacing

1. The change in tension as it occurs throughout a story.
2. The change in difficulty as it occurs throughout a game.

Package diagram

A collection of class diagrams used in UML that are designed to provide a simplified view of the larger, more detailed collection of class diagrams that have been assembled.

Packaging

The materials used to protect and promote a product while being shipped and displayed.

Packet

A small collection of data bound together and sent from one system on a network to another.

Packet loss

The dropping and subsequent loss of a section of data while being transferred through a network.

Page file

A portion of the hard drive reserved for temporary data storage.

Page flipping

An animation method that stores two or more consecutive versions of a scene in memory so that the scene can be quickly updated.

Paidea

"*Child education*" (Greek). On Caillois' scale, games with an affinity for free-formed, loosely codified play. ⊞

Painter's algorithm

A method of 3D graphics rendering in which objects are drawn in an order of farthest to nearest, with any obstructing objects being rendered directly over any objects they block from view. ▘ ▦

Pair programming

The partnering of programmers during the writing or rewriting of code. ▦ ♪

PAL

Phase Alternating Line. The standard set for analog video signals in Europe, Australia, the Middle East, and others. Among other things it determines the display ratio of a television monitor. ♪

Palette swap

A rendering technique in which the range of colors an object is assigned is replaced en masse so that the object's coloring dramatically changes and makes the object appear substantially different. ▘

Pan European Game Information (PEGI)

The organization that provides content and suggested age ratings for video games released in Europe. See also **CERO** and **ESRB**. ♪

Paper doll

A 2D representation of a player's character often used by inventory systems to show where items are equipped. ▘ ⊞

Paper launch

A limited release of a product to a select group, such as a media outlet or testing facility, often to garner positive reviews that are then used for marketing. ♪

Parallax mapping

A mapping technique that creates a greater sense of depth within the texture by altering the texture based on the angle at which it is viewed. Also known as **Offset Mapping** and **Virtual Displacement Mapping**. ▘

Parallax scrolling

A method of using multiple layers of 2D artwork and scrolling them across the screen at different speeds to create a sense of depth. ⁛▮

Parallel narrative structure

The separation of a story into several coexisting threads, any one of which the protagonist may choose to divert to or from. ⚒

Parallel projection

A method of displaying objects inside clip space so that the objects maintain their size regardless of distance. ⁛▮

Parallel streaming

The diverting of a transmitting process into multiple paths in which each process is handled independently by the system's resources before being merged together again, thereby allowing quicker processing of the application's instructions. ▦

Paralysis by analysis

1. The inability to move past the analysis stage due to a fear of misinterpreting the data, thereby resulting in a lack of decisions being made. ♪ ▣

2. A reduction in a player's ability to choose an action because of an overload of options and data to sift through. ▣

Parametric decision

A choice in which the chance of success can be calculated using only known and consistent factors. See also **Non-Parametric Decision.** ▣

Parametric surface

A form created using precise mathematical relationships. See also **Freeform Surface.** ⁛▮

Parent

1. An object that passes some or all of its behaviors and attributes to a subordinate object. See also **Child.** ▦

2. A joint or bone in an animated skeletal system that influences the movements of a subordinate bone. See also **Child.** ⁛▮

3. A node that controls at least one subordinate node. See also **Child.** ▦ ⁛▮

Pareto principle

A mathematical generalization, named after Pareto and publicized by Juran, that 80% of benefits come from just 20% of the resources. Also known as the **80/20 Rule**. ♪

Parkour (PK)

A form of personal movement through an obstacle-filled environment that emphasizes speedy and efficient actions such as leaping through, swinging between, and scaling over the obstacles. See also **Freerunning**. ▣

Parlor games

A classification of games popular in the 1800s that focused on group play in an indoor setting. ♪

Parse

The process of subdividing and analyzing text to categorize its purpose so that the data can be used properly. ▮

Particles

The visual representation of dynamic and fluid elements that often dissipate over time, such as rain, smoke, glitter, and sparks. ▮

Party

1. A group of player characters, controlled individually or as a group, that have joined together to accomplish tasks within a game world, most often used in reference to RPGs. ▣ ♪

2. A person, company, or other entity that is part of an agreement or potential agreement. ♪

Party game

A classification of games that are intended to be played between a large number of players at the same physical location and which often emphasizes social interaction over competitiveness. See also **Group Gaming**. ♪

Pass

1. Any one of a series of progressive steps within the rendering process that applies its effect to the scene being rendered. ▮

2. To move values from one section of code to another. ▮

3. The approval of a submission. See also **Fail**. ♪

4. A build. ▮

5. A cycle spent on reworking a section or item. ♪

6. A player action in which the player elects to skip a turn or a section of a turn. ⌨

Passive ability

A power that does not need to be triggered by the player. ⌨

Passive optical marker

A reflective surface that is mounted on an object so that a camera can track its movements when filming. ▚▌

Patch

1. A post-release section of code distributed to fix known issues with a game. ♪ ▧

2. A four-sided geometrical section created by the intersection of splines during NURBS modeling. ▚▌

Patch modeling

A NURBS-based modeling method of creating a mesh by making a series of intersecting splines. ▚▌

Patent

Exclusive ownership and usage rights granted to the inventor of a product for a limited period of time. ♪

Pathfinding

The plotting of a route through an environment by the AI. Also known as **Pathing**. ▧ ⌨

Pathing

The plotting of a route through an environment by the AI. Also known as **Pathfinding.** ▧ ⌨

Patrol

1. An individual or group of AI entities that travel a predetermined path within a game world. ⌨ ▧

2. The movement of an individual or group of characters through the environment in an organized, often cyclical, manner to serve as a deterrent or to expose threats. ⌨

Pattern recognition

The ability to spot and evaluate reoccurring events and use that knowledge to make predictions. ▱

PBEM

Play by Email. A mode of play in which players send their actions or a saved file containing their moves to each other through electronic correspondences. ▱

PBW

Play by Web. A mode of play in which players submit their actions on an online forum or Internet-connected utility program. ▱

PC

1. *Personal Computer.* Any computer designed for individual use in primarily a desktop environment. ▰ ♪

2. *Personal Computer.* A computer designed for individual use based on a variation of the standards for the IBM PC as opposed to other systems, such as the Apple Macintosh. ▰ ♪

3. *Player Character.* The character a player controls during gameplay. ▱

Peeling

An enemy's change of focus from one character to another as a result of the second character's intervention. ▱

Peer-to-peer

A networking method that allows two systems to communicate without a designated server. ▰ ♪

PEGI

Pan European Game Information. The organization that provides content and suggested age ratings for video games released in Europe. See also **CERO** and **ESRB**. ♪

Penumbra

The light, outer part of a shadow. ▮

Perceived value

The worth that an individual assigns a product based on the level of satisfaction they receive from it. ♪

Percentage closer filtering shadow mapping

The application of a hazy distortion to an existing shadow map based on information stored in the light space thereby creating a softer shadow. 🖉

Perfect information

Complete knowledge of the current state of a game that is available to all players. See also **Imperfect Information**. 🖳

Performance analyzer

Software used to evaluate how much of a processor's resources are spent on executing a specific section of code. Also known as a **Profiler**. 🖳

Performance capture

Highly detailed recordings of the movements that make up an actor's facial expressions to reproduce them digitally. See also **Facial Capture**. 🖉

Performance level

The actions and reactions of the characters to the events within a story. Also known as the **Actants Layer**. ✒

Performance requirements

The technical specifications that the software or hardware is required to meet. ♪ 🖳

Performance review

An administrative evaluation of a team member's contribution to the organization, often used as a guide to increasing compensation. ♪

Permadeath

A lose condition in which a player's current avatar is considered dead and cannot be brought back. See also **Dead** and **Respawn**. 🖳

Persistent world

A changing world environment, almost exclusively online, in which time passes or appears to have passed regardless of whether the player is in the game or not, thereby allowing changes to the game world even while the player is away. 🖳

Personification

The giving of human attributes to a nonhuman entity. ✒

Perspective

1. The depiction of depth in a 2D environment by having objects converge toward a common point as they become more distant. 🖊

2. The view from which the player sees the game world. See also **Point of View**. 🖻

3. The view from which an author tells a story. 🖋

Perspective correction

The stretching of an image's corner or corners so that they correctly match the viewing angle. 🖊

Perspective projection

A method of displaying objects inside clip space so that the objects appear smaller the farther away they are. 🖊

PERT analysis formula

Project Evaluation and Review Technique analysis formula. A formula that predicts the amount of time needed to finish a project based on weighted values for the best-, worst-, and most-likely case scenarios. Defined as Time = (Optimistic + Pessimistic + (4xExpected))/6. ♪

PERT chart

Project Evaluation and Review Technique chart. A diagram that represents the dependency of tasks within a project with a focus on events rather than durations. See also **Critical Path Methodology**. ♪

Pet

An AI character that serves as a companion to the player's avatar. 🖻

Phishing

The practice of creating official-looking electronic communications, such as emails and websites, for the purpose of gaining private information from an unsuspecting user. ♪

Phong

A shader that uses a pixel-based interpolation to achieve more realistic specular lighting. 🖊

Physics Processing Unit (PPU)

A microprocessor dedicated to performing the necessary calculations to aid in the efficient implementation of dynamic forces that occur within the game world. ▨

Pickup Group (PuG)

A team of players that has been formed randomly. ♪ ▣

Pickup session

An additional recording session scheduled to add last-minute changes to the voice-over work. ♣

Pillar

The key concept a game is based on and which all other features are designed around. ▣

Pipeline

1. A process of passing instructions through hardware in a particular order so that the results of one pass serve as the input for another, with multiple instructions often handled in parallel between multiple parts of the CPU in order to improve performance. ▤

2. The flow of work between teams and individuals. ♪

3. The order in which rendering in the game environment occurs. ▮

Piracy

The illegal duplication and distribution of someone else's work. ♪

Pitch

1. A presentation designed to garner interest in a project. ♪

2. The perceived frequency of a sound. ♣

Pixel

Picture Element. The smallest unit of a digital raster image, and composed of a single color, and when combined with others gives an image its appearance. ▮

Pixel fog

A fog effect created on a per-pixel basis thereby giving it better image quality at the cost of processing speed. ▮

Pixel popping

The sudden appearance of a texel as the camera moves closer to it. ▮

Pixel shading

The application of lighting effects to each individual pixel on the lit surface. ▮

Pixelation

An undesirable effect in which the pixels of a rendered object have been enlarged allowing the single-colored squares that made up the original pixels to become easily visible and resulting in a loss of image quality. 🔹

PK

1. *Player Killing.* The act of intentionally killing another player's character solely for the enjoyment of doing so even when it provides no actual advantage in a game. See also **Griefing**. 🎲

2. *Player Killer.* A person who engages in player killing. 🎲

3. *Parkour.* A form of personal movement through an obstacle-filled environment that emphasizes speedy and efficient actions such as leaping through, swinging between, and scaling over the obstacles. See also **Freerunning**. 🎲

Place of performance

A contractually agreed-upon location or locations where the work will be performed. Particularly of interest in regard to work that might be subcontracted. 🎵

Placeholder

An object in a prerelease version of a game intended to represent an asset that has not yet been implemented. 🎵 🔹 👥 🎲

Planned obsolescence

A design approach that intentionally limits the useful life of a product so that future versions or products can be marketed without the older version competing against them. 🎵 🎲

Plant

The placement of an object in a scene so that its later use will seem natural to the audience. ✎

Platform

The hardware system a game is designed to be played on. 🎵 ▪

Platform transition

The phase in the life cycle of a newly introduced console between when it is announced and when it is released that affects the marketability of the current console and related products. 🎵

Platformer

A genre of video games that involves getting from one point in the game world to another by jumping from ledge to ledge. ♪

Play

1. The activity of make-believe. ▣

2. To participate in a game. ▣

3. To engage in a recreational activity. ▣

4. To voluntary take on a challenge for entertainment. ▣

5. The specific action a player performs during her or his turn. Also known as a **Move.** ▣

Play by Email (PBEM)

A mode of play in which players send their actions or a saved file containing their moves to each other through electronic correspondences. ▣

Play by Web (PBW)

A mode of play in which players submit their actions on an online forum or internet-connected utility program. ▣

Play-life

The lifespan of a game expressed by how long a player will actively continue to play it. ♪ ▣

Play nice rules

Rules of social conduct for players while in a game that are enforced by means other than the game's mechanics. See also **Honor System.** ♪ ▣

Play sequence

The rules that dictate the sequence in which the player can perform his or her actions. Also known as **Order of Execution, Sequence of Play, Turn Order,** or **Turn Sequence.** ▣

Play session

1. The investment of time a player makes in one sitting. ▣

2. The minimum amount of time a player must invest at each sitting to make progress in a game. ▣

Play testing

An evaluation of the game from the point of view of the player. ♪

Play-through

An evaluation made by playing the game from start to finish to determine if it can be completed and if it functions at its most basic level. ♪

Play time

The total amount of real time a player has spent within a game. ▣ ♪

Player

1. A person who voluntarily engages in a game's activity. ▣

2. A competitor within the game, who may be an actual person or an artificial opponent. ▣

Player acknowledgement

Recognition by the game environment that the player has performed an action, as described by Birdwell. ▣ ▪

Player advocacy

The support and defense of a player's interests and points of view during a game's development. ♪ ▣

Player Character (PC)

The character a player controls during gameplay. ▣

Player input module

The section of code that reads the selections made by a player via keyboard or other controller. ▪

Player intentionality

A game's capability to allow players to formulate and carry out their own strategy. ▣

Player interaction pattern

How players act upon and react to each other and to the game environment. ♪ ▣

Player Killing (PK)

The act of intentionally killing another player's character solely for the enjoyment of doing so even when it provides no actual advantage. See also **Griefing**. ▣

Player procedures

Activities that a real or AI player can initiate or resolve. ▣

Player restriction module

The section of code that deals with the available actions and collision detection for the player's object. ▦

Player update module

The section of code that adjusts the current state of a player's object to account for any interactions with the game environment or opponents. ▦

Player versus Environment (PvE)

A classification of multiplayer gameplay in which players compete against the artificial elements of a game world instead of each other. ▣

Player versus Player (PvP)

A classification of multiplayer gameplay that allows players to directly compete against each other. ▣

Playtester

A tester whose primary means of evaluation is through interaction with the game. ♪

Plot

The series of events within a game or story that have a direct impact on the course the game or story takes. ⚖

Plot coupon

1. One item in a set of items that needs to be collected to trigger a story's climax. ⚖

2. One task in a series of tasks that needs to be completed to trigger a story's climax. ⚖

Ply

1. A single turn taken by one player during a turn-based game. ▣

2. The depth, in terms of the number of turns, through which a potential move is evaluated. ▦

POGE

Principle of Good Enough. A design principle that the primary goal is to get a quick and testable system in place and then allow more extensive design requirements to evolve. ♪ ▦

Point light

A light source that emits in all direction with its strength at its center. 🖊

Point of no return

The point at which a hero can no longer afford to abandon their adventure. ✍

Point of Purchase (POP)

The location where a consumer can acquire the product. ♪

Point of View (POV)

1. The camera's placement within a scene. 🖵 🖊

2. The perspective, usually belonging to one of the characters, from which a scene or story is viewed. See also **Perspective**. ✍

Point release

A software update often issued to the public on a regular or semi-regular basis and noted by incrementally adjusting the decimal number of the software's version. ▣ ♪

Point sampling

A technique of texture filtering in which the color value assigned to the new pixels that are created when scaling are based on the pixels nearest them, thereby resulting in extremely efficient computation but introducing aliasing errors. Also known as the **Nearest Neighbor Method**. 🖊

Poison pill

A strategy, often used as a deterrent, in which a player intentionally weakens a resource they control in order to make it a less desirable target to an opponent. See also **Nuclear**. 🖵

Polish

The application of minor adjustments to a product that is functionally solid. ♪ 🖵

Poly

Polygon. A multiedged surface that is used as a basic unit for polygonal modeling and, when combined with other polygons, gives a model its 3D appearance. 🖊

Polycurve

A line composed of multiple curves joined together. 🖊

Polygon (Poly)

A multiedged surface that is used as a basic unit for polygonal modeling and, when combined with other polygons, gives a model its 3D appearance. 📍▮

Polygonal modeling

A modeling method in which multiedged surfaces are compiled together into a mesh that allows for fast real-time rendering but lacks smooth curves and requires a large amount of data to create highly detailed geometry. See also **NURBS Modeling**. 📍▮

Polyhedral

The characteristic of having multiple sides to create a shape. 📍▮

Polymorphism

The technique of making objects of different types respond to the same triggering method. ▦

Polyphony

A characteristic of a sound channel that describes how many notes it can carry at one time. ♣

Polysurface

An object composed of multiple surfaces joined together. 📍▮

POP (*Pee-oh-pee*)

Point of Purchase. The location where a consumer can acquire the product. ♪

Pop-up

A window that appears in order to provide updated information or a prompt for the player. ▣ ◀ 📍▮

Populate

The placement of instances of an object into the game environment. ▦ ▣

Port

1. The process of converting the code and assets designed for one platform over to another platform. Also known as **Conversion**. ♪ ▦ 📍▮

2. *Teleport.* The direct transportation of a character from one spot in the game world to another. Also known as **Gate**. ▣

3. A hardware component designed to allow other devices to plug into the system. ♪

Portability

The ease at which code can be transferred from platform to platform. ▧

Portal

An opening in a virtual environment that exposes another section of the environment to the player. See also **Occluder**. ▣

Portfolio

1. A collection of representative work of an individual. ▎ ♪ ✍

2. A bound physical collection of an individual's work often submitted during the employment interview process. ▎ ♪ ✍

Positional continuity

The connection of two curves or surfaces so that they meet at a common point or edge without gaps. Also known as **G0 Continuity**. ▎

Positive feedback loop

A control mechanism that grants a beneficial or punitive effect that also reinforces itself, thereby resulting in an amplification of that effect over time. Providing a player with more advantages the better he or she does is an example of a positive feedback loop. See also **Negative Feedback Loop**. ▣

Positive sum game

A win-win game in which all players can exit with gains. See also **Variable Sum Game** and **Zero Sum Game**. ▣

Positive testing

A QA philosophy in which the focus is on evaluating the software's ability to perform correctly when encountering anticipated situations. Also known as **Testing to Pass**. ♪

Post

1. The placement of a message in a forum. ♪

2. The period after the main activity of a project or segment of a project has finished and the results are evaluated and adjusted as needed. Also known as **Post-production**. ♪

Postmortem

The practice of reviewing the successes and failures of a project after its completion with a focus on finding ways to improve the process. ♪

Post-production

1. The period in a design cycle after the product has shipped. ♪

2. The period after the main activity of a project or segment of a project has finished and the results are evaluated and adjusted as needed. Also known as **Post.** ♪

3. The period in a film production cycle when filming has finished and the focus shifts to editing and compositing. ♪

Post-release

The period in a game development cycle when the project has been released to consumers and the emphasis focuses on customer satisfaction and closing the project. ♪

POV

1. *Point of View.* The camera's placement within a scene. ▣ 🕯

2. *Point of View.* The perspective, usually belonging to one of the characters, from which a scene or story is viewed. See also **Perspective**. ♪

Power gamer

A player dedicated to achieving a high player ranking. ♪ ▣

Power leveling

The act of a high-level character teaming up with a low-level character so that the low-level character gains experience at a faster-than-normal rate. ♪ ▣

Power up

An object in a game that, when collected by a player, immediately increases a stat or ability temporarily. ▣

PPU

Physics Processing Unit. A microprocessor dedicated to performing the necessary calculations to aid in the efficient implementation of dynamic forces that occur within the game world. ▪

PR

Public Relations. The managed communication between an organization and the general public with the intent of presenting the best image of the organization and their products. ♪

Practical

A special effect that is created without the use of CGI. 🕯

Pre-production

1. The period in a design cycle in which work has begun but a full team has not been assembled. ♪

2. The period in a design cycle in which work on a project has been approved but has not started. ♪

3. Any period in a design cycle between project approval and the alpha phase. ♪

Pre-production plan

A foundational strategy, established before teams are created, that explores the goals of a project and ways to achieve those goals. ♪

Predator

An object assigned to react to another object by following and catching up to it. See also **Prey**. ▪ ▱

Predefined models

A 3D mesh whose animation is locked and cannot be deformed. ⬆

Prediction code

Network code used to evaluate if a collision between two objects in the game should occur, and then forcing its occurrence when predicted instead of allowing the collision to be simulated thereby freeing up the network from having to transmit all of the necessary data, such as player position updates. ▪

Prefab

An object template from which instances of the object can be formed. ▪

Prefetch

The storing of instructions in a cache instead of in standard memory to speed up how quickly the processor can access the data. ▪

Premise

1. The underlying concept of a game or story. ✦

2. A proposed or assumed fact from which a conclusion can be drawn. ♪ ▱

Preorder

A marketing strategy of encouraging customers, often by including bonus content, to place orders before the product has been manufactured. ♪

Presentation level

The presentation of the game world and the events taking place within it to the player. See also **Simulation level**. ⚔

Preview

An article written by the press describing a game before it is released. ⚔ ♪

Prey

An object assigned to react to another object by running from it. See also **Predator**. ▣ ▨

Price point

A potential retail price of a product based on an evaluation of the demand for such a product within the marketplace. ♪

Primitive

Any of the basic geometric shapes, such as sphere, cube or cone, as determined by a specific modeling software package. ▜

Primitive modeling

The method of creating complex models by combining and altering basic primitive shapes. ▜

Principle of Good Enough (POGE)

A design principle that the primary goal is to get a quick and testable system in place and then allow more extensive design requirements to evolve. ▣ ♪

Prisoner's dilemma

An illustration of the conflict created when perfect information is unavailable. In the example, two prisoners must each decide whether or not to take a deal by implicating the other prisoner without knowing if the other is considering it. ▨

Privileged information

Information granted to some players but not to others. ▨

PRNG

Pseudo-Random Number Generator. A section of code that produces a random value via a seeded mathematical algorithm, often used to simulate the results of a die roll or other similar randomizing mechanic. When given the same seed value, however, it will produce the same result. See also **Random Number Generator**. ▣

Probability curve

The mathematical representation of a result's statistical variation. 🗔 ▰

Proc

Special Procedure. An additional or alternative effect for a commonly repeated activity that is triggered only when a specified condition is met. 🗔 ▰

Procedural animation

The illusion of movement given to an object by defining the rules and data set that the system uses when calculating and rendering results, as opposed to adjusting the objects position manually. ▰

Procedural generation

The automated creation of an element or asset from code or formulas instead of by hand. ▰ 🗔

Process

1. An instance of a computer program. ▰

2. The series of steps utilized in the creation of a product. ♪

Producer

A person tasked with the overall daily supervision of a project, particularly on business aspects. ♪

Product description

A structured listing of the critical information related to a product, such as its features, benefits, and price. ♪

Product placement

The utilization of a real-world product within a story or game for advertising purposes. ♪

Product plan

A publisher's listing of products they would like to have or are currently developing. Also known as an **SKU Plan**. ♪

Product research

The evaluation of potential goods or services in regard to the needs, wants, and desires of potential consumers. ♪

Production plan

The formalized set of documented strategies and schedules that a project is expected to follow. ♪

Profiler

Software used to evaluate how much of a processor's resources are spent on executing a specific section of code. Also known as a **Performance Analyzer.** ▪

Profit and Loss statement (P & L statement)

A financial disclosure that summarizes a company's expenses, costs, and earnings. ♪

Programmer

1. A person tasked with writing code for software. ♪ ▪

2. A person tasked with designing the software's architecture from an engineering perspective. ♪ ▪

Progression

1. The advancement of a player through a game or a level toward her or his objective. ▣

2. The order in which players perform actions within a turn-based game. ▣

Progression bar

A UI element that allows a player to gauge how far they are into a process. ▣ ▪

Progressive scan

A method of displaying an image on a monitor by drawing it in one pass. See also **Interlaced Scan.** ▮ ♪

Project manager

A person tasked with the overall leadership of a title. ♪

Project plan

The schedule and related documents that lists all responsibilities, timelines, tasks, schedules, and milestones of a game's production. ♪

Project triangle

A visual representation of a project in which three competing goals are weighted to depict a bias. ♪

Projective shadow

A texture designed to replicate shadows in an environment. Also known as a **Shadow Map**. ▯▮

Projective texture

A method of dynamic mapping in which a texture is displayed onto a 3D object, much like film projected onto a screen. ▯▮

Proof

1. A printout of art or text in its anticipated final form and intended for evaluation. ♪ ✍

2. The process of evaluating a submission for errors. ♪ ✍

Proof of concept

A work produced with the intention of showing that an untested idea can be successfully implemented. ▱ ▮ ♪

Proof of technology

A work produced with the intention of showing that specific current technological options are feasible as solutions. ▮ ♪

Prop

An object in a game that is not intended to be utilized by the character for gameplay purposes. ▯▮ ▱

Prophylaxis

A strategy that provides no advantage to the player making the play but instead is used to prevent opponents from making plays that would be to their advantage. ▱

Proposal doc

1. A description of the project, its expected budget, team composition, and company background that is often used as part of the pitch process. Also known as a **Concept Doc** or **Vision Doc**. ♪

2. A description of the project at its earliest stages that is used in team communications. Also known as a **Concept Doc** or **Vision Doc**. ♪ ▱

3. Any summary of the project that emphasizes its viability and is distributed to potential investors or publishers to increase their interest. Also known as a **Proposal Doc** or **Vision Doc**. ♪ ▱

Proprietary

A technology, design, or mark that is owned exclusively by one party and cannot legally be used by another party without the consent of its owner. ♪

Protagonist

1. The central character of a story. ⚔
2. The identity the player assumes within a game. ⚔

Protocol

Any one of several criteria that regulates how a network of systems communicate and interact with each other. ▬

Prototype

An early version of a product used for evaluation and from which future versions are modeled. ▨ ♪

Proxy

An element that is designed to be used temporarily in place of the finalized element for efficiency purposes. ▬ ⚑ ♣ ▨

Pseudo-3D

An art style that gives the impression that objects are three dimensional despite being displayed inside a 2D environment. Also known as **2.5D**. ⚑

Pseudo code

A simplified version of code used to layout the logic and components necessary to build a specific program before fully writing it in a true programming language. ▬

Pseudo-Random Number Generator (PRNG)

A section of code that produces a random value via a seeded mathematical algorithm, often used to simulate the results of a die roll or other similar randomizing mechanic. When given the same seed value, however, it will produce the same result. See also **Random Number Generator**. ▬ ▨

Public beta

A testing and marketing phase, generally occurring late in an MMO's beta phase, in which the public is invited to play a pre-released version of the game and in which testing focuses on server stability, load handling, and balance. ♪

Public domain

A legal concept that, under specific circumstances, the rights to a work become the property of the general public. ♪ ⚞

Public Relations (PR)

The managed communication between an organization and the general public with the intent of presenting the best image of the organization and their products. ♪

Publisher

A company tasked with handling, either directly or through a third party, the business activities of developing, marketing, and distributing a game and who often provides the developers with the majority of the financing needed. ♪

PuG

Pickup Group. A team of players that has been formed randomly. ♪

Pull

1. The changing of the focal depth of a camera to bring an object in or out of focus. ⚞ ▮

2. A strategic action of encouraging an opponent, usually an AI, to pursue the player into an environment where the player has an advantage. ▣

Pulling focus

The use of lighting, texture, composition, or other means to attract the attention of the viewer to a certain element in a scene. ▮ ⚞ ▣

Punch

1. An attack made with the hands. Also known as a **Blow**. ▣

2. The pressing of a key or button. ▣ ▬

Pure strategy

The optimal application of any particular strategy. ▣

Push

1. A strategy that is intended to force the action by moving aggressively toward a target location. ▣

2. A situation in which the game ends without either player achieving a victory condition. Also known as a **Draw**. ▣

Puzzle

1. A challenge, often intellectual, in which the correct number of solutions is limited, usually to one. ▣

2. A genre of video games in which the player is expected to complete challenges that focus on mental acuity, visual acuity, or wordplay. ♪

PvE

Player versus Environment. A classification of multiplayer gameplay in which players compete against the artificial elements of a game world instead of each other. ▣

PvP

Player versus Player. A classification of multiplayer gameplay that allows players to directly compete against each other. ▣

Pyrrhic victory

A victory over an opponent that leaves the victor too weak to challenge the other remaining players. ▣

Q & A

Questions and Answers. A conversation format in which one participant answers inquiries from others. ♪

Q & A doc

A manuscript prepared for PR representatives that provides central information about a product in anticipation of their being interviewed about it. ♪

QA

1. *Quality Assurance.* The department tasked to ensure that a product's minimum standards are met. ♪

2. *Quality Assurance.* The process of evaluating a product for negative issues. ♪ ▣

QOL

Quality of Life. The focus on providing team members with the means and methods of achieving a state of personal fulfillment and enjoyment. ♪

QTE

Quick Time Event. A cut-scene in which a player is challenged to advance the scene by correctly responding to prompts. See also **Interactive Cut-scene.** ▮ ▣ ✦

Quad

A polygon with exactly four edges.

Quality Assurance (QA)

1. The department tasked to ensure that a product's minimum standards are met.

2. The process of evaluating a product for negative issues.

Quality of Life (QOL)

The focus on providing team members with the means and methods of achieving a state of personal fulfillment and enjoyment.

Quantification

1. The assignment of numerical values to the elements of a game.

2. The measuring and sorting of empirical data into a usable and analytical format.

Quantization

1. The compression of a range of data into a single value.

2. The compression and subsequent uncompression of data on an as-needed basis.

Quaternion

A series of dimensional parameters for orientating and rotating rigid bodies in a 3D environment thereby allowing for smoother and more predictable results. See also **Euler Angles.**

Quest

An objective or series of objectives the player must meet to either receive a benefit or progress through the game.

Quest chain

A series of missions that a player must complete in a particular order.

Quest ender

The person or object that acknowledges the completion of a character's mission, most often an NPC.

Quest giver

The person or object that assigns a mission to a character, most often an NPC.

Queue

1. A listing of events or actions waiting to take place.

2. A list of players waiting to join the game.

Quick Time Event (QTE)

A cut-scene in which a player is challenged to advance the scene by correctly responding to prompts. See also **Interactive Cut-scene**.

Race condition

A situation in which two or more threads or processors may attempt to concurrently retrieve or manipulate data without being aware of each other's attempts.

Radial fog

A technique for creating a realistic fog effect that remains consistent when the camera rotates by basing the calculations on precise distance measurements.

Radio button

A user interface element that allows only one choice to be active at a time, when another choice is made it overwrites the earlier choice.

Radiosity

The property of virtual light that allows it to carry with it the color of the surface it has bounced off of. Also known as **Color Bleeding**.

Ragdoll physics

A procedural animation process that calculates the movements of jointed objects so that they move in a natural and unscripted way when a force is applied to them.

Rage quit

To leave a game before it ends because of anger toward another player or the game itself.

RAI

Rule as Intended. An interpretation of a rule made by considering the possible intentions of the designer.

Rail

A path or section of paths to which a NURBS can be applied to create a surface.

Rail shooter

A subgenre of shooters in which the player follows a predefined path from which he or she is unable to veer. Also known as an **On-rails Shooter**. ♪

Ramping

A range of values and the rate at which the lower value transitions to the higher value thereby creating a gradient. ⬛ ⛏ ⬛

Random encounter

A combat sequence that occurs at a nonscripted time and often includes randomly chosen opponents. ⬛

Random Number Generator (RNG)

1. A section of code that allows a computer to simulate the process of selecting a value at random. See also **Pseudo-Random Number Generator**. ⬛

2. A section of code that receives some type of true random input that is, in turn, used to seed an algorithm to generate a true random number. Of limited use within the game industry, often limited to gambling equipment. ⬛

Ranged combat

Combat between units or characters that takes place while they are not adjacent to each other. See also **Melee**. ⬛

Rapid prototyping

A process of creating an early version of a product and repeatedly modifying it until it meets its goal. ⬛

Raster

An image format in which the image is made up of pixels arranged in a grid. Also known as **Bitmap**. ⬛

Rate of fire

The speed at which attacks can be made, particularly in relation to the weapon used. ⬛ ⬛

RAW

1. *Rule As Written*. An interpretation of the rules by considering only the exact text as it was published. ⬛

2. A data storage format that is largely unprocessed, often used by digital cameras. ⬛

Ray casting

A technique that simulates the path of light waves but, to increase the speed of its renders, does not handle reflections, refractions, or shadows as accurately as other methods, such as ray tracing. See also **Ray Tracing**.

Ray tracing

An automated, processor-intensive technique of simulating a path of light waves and having them affect modeled objects to produce photorealistic results in a virtual 3D environment.

RC

1. *Release candidate.* A build that is being evaluated for distribution. Also known as a **Code Release Candidate** or **Final Candidate**.

2. *Release candidate.* The third phase of software development in which, traditionally, all of the features and assets have been tested and the emphasis is on confirming the fixes. Also known as **Code Release** and **Gamma**.

Reactive strategy

A strategy that is entirely dependent on an opponent's previous move.

Reagent

An item a character is required to have in inventory to use a skill or ability.

Real time

1. A classification of games in which the action never pauses for player input. See also **Turn Based**.

2. The displaying of an output immediately after input.

3. The depiction of an event at the same time and rate at which it occurs.

4. The passage of time within the real world as opposed to within the game.

Real-time sequence

A series of events that are executed and rendered as they are encountered, such as in-game cinematics.

Real-time shading

The creation of shadows when light is applied to an environment, as opposed to having them preplaced.

Real-time speech

The creation of sounds on an as-needed basis, as opposed to having them prerecorded. ♣

Real-Time Strategy (RTS)

A subgenre of strategy games in which the game action continues without waiting for the players' input or interaction. ▣ ♪

Realization relationship

A class reliance in which one class enacts the behavior supplied by another class. ▦

Recipe

A formula for combining objects via a crafting system to permanently create a specific object. See also **Ingredient**. ▣

Recoupable

An expense that can generate a reimbursement for the party that has incurred a cost or loss. ♪

Refactoring

The modification of code to improve its efficiency. ▦

Reference sheet

A small card or piece of paper, often included with the manual, that provides a synopsis of the important elements of a game. Also known as a **Cheat Sheet** or **Crib Sheet**. ▣ ♪

Reflection

1. The bouncing of an environment's image off an object. ▨
2. The bouncing of a sound off an object. ♣

Reflection map

A technique of simulating a reflection by creating a texture that is a mirror image of the environment and placing it where the reflected image would normally be seen. ▨

Refrast

Reference Rasterizer. A software-emulated video card used as a baseline to test the compatibility of a game's 3D rendering. ▨

Refresh

1. The redrawing of information on the screen. ▪

2. The process of reading a section of memory and then rewriting it without making any modifications to the data. ▪

Refusal of the call

An element of the hero's journey in which the hero demonstrates a reluctance to undertake the adventure. ▪

Registry

Window's database of settings and options that an end user is not expected to have direct access to and which is often used to track installation paths and verification information. ▪

Regression list

A complete cataloging of all of the changes within each version of the software throughout a project. See also **Build Notes**. ♪ ▪

Regression testing

1. The examination of an earlier version of a program or code to determine at what point an issue was first introduced or reintroduced. ♪ ▪

2. The examination of the current version of a program or code to ensure that any recent changes have not created any new errors. ▪

3. The evaluation of a current version of a program with a focus on previously fixed issues to ensure that those issues have not been reintroduced. ♪

Reinforcer

A reward given to a player to encourage the continuation of a desired behavior. ▪

Relationship management

The coordination of the interactions between the game's various elements. ▪ ▪

Release Candidate (RC)

1. A build that is being evaluated for distribution. Also known as a **Code Release Candidate** or **Final Candidate**. ♪

2. The third phase of software development in which, traditionally, all of the features and assets have been tested and the emphasis is on confirming the fixes. Also known as **Code Release** and **Gamma**. ♪

Remedy

A prearranged compensation described in a contract for reimbursing any specific damages suffered by a party. ♪

Render

1. The production of an image from a source. 📷

2. The assembly of an image for display on a monitor. 📷 💻

Render budget

The amount of geometry, usually expressed as tris or polys, that a scene can contain and still render within specifications. 📷

Rendering-to-texture

A technique of creating a new, more efficient texture by first rendering the surface of an object with its existing texture and lighting and then converting the resulting render into its own texture. Also known as **Baking** and **Texture Baking**. 📷

Replayability

A game's ability to retain interest after having been played through once. ♪ 🎮

Reproducibility

The capability of generating identical results by following identical steps. ♪ 💻

Request for Proposal (RFP)

A formal invitation to submit potential game projects to be considered for publication. ♪

Requirement analysis

An early stage in development, often done during the technical design documentation, in which game concepts are evaluated in terms of how they can be technically implemented. ♪ 💻

Requirement capture

The process of listing all of the expectations for a project and its related product. ♪

Reroll

1. The recreation of a character from scratch, originally limited to characters with randomly generated stats but more recently applied to characters with any type of customizable stats. 🎮

2. A mechanic that allows a random result to be ignored and replaced with a new random result. 🖫

Research proposal

A documented request for funding to explore a new idea or technology, often independent of any specific application. ♪

Resolution

1. The number of pixels that can be displayed on a screen at its current setting. ᐟᖶ

2. A measure of how much detail an image holds as described by the number of units of a specific type that makes up the image. ᐟᖶ

Resource

A game element that a player can collect and expend to gain an advantage. 🖫

Resource-constrained model

A scheduling pattern that initially considers the availability and potential availability of the assets needed to complete a project, and then extrapolates a timetable based on those limitations. ♪

Resource curve

The progression in which resources are distributed to the players over time. 🖫

Resource management

A player's collection and deployment of advantageous items. 🖫

Respawn

The reintroduction of a character to the game world after it has died. See also **Dead** and **Permadeath**. 🖫

Resurrection sickness

The temporary effects applied to a character when he or she respawns. 🖫

Reticle

A UI element used for aiming, such as crosshairs. ᐟᖶ 🖫

Return on Investment (ROI)

The relationship between the profit generated from a project and the amount invested into it. ♪

Returns

Unsold product that a retailer sends back to the publisher for a refund. ♪

Reusability

The ability of code to be easily moved into other projects while retaining their functionality. ▰

Reveal

A moment in a story in which some crucial information, previously hidden from the audience, is suddenly disclosed, resolving a key mystery and clarifying the story. ✦

Reverse engineering

The design method of taking an existing system or product and breaking it down to gain an understanding of its components and how they function. ▰ ▣ ♪

Review

1. An article written by the press evaluating a game after its release. ✦ ♪
2. A meeting in which the development of a specific aspect of the game is evaluated, often named after the particular element being examined, such as an art review or a code review. ♪

Revision control

The maintenance of a project's files as they change over time. Also known as **Version Control**. ♪ ▰

Revision control system

A procedure, often automated, that tracks all changes made to the files during the life of a project. Also known as a **Version Control System**. ♪ ▰

Revolve

The creation of a surface by rotating a NURBS around a fixed axis. ▰

Reward

1. The potential positive consequence of a strategy. ▣
2. The benefit given for completing a challenge. ▣

RFP

Request for Proposal. A formal invitation to submit potential game projects to be considered for publication. ♪

RGB

Red, Green, Blue. A digital coloring method that blends lights in various amounts of red, blue, and green, producing a desired color.

Rhizome structural model

A division of a story into nonhierarchal interweaving nodes.

Rhythm game

A genre of video games in which a player is challenged to match the timing and sequence presented to him or her.

Ride path

A predetermined path that a character travels on while moving from one location in the world to another, particularly when the simulated mode of travel is on the ground. See also **Flight Path**.

Rigging

The creation and manipulation of a skeletal hierarchy within a model to drive its animation.

Right-hand rule

A physical means of representing an XYZ location by positioning the hand so that the thumb points in the X-axis, the forefinger points in the Y-axis, and the middle finger in the Z-axis.

Right of first refusal

A negotiated legal right to be the first party to which a specific proposal is offered.

Right of first sale

The right of a consumer to resell products they have legally purchased without requiring the permission of or paying reimbursement to the original copyright holder. Also known as the **Exhaustion Rule** and **First-Sale Doctrine**.

The Right Thing

A design approach, described by Gabriel, that ranks correctness, consistency, and completeness higher than simplicity. Also known as the **MIT Approach**.

Rigid body

A solid form that cannot be deformed.

Rim light

A light source that hits the back of an object thereby separating it from the background. Also known as a **Backlight**, **Hair Light**, or **Kicker Light**.

Rising action

The sequence of complications within a story that leads to its climax.

Risk

The potential negative consequence of a strategy.

Risk analysis

An evaluation of the threats to and negative consequences of a specific course of action.

Risk aversion

1. The resistance by investors to contribute to a project based on the likelihood of it not returning a sufficient profit.

2. A characteristic of a strategy that favors safe, low risk options over more speculative options that may yield higher rewards.

Risk mitigation plan

A document outlining responses to specific areas of concern and under what conditions those responses are to be triggered.

RNG

1. *Random Number Generator*. A section of code that allows a computer to simulate the process of selecting a value at random. See also **Pseudo-Random Number Generator**.

2. A section of code that receives some type of true random input that is, in turn, used to seed an algorithm to generate a true random number. Of limited use within the game industry, often limited to gambling equipment.

3. *Random Number Generator*. Randomness; often in terms of the perceived degree of randomness that a pseudo-random number generator produces.

Robustness

The ability of code to handle a variety of circumstances and unexpected inputs without affecting its performance.

Rock-paper-scissors

1. A game in which each player simultaneously reveals a shape made by their hand representing rock, paper, or scissors with each shape beating one of the other shapes and losing to the third. 🖽

2. A balancing mechanic that relies on every element having an opposing element it can trump and an opposing element which trumps it. See also **Triangularity**. 🖽

ROI

Return on Investment. The relationship between the profit generated from a project and the amount invested into it. ♪

Role name

An indicator used in UML modeling to specify the purpose of a relationship between two classes. ▦

Role-Playing Game (RPG)

1. A genre of video games in which the emphasis is on tactical combat and defined characters whose abilities grow throughout the game. ♪

2. A genre of tabletop games that focus on storytelling and in which each player takes on the role of one of the game's characters with nearly complete autonomy as to how that character reacts. ♪

Room tone

A recording of the ambient sounds of the space in which dialog has been recorded and used to bridge clips of dialogue together when the absence of the ambient sound would be noticeable. ♟

Rotated grid

A supersampling method in which the samples are taken from nonaligned areas. ▮

Rounding

1. Altering a number by adjusting its value based on how close it is to a more convenient version of itself. ▦

2. Smoothing an edge so that the transition from one angle to another is more gradual. ▮

Royalties

A payment structure in which the artist or developer is paid a percentage of the revenue generated by the sales of a product they created or help create. ♪

RPG

1. *Role-Playing Game.* A genre of video games in which the emphasis is on tactical combat and defined characters whose abilities grow throughout the game. ♪

2. *Role-Playing Game.* A genre of tabletop games that focus on storytelling and in which each player takes on the role of one of the game's characters with nearly complete autonomy as to how that character reacts. ♪

RTFM

Read the F'n Manual. A rationale that states if an issue is addressed in the manual it is unnecessary for the design team to address it within the game. ▪

RTS

Real-Time Strategy. A subgenre of strategy games in which the game's action continues without waiting for the players to interact. ▣

Rubber banding

1. An error due to latency in which a moving object pops back to a location it was at earlier. ♪

2. Providing benefits to an AI opponent when the player has gained a significant lead thereby allowing the AI to catch up. See also **Negative Feedback Loop.** ▪

3. The controlled stretching or shrinking of a line or shape from a fixed point within a computer graphics program. ▮

Rule as Intended (RAI)

An interpretation of a rule made by considering the possible intentions of the designer. ▣

Rule as Written (RAW)

An interpretation of the rules by considering only the exact text as it was published. ▣

Rule lawyer

A player who often looks for obscure information or imprecise terminology in the rules' description in order to argue for an advantage. ▣

Rule system

A system whose behavior is derived from a list of restricted, allowable, or required actions. ■ ▣

Ruled surface

A shape that can be created by moving a straight line along a path. ▮

Rules

A set of nonnegotiable instructions that govern gameplay. ▣

Runner

An enemy that breaks from combat and attempts to flee. ▣

Runtime sequence

A series of activities that a computer performs during the execution of its code. ■

Saddle point

The section of a graph or surface where the contour curves up on one axis and down on the other, thereby creating a form that resembles a saddle. ▮

SAG

Screen Actors Guild. A labor union that represents actors. ♪

Sampling

1. Collecting and reusing a sound or snippet of sound. ♣

2. The process of taking a portion of an element to use as representative of a larger area or collection. ■ ▮

Sandbox

1. A genre of video games in which the emphasis is on free-form play and that often provides players the capability to interact with the game's environment in the absence of any goals. ▣ ♪

2. A mode of gameplay in which a player can interact with the game environment outside of its established rules and goals in a free-form manner. ▣

Sandbox design method

A development process in which a working, nearly featureless version of the game is created and experimented with first and then new features are implemented on an as-needed basis. Also known as **Evolutionary Prototyping** or the **Testbed Design Method.** ▣

Satisficing

A design strategy, initially described by Simon, focused on meeting the minimally acceptable outcome as opposed to the optimal outcome. 🎲

Saturation

The purity of the chromatic content within a color. 🖌

Save anywhere

A saving scheme that allows a player to save the current game state anytime they wish. 🎲

Save game system

The mechanics for recording and restoring the current state of the game. 🎲 ▦

Save point

A saving scheme that allows saving the current game state only when the player reaches a predetermined location. 🎲

Save scumming

A strategy that relies on the use or duplication of saved game files to beat the game. 🎲

Say

The player's input, through actions, into the game state. 🎲

Scale

1. To increase or decrease an object's size while retaining its proportions. 🖌

2. To adjust a value by an incremental amount. 🎲 ▦

3. The use of a character's stats to determine the effectiveness of a power or ability the character has, often expressed as a ratio. 🎲

Scan data

The collection of data points generated from scanning a 3D object into a storage device. 🖌

Scanline rendering

A rendering method that draws the scene from top to bottom, one row at a time. 🖌

Scene

1. The specific setting in which the action of a story takes place. ✎

2. A unit of action taking place in a single location. ♣

3. The arrangement of elements in a 3D environment. 🐾

Scene graph

A branching tree structure that assigns a parent-child relationship to objects in a collection so that they can be adjusted dependently or independently of each other as desired. ▪️ 🐾

Scope

1. The range of experiences the game will cover. 🖳

2. The anticipated size of a proposed project, often expressed in terms of man hours or cost. ♪

3. An item designed so a player can focus more closely on a target. 🖳

Score

1. A designation, usually numerical, that represents how successful a player was at meeting the game's challenge. 🖳

2. The musical arrangement used in the background of films, television, and games. ♣

Screen capture

A capture of an image being displayed onscreen. Also known as a **Capture** and **Screenshot**. ♪ 🐾

Screen space

A 2D environment in which object locations are given in terms of their relation to the center of the screen on which they are displayed. 🐾

Screen space blurred shadow mapping

The application of a hazy distortion to an existing shadow map based on information stored in the screen space thereby creating a softer shadow. 🐾

Screen splatter

An effect such as mud, gore, or water droplets that are applied to a plane in front of the game's virtual camera to obscure its view and simulate the environmental hindrances to the character's view. 🐾

Screenshot

A capture of an image being displayed on screen. Also known as a **Screen Capture**. ♪ ☝

Script

1. A detailed, written description of the actions and dialogue within a film, show, or game. ✍

2. Instructions that have been written outside of the program's code but which the code can access and execute. ▰

Scripted testing

A testing methodology in which player interaction is replaced by computer-driven instructions. Also known as **Automated Testing**. ▰ ♪

Scrubbing

The rapid movement of audio or video through a timeline by means of a UI element. ☝

Scrum

1. An adaptive, iterative, project management framework that focuses on brief, daily, team-centered meetings. ♪

2. The daily meeting within a scrum framework. ♪

Sculpting

1. The use of clay or other moldable material to fashion a model of an object. ☝

2. A method of creating highly detailed textures or models in a virtual environment with paint-like tools. ☝

SDK

Software Development Kit. A series of prepackaged tools by the creators of a particular platform, engine, or framework to facilitate the use of their standards and properties. ♪ ▰

Seamless texture

A texture that, when repeated, allows its edges to merge uniformly with itself. ☝

Section 86

The section of Germany's criminal code that makes it illegal to distribute games or other forms of media that have Nazi symbols or depictions regardless of context. ♪

Section 131

The section of Germany's criminal code that makes the depiction of gratuitous violence illegal. ♪

Seeding

The placement of a number into an algorithm. Often utilized in pseudo-random number generators due to the fact that inputing the same number will consistently yield the same result, but varying the number creates the impression of randomly generated results. ▨

Segue

1. The transition from one scene to another. ⬛ ✄
2. The transition from one gameplay sequence to another. ⬛ ✄
3. The transition from one sound to another. ⚒

Self-balancing

Any mechanic designed to keep players competitive regardless of differing skill levels. ▣

Self-shadowing

The capability of an object to cast a shadow upon itself. ⬛ ▣

Sell ins

The number of units shipped to retailers for which they are being billed. See also **Sell Throughs**. ♪

Sell sheet

A single-page flyer released to distributors and retailers highlighting the unique selling points of a game. ♪

Sell throughs

The number of units sold by retailers to consumers. See also **Sell Ins**. ♪

Sensory-motoric immersion

The capture of a player's focus with the immediate activity occurring within a game, as described by Björk and Holopainen. Also known as **Tactical Immersion**. ▣

Sequel

A game that builds on a previously released game and often has the earlier game's title embedded into its own. ♪

Sequence

1. A series of events or scenes. ♩

2. The order in which players take their turn. ▣

3. The order in which actions are taken and effects are resolved. ▣

4. The logical order in which instructions are carried out. ▆

Sequence diagram

A chart used in UML to illustrate the order in which the processes interact with one another. Also known as an **Event Diagrams**, an **Event Scenario**, and a **Timing Diagram**. ▆

Sequence of play

The rules that dictate the sequence in which the player can perform his or her actions. Also known as **Order of Execution**, **Play Sequence**, **Turn Order**, or **Turn Sequence**. ▣

Sequencer

A program or system that is designed to maintain and control computer-generated music. ♣

Sequential reasoning

The ability of a player to apply a strategy in a step-by-step progressive manner so that a desired end result can be achieved. ▣

Serious game

A game created with an overt secondary objective besides entertainment, such as education or promotion. ▣ ♪

Server

A dedicated host computer that provides data to a series of client computers, often in a secure manner so that none of the users have access to parts of the program that might be technologically exploited. ▆ ♪

Setting

The spatial, temporal, and circumstantial environment in which a story takes place. ♩

Setup

1. The process of placing all conditions and states to their defaults before the game starts. ▣

2. A game's initial state at startup. ▣

Severity

A measure of the impact of a bug on gameplay. ♪

Shader

1. Instructions that provide information on a pixel's or vertex's traits for rendering purposes. ⛏

2. The method used for customized rendering of textures and lighting effects within the graphic processing pipeline. ⛏

Shading language

A programming language that has data types designed specifically for rendering processes. ⌨ ⛏

Shadow character

An archetype NPC, almost always the villain, that represents the inverse of the game's hero in terms of character and serves to illustrate the corollary to the theme. ✍

Shadow map

A texture designed to replicate shadows in an environment. Also known as a **Projective Shadow**. ⛏

Shadow patch

An update released without an announcement or a description of what it addresses. ♪

Shadow volume

The 3D shape that a shadow creates, often through use of a stencil buffer. ⛏

Shape

A design element that is created when a line encloses a 2D space. ⛏

Shareware

A distributed version of software, often with limited capabilities, whose developer relies on the consumer paying for it after they have used it. ♪

Shell

1. The parts of a video game, such as the menu system, that exist outside the gameplay environment. 🖥 ⛏ ⌨

2. The outer layer of a hollowed out solid model. ⛏

Shield

A protective layer, such as confirmation screens, designed into a product to prevent the accidental implementation of an effect that may be undesirable to the user. ▪ ▱

Shimmering

The blinking of a texture while a camera is moving, caused by changes in the colors assigned to that texture's pixels. ▪

Ship date

The date a product is sent out to distributors or consumers. ♪

Shoot 'em up

A subgenre of shooter games in which the player constantly fires at large numbers of opponents while dodging their incoming attacks. Also known as a **Shmup**. ♪

Shovelware

Software that has been rushed through production with little or no quality control, often to capitalize on a popular trend. ♪

Shmup

A subgenre of shooter games in which the player constantly fires at large numbers of opponents while dodging their incoming attacks. Also known as a **Shoot 'em up**. ♪

Side quest

A mission that is not part of the critical path of a game. ▱

Sign off

To provide written approval. ♪

Signature move

An animation, usually an attack in a fighting game, that is unique to a specific character and is designed to separate that character's style from all others. ▪

Silence

A power or ability that prevents other characters from using their skills or abilities. ▱

Silent protagonist

A player character that has no dialogue. ◢

Sim

1. *Simulation.* A genre of video games that has a strong correlation between the activity it represents and its real-world counterpart. ▦

2. *Simulation.* A characteristic of a game, or portion of a game, that emphasizes mimicry of a real-world activity over abstraction. ▦

3. *Simulation.* A representation of an idea or object that attempts to match its real-world counterpart. See also **Abstraction**. ▦

4. *Simulation.* Training software that replicates a real-world environment to allow the user to develop skills related to that environment at a reduced risk or cost. ▦

5. *Simulation.* Software designed to replicate a real-world phenomenon to observe or experiment with it when such a phenomenon would be impossible, extremely risky, or too cost prohibitive to observe in real life. ▦

6. *Simulation.* The reduction of a complex system to a more abstract version. ▦

7. *Simultaneous Release.* The concurrent release of a product alongside another product. See also **Day and Date**. ♪

Simplification

A play that reduces the complexity of a game without changing the inherent strengths and weaknesses of the players, such as exchanging pieces of equal value in chess. ▦

Simulation (Sim)

1. A genre of video games with a strong correlation between the activity it represents and its real-world counterpart. ▦

2. A characteristic of a game, or portion of a game, that emphasizes mimicry of a real-world activity over abstraction. ▦

3. A representation of an idea or object that attempts to match its real-world counterpart. See also **Abstraction**. ▦

4. Training software that replicates a real-world environment to allow the user to develop skills related to that environment at a reduced risk or cost. ▦

5. Software designed to replicate a real-world phenomena to observe or experiment with it when such a phenomena would be impossible, extremely risky, or too cost prohibitive to observe in real life. ▦

6. The reduction of a complex system to a more abstract version. ▦

Simulation baking

The solidifying of the results of a simulation process thereby no longer requiring the system to perform calculations and, in doing so, increases its performance. Also known as **Baking**. 🖊 ▨

Simulation level

The implementation of the actions within the game as defined by the game's rules. See also **Presentation Level**. ✦

Simultaneous game

A game in which all players make their moves at the same time. ▨

Simultaneous release (Sim)

A release date that is concurrent with a release of another product. See also **Day and Date**. ♪

Single player

1. A mode of gameplay intended for only one player. ▨

2. A classification of video games in which the chief mode of play is against AI opponents. ♪

Singleton pattern

A software design pattern in which only one instance of an object is needed and therefore instancing is restricted. ▨

Sink

A game mechanic whose purpose is to remove resources from players. Also known as a **Drain**. ▨

Sizzle

The elements of a product that create the greatest amount of interest in it. ♪

Skeletal animation

An animation method that utilizes bones and joints to guide the movements of a model. 🖊

Skill

1. The player's ability to overcome challenges by means of his or her own talents. ▨

2. An ability that the player's character may acquire or improve on during gameplay. ▨

3. A classification of any mechanic that relies on the player's judgment and ability instead of statistical probability. See also **Chance**. 🖪

Skill point

A reward given to a player that he or she can use to increase their character's abilities. 🖪

Skill showcase

A portion of the game in which a character has temporary access to many, if not all, of the abilities within the game to provide an incentive for acquiring them permanently. 🖪

Skill tree

An advancement structure for the capabilities that a character or player can earn in which progression is in one direction but often branches. Furthermore, before players can choose a particular advancement, they must have access to any underlying nodes. Also known as a **Node Tree** or **Tech Tree**. 🖪

Skill web

An advancement structure for the capabilities that a character or player can earn in which progression can come from several different directions. Furthermore, before players can choose a particular advancement, they must have access to any or all of the connecting nodes. Also known as a **Node Web** or **Tech Web**. 🖪

Skinned skeleton

A 3D mesh whose animation can be deformed by manipulating the skeleton it surrounds. ▌

Skinning

1. Creating and wrapping a 2D texture around the geometry of a 3D model. ▌

2. Applying the bones and joints to a model. ▌

3. The process of using a loft action to create a surface. ▌

SKU

Stock Keeping Unit. The unique number given to each version of a product to allow for easier inventory management. ♪

SKU plan

A publisher's listing of products they would like to have or currently have in development. Also known as a **Product Plan**. ♪

Skybox

A modeled 3D enclosure that has sky and horizon textures applied to its interior faces to simulate a vastly distant environment while the player is inside that model.

Slot

A location within a character's inventory panel in which items can be placed to indicate that they are currently equipped. Also know as a **Socket**.

Slug

A concise header, written in all caps, meant to attract the reader's attention to an important detail within a script. Also known as a **Slug Line**.

Slug line

A concise header written in all caps meant to attract the reader's attention to an important detail within a script. Also known as a **Slug**.

Smoke test

A quick test to evaluate if a version is functional enough to undergo further testing.

Snake draft

A method of selecting resources in which the order of selection reverses each round, so that the last player to make a selection in one round makes the first selection in the next.

Snowballing

1. The exponential growth of a player's strength due to the ease of accumulating further benefits once a pivotal level of benefits is achieved.

2. A rapid, unintended growth in a project's scope or expense.

Soak test

An evaluative procedure that focuses on how well the software reacts to being in an idle state for long periods of time.

Social game

A classification of games based on the ability to casually interact with other players, often through a social media portal.

Social media

The means and channels of communication designed to allow members of the general public to target their message to a larger community. ♪

Social reasoning

The ability of a player to perceive another player's state of mind and make predictions when interacting with them. ▣

Socket

1. Software that allows a specific piece of hardware to interact with the operating system and its applications. Most often used in reference to Mac computers. See also **Drivers** and **Firmware**. ▦

2. A numeric identifier assigned to a specific service on a particular node on a network. ▦

3. A location within a character's inventory panel in which items can be placed to indicate that they are currently equipped. Also known as a **Slot**. ▣

Soft architecture

A project structure that is flexible and fairly easy to adjust. ♪

Soft body

A dynamic form capable of being deformed by forces. ▚

Soft cap

1. A limit that is achieved based on the mechanics of the game and if the mechanics are altered, the current limit may be altered as well. ▣

2. A limit created by applying diminishing returns so that once the limit is exceeded the benefits of expanding beyond the cap are minimal and inefficient. ▣

Soft fraud

The deception for gain by means of exaggerated or hard-to-verify claims. ♪

Soft modem

Software used to emulate the functionality of a modem. ▦

Software

An independent application designed for use on a computer. ▦

Software architecture

The creation of an outline of the components and layers of a software project that occurs early in the development process. Also known as **High-Level Software Design**. ▧

Software bloat

The tendency of developers of new software to include more features and use more resources than are needed to meet the demand of users. ♪ ▧ ▣

Software designer

A person tasked with the overall creation of the systems an application contains. ♪

Software Development Kit (SDK)

A series of prepackaged tools by the creators of a particular platform, engine, or framework to facilitate the use of their standards and properties. ♪ ▧

Software factory

A software development methodology, proposed by Adams and Rollings, in which the processes and tools used in development are designed to be interchangeable with multiple projects, thereby allowing future products to be more easily assembled. ♪

Software planner

A person tasked with the breakdown of a game's design into its technical elements. ♪

Solid model

A virtual object that possesses an internal density thereby allowing the subtraction of material from the object without exposing a cavity. ▮

Solvability

How easily the solution to a game's challenge can be determined. ▣

Sound designer

A person tasked with planning the implementation of a game's auditory elements in order to achieve a desired auditory experience. ♪

Source code

The uncompiled instructions that constitute a computer program. See also **Code**. ▧

Source code management

A system that manages all of the revisions of various files. ▧ ♪

Space

A design element created by the distance and area between the objects in a scene. 📍

Spamming

1. Repeatedly using the same skill, attack, or ability over and over again by rapidly hitting the same button or key. See also **Button Mashing**. ▣

2. Broadcasting the same message over and over again. ▣

Spatial immersion

Capturing a player's focus with the sense of reality created by the game world, as described by Björk and Holopainen. ▣

Spatial index pattern

A software design pattern intended to efficiently evaluate large 3D areas and locate objects within that field. ▰

Spatial reasoning

The ability of a player to recognize, manipulate, and transform objects in a 3D environment. ▣

Spawn point

A specific location within the game from which a character emerges when it enters or reenters the game world. ▣

Spec

1. *Speculation*. A piece of work produced without any promises of consideration. ✎

2. *Specification*. The precise qualities and attributes that a product is required to meet. ♪ ▣

Special effect

The elements in a scene that are simulated, either while the action is recorded or added in afterward. Also known as an **Effect**. 📍

Specification (Spec)

The precise qualities and attributes that a product is required to meet. ♪ ▣

Specular light

A bright reflection off of a reflective surface. Also known as a **Highlight**. 📍

Specular light mapping

The placing of a map onto a model to simulate the highlights on a reflective surface. 📷📖

Speculate stage

A phase of Agile Software Development in which a project's goals are set, plans are developed, and limitations are drawn. ♪

Speculation (Spec)

A piece of work produced without any promises of consideration. ✍

Spherical environmental mapping

A technique of creating a distant environment by placing the camera within a large sphere and attaching a texture representing the environment onto the inner face of the sphere. 📷📖

Spiritual successor

A game designed to be very similar to a previously released game while distinguishing itself as a separate IP, often made by many of the same team members who worked on the earlier game. ♪

Splash damage

Damage applied to a unit or entity because of its closeness to a target that has been hit. 🎮

Splash screen

A full-screen image often used to inform a user that the software has launched or is loading. See also **Title Screen**. 📷📖 ♪ 🎮

Spline

1. A series of basic curves connected together to form a single complex curve. 📷📖

2. A curved line that passes through fixed points and which is used in the creation of NURBS models. 📷📖 ♪

3. Any curve. 📷📖

Split screen

A mode of multiplayer gameplay that allows two or more players to view the game on a common screen that has been divided into sections. 🎮

Sports game

A classification of video games in which the players engage in a simulated athletic competition. ♪

Sports management sim

A simulation in which the player is placed into a decision-making position similar to that of an owner, manager, or coach of a sports team. ♪

Sports sim

A genre of video games in which the player takes on the role of an athlete during a simulated athletic competition. ♪

Spotlight

A light source that emits as a cone in one direction with its strength at its center. 🕯

Sprite

A two-dimensional image, often with a transparency channel, intended to be animated over a backdrop. 🕯

Spun surface

A surface created from using a revolve action on a spline. 🕯

SRP

Suggested Retail Price. The market price that the manufacturer states its product can be sold for under current market conditions. Also known as **MSRP**. ♪

Stack

1. A virtual linear storage structure designed so that data can be retrieved in an orderly manner. ⌨

2. The collection of data into a structure that retrieves data in a last in, first out methodology. ⌨

3. A dedicated structure for storing information related to the currently active subroutines. Also known as a **Call Stack**. ⌨

4. An orderly arrangement of events waiting to be resolved. ▣

5. A random or prearranged assortment of resources that the player can access. ▣

6. An incremental counter applied to an ability or effect that increases its influence for each counter applied. ▣

Stag hunt

A game in which the optimal strategy is for players to choose to cooperate. Originally posed as a scenario in which two hunters team up to collect bigger prey. Also known as an **Assurance Game**. ▣

Stamper

A metal plate used to stamp out copies of a disk. ♪

Startup

1. A company that is in the process of its initial development and therefore has not yet created a track record. ♪

2. The boot up sequence for a platform that provides it with instructions to execute when first turned on. ▪

State

1. The visual representation of the current status of an element. ▪ ♪▮

2. The currently assigned status of an issue. ♪

3. The current condition of an object. ▪

State pattern

A software design pattern in which objects transition to other sets of behaviors based on their current status. ▪

State space search

An algorithm that predicts all possible variations of a solution then chooses the one that leads to the best result. ▪

Static bot

An AI entity that is programmed to move along a preestablished route. ▪

Static budget

A firm limitation on the amount of financial resources that a project can spend. Also known as a **Fixed Budget**. ♪

Static modeling

The expression, used in UML, of a system's components that do not change over time. Also known as **Structural Modeling**. ▪

Static structure diagram

A UML chart that illustrates the implementation of the components of a system. Also known as a **Structure Diagram**.

Steering committee

A group of experts in an organization that provides guidance on a project's key issues and evaluates the team's performance.

Stencil buffer

A temporary data storage location used to determine rendering effects, most commonly during the creation of shadows.

Stereo

Stereophonic. An audio signal that travels through multiple channels giving the listener the impression that it is originating from a variety of locations. See also **Mono**.

Stereophonic (Stereo)

An audio signal that travels through multiple channels giving the listener the impression that it is originating from a variety of locations. See also **Mono**.

Stereotype

A type of character whose similarity to other characters that have filled a comparable role has become cliché and sometimes derogatory.

Stitch line

The edges where two textures are attached.

Stock Keeping Unit (SKU)

The unique number given to each version of a product to allow for easier inventory management.

Story

A telling of events usually involving characters in conflict.

Story arc

The logical progression of a story. Also known as an **Arc**.

Story mode

A mode of play that imposes a narrative into the game.

Storyboard

A shot-by-shot illustration of a cinematic or other visually observable series of events, primarily used in preproduction. 🍖 📖 ♪ ⚔

Strafing

The sideways movement of a character while performing an action, such as firing a weapon. 📖

Strategic balancing

A method of balancing by assigning various long-term consequences to different options so that a player must choose between the immediate and the eventual. 📖

Strategic immersion

The capture of the player's focus by the mental challenges presented within a game, as described by Adams. Also known as **Cognitive Immersion**. 📖

Strategic map

A small version of the play field that shows the immediate area, the orientation of the player's avatar, and its current position. Also known as an **Inset Map** or a **Mini-map**. 📖 🍖

Strategic scale

A high-level, army-by-army scope that simulates an entire war, particularly used in reference to wargames. See also **Operational Scale**, **Grand Strategic Scale,** and **Tactical Scale**. 📖

Strategy

An overarching plan or combination of plans decided on by a player to gain an advantage in achieving a victory condition. 📖

Strategy game

A genre of video games that emphasizes decision making and resource management over chance and hand-eye coordination. ♪

Strategy guide

A publication that provides hints, strategies, and sometimes exclusive information about a game. ♪ 📖

Strategy pattern

1. A software design pattern in which behaviors are encapsulated as objects to allow their algorithms to be dynamically swapped in and out. ▆

2. The encapsulation of behaviors so that the AI's algorithms can be switched in and out to find the most effective one for its current situation. ▦

Stress test

An evaluative procedure that focuses on how well the network code supports a large amount of simultaneously connected users. ♪ ▦

Stressor

A challenge that creates tension in the player. ▣

Stroboscopic effects

The use of a pulsating light or mechanical device to interrupt observation of an object thereby causing a moving or animated object to appear stationary. Also known to cause seizures and therefore games with such effects often carry warnings to that effect. See also **Temporal Aliasing**. ▘

Structural modeling

The expression, used in UML, of a system's components that do not change over time. Also known as **Static Modeling**. ▦

Structural substrate

The underlying order and sense of the world contained within a story. ✄

Structure diagram

A UML chart that illustrates the implementation of the components of a system. Also known as a **Static Structure Diagram**. ▦

Structured conflict

The opposition in goals that is inherent in a system's core design. ▣

Stun lock

To prevent another character from moving or using their attacks by continually applying effects that negate their ability to engage in combat. ▣

Style guide

1. An authoritative reference work that dictates publication standards. ✄

2. An authoritative reference work that dictates the standards and canon for an IP across multiple media. ♪

Sub-D modeling

Subdivision modeling. A method of polygonal modeling in which details are added by increasingly dividing the existing polygons in half thereby providing a greater resolution to a basic, sometimes primitive, mesh. 🔧

Subdivision modeling (Sub-D modeling)

A method of polygonal modeling in which details are added by increasingly dividing the existing polygons in half thereby providing a greater resolution to a basic, sometimes primitive, mesh. 🔧

Subfaction

A coalition of NPCs that derives the amount of favor it has toward a character based on that character's existing standing with another, broader coalition, such as a city whose residents determine their tolerance for a character based on that character's current standing with the empire. See also **Faction**. 🖼

Submission

1. A build distributed to another department for evaluation. 🎵

2. A win achieved by an opponent yielding. 🖼

Subplot

A secondary series of events that complicate the story and which often reinforces or contrasts the theme of the main plot. Also known as a **B Storyline**. ✍

Subscription based

A payment model that utilizes a cyclical fee. 🎵

Subsurface light scattering

A method of creating the realistic depiction of light as it reacts to the translucency of an object. 🔧

Subtext

The underlying intention that a character conveys through a piece of dialogue that often differs from the literal meaning of what was said. ✍

Subtitles

The display of spoken dialogue or other pertinent information as text, which is often translated for the target audience. See also **Closed Caption**. ✍ ♟

Subversive play

Emergent gameplay that is contrary to the intent of the designer. 🖼

Suggested Retail Price (SRP)

The market price that the manufacturer states its product can be sold for under current market conditions. Also known as the **Manufacturer's Suggested Retail Price**. ♪

Suicide cheat

An emergent strategy in which a player intentionally kills her or his own character to prevent an opponent from getting credit for the kill. 🖾

Summoning sickness

A temporary effect that imposes restrictions or negative attributes onto units when they are brought into the game. Most often used in collectable card games. 🖾

Super storyboard

An illustrated document that functions as a flowchart for coordinating all of the individual elements of an interactive media project. ♪

Supersampling

An antialiasing technique of sampling multiple locations that would all fall within the same displayed pixel and averaging their colors to provide a smoother blending between the displayed pixels. 🖈

Supportive balancing

A method of balancing by providing indirect advantages to what would otherwise be weak options. 🖾

Surgical team

A collection of employees who are highly skilled at very specific tasks. ♪

Survival horror

A genre of video games, often set in an isolated and terrifying environment, that emphasizes caution and resource management over aggressive combat. ♪

Suspension of disbelief

The voluntarily concession of some demands for realism by the player as long as the normally unbelievable portions of the story are crucial and sufficiently established. 🖋 🖾

Swag

Promotional material handed out for free at conventions and expos. ♪

Switching cost

The inherent disadvantage that occurs when a player alters her or his strategy. 🖾

Symbolism

The use of an item, color, character, or icons to represent something else. ♟

Symmetrical game

A game in which each player's starting position, resources, win conditions, and available actions are exactly identical thereby giving no player an advantage. ⬚

Sync

1. *Synchronization.* The ability of two interconnected systems that share common data to maintain the continuity and sequencing of that information. ■ ♪

2. *Synchronization.* The temporal correlation between sound and the object creating the sound. ♣

Synchronization (Sync)

1. The ability of two interconnected systems that share common data to maintain the continuity and sequencing of that information. ■ ♪

2. The temporal correlation between sound and the object creating the sound. ♣

Synchronization license

The right to use music owned by someone else in a medium that is different from that for which it was originally recorded. ♣

Synergetic balancing

A method of balancing by allowing certain decisions to interact positively with other separate decisions thereby making the use of complex strategies more beneficial than simple ones. ⬚

Synopsis

A concise description, often just one or two pages long, of the events that will take place within a game or story. ♟ ⬚

Syntax error

An error in the program's code that originates from the use of a word, number, or operator not recognized by the compiler. ■

System design

1. The process of creating and refining the core rules of a game. ⬚

2. The creation and implementation of a specific interactive feature or process in a game, such as combat, crafting, or chat. ⬚

3. The creation of the architecture, components, and information flow of interrelated elements into a cohesive unit. ▦

System procedures

Activities that a game program or system initiates and resolves independent of a real or AI player. ▣

System requirements

The specifications a user's computer must meet or exceed in order for the software to function properly. ♪ ▦

System testing

The stage of testing that occurs once the entirety of the project has been integrated. ▦

Tab

1. A visual UI element that allows a user to quickly change what options or data sets are available. ▣

2. A key by the same name that is often used within a program to change the current focus of a UI element. ▣

Table

A series of prearranged data fields laid out in a logical order to facilitate looking up the information they contain. ▣ ▦

Tabletop games

A classification of games that can be played on a table or similar flat surface. ♪

Tabula rasa

"Blank slate" (Latin). A premade player character that is created with little to no inherent personality or background. ◢ ▣

Tactical immersion

The capture of a player's focus with the immediate activity occurring within a game, as described by Adams. Also known as **Sensory-Motoric Immersion**. ▣

Tactical scale

A low-level, unit-by-unit scope that simulates a battle or series of battles, particularly used in reference to wargames. See also **Grand Strategic Scale**, **Operational Scale**, and **Strategic Scale**. ▣

Tactics

The actions undertaken to execute a grand strategy. ▣

Tag

1. A method of claiming the rights to an enemy or resource by engaging or otherwise interacting with it. ▣

2. A keyword that labels an asset so that it can be easily identified and classified, often with the intent of allowing rapid retrieval of such assets when they are searched for. ♪

Tagged animation

An animation technique that divides an object into sections and animates each of them individually. ▮

Talking heads

A shot or series of shots in which the characters recite dialogue for an extended period with little other action taking place. ◀

Tangency continuity

The connection of two curves or surfaces in such a way that they share a common direction at the point of connection. Also known as **G1 Continuity**. ▮

Tangent

An orientation in which an object is in contact with another element but not intersecting it. ▮

Tangent space

A virtual 3D environment in which a 2D map's coordinates are given in relation to a 3D model's location. ▮

Target market

The demographics of potential consumers to which a product is expected to be of interest. ♪

Target render

A conceptual simulation of what a game's graphics should look like, often made before the game engine or rendering hardware are available and included as part of the pitch to publishers and investors. ▮ ♪

Task rejection

A worker's refusal to fully take on an assigned duty, as proposed by Bethke. ♪

TCR

Technical Certification Requirements. Microsoft's list of technical guidelines for third-party publications on their consoles. ♪

Team killing

The intentional destruction of an allied player's character by friendly fire. ♪

Tearing

A rendering flaw that causes gaps to appear in a texture applied to an object.

Tech support

Technical support. The personnel assigned as a point of contact for the public and tasked with increasing customer satisfaction by providing them with solutions to technical issues, such as installation, system stability, and performance. ♪

Tech tree

An advancement structure for the capabilities that a character or player can earn in which progression is in one direction but often branches. Furthermore, before players can choose a particular advancement, they must have access to any underlying nodes. Also known as a **Node Tree** or **Skill Tree**.

Tech web

An advancement structure for the capabilities that a character or player can earn in which progression can come from several different directions. Furthermore, before players can choose a particular advancement, they must have access to any or all of the connecting nodes. Also known as a **Node Web** or **Skill Web**.

Technical Certification Requirements (TCR)

Microsoft's list of technical guidelines for third-party publications on their consoles. ♪

Technical design doc

A detailed description of the means and methods the programmers will utilize to code the game. Also known as the **Technical Specifications**. ■ ♪

Technical Requirements Checklist (TRC)

Sony's list of technical guidelines for third-party publications on their consoles. ♪

Technical review

1. An evaluation of the code by either the programming team or programmers unrelated to the product. ■

2. An evaluation at the beginning of development to determine which methods and tools are the best fit for each team. ■ ▮ ♪

Technical Review Group (TRG)

A collection of employees tasked with the peer-review of a product or process. ♪

Technical specifications

A detailed description of the means and methods the programmers will utilize in the coding of the game. Also known as the **Technical Design Doc.** ■ ♪ ▣

Technical support (Tech support)

The personnel assigned as a point of contact for the public and tasked with increasing customer satisfaction by providing them with solutions to technical issues, such as installation, system stability, and performance. ♪

Telecine (TK)

The process of transferring film to video. ▮

Teleport

The direct transportation of a character from one spot in the game world to another. Also known as a **Gate.** ▣

Template method pattern

A software design pattern in which algorithms exist as a framework and to which templates can be applied to redefine how they function thereby allowing one module to produce a variety of results depending on which template is applied to it. ■

Temporal aliasing

A visual phenomenon in which the frame rate of the capture device causes any movement or animation to appear at a notably different speed than it actually occurs. See also **Stroboscopic Effects** and **Wagon Wheel Effect.** ▮

Temporal balancing

A method of balancing by giving stronger advantages a shorter lifespan than weaker ones. ▣

Tension

The conflict generated by opposing forces. ◀ ▣

Termination

1. The means and methods by which an agreement can come to an end. ♪

2. The ending of a project before it is completed. ♪

3. The ending of an employee's contract. ♪

Terrain editor

A software tool used to create and alter the geometry of a game's exterior land environment. ⬛ ▣

Tessellation

1. The creation of a pattern that fills a surface without gaps or overlays. ⬛

2. The conversion of 3D geometry into a series of standardized polygons. ⬛

Test harness

The data and software used for automated testing. ⬛ ♪

Test plan

1. A documented outline of the budget, schedule, scope, and tasks for the evaluation of a product. ♪ ⬛

2. The scheduling and assignment of evaluative tasks to members of the QA team. ♪

Testbed design method

A design process in which a working, nearly featureless version of the game is created and experimented with first and then new features are implemented on an as-needed basis. Also known as **Evolutionary Prototyping** or the **Sandbox Design Method**. ▣

Testing

An evaluation process for a product to ensure that it achieves its functional and marketability goals. ♪ ⬛

Testing plan

The formal listing of the methodologies and schedules used by the QA team during the project. ♪

Testing to fail

A QA philosophy in which the focus is on evaluating the software's ability to perform correctly when encountering unexpected situations. Also known as **Negative Testing**. ♪

Testing to pass

A QA philosophy in which the focus is on evaluating the software's ability to perform correctly when encountering anticipated situations. Also known as **Positive Testing**. ♪

Tet

Tetrahedron. A 3D shape composed of four triangular faces. See also **Tetrahedral Modeling**. ⬛

Tetrahedral modeling

The division of a mesh into 3D triangular shapes known as tets, often to simulate physics and fluid movements. See also **Tetrahedron**. ⬛

Tetrahedron (Tet)

A 3D shape composed of four triangular faces. See also **Tetrahedral Modeling**. ⬛

Texel

Texture Element. The smallest unit of a texture that can shrink or grow in relation to the pixels used to make up its image. ⬛

Text

Any displayed alphanumeric characters or marks. ⬛ ✦ ⬛

Text-based games

A genre of video game in which the player is provided a written description of the environment and events instead of their graphical representation. ♪

Text box

A user-interface element that allows text and numbers to be entered into a prede-fined area. Also known as a **Field**. ⬛ ⬛

Texture

1. A layer applied to the surface of a polygon that can imitate the lighting, texture, color, and material of the 3D object. ⬛

2. A design element that creates the impression of the tactile quality of an object's surface. ⬛

Texture baking

A texturing technique for creating a new, more efficient texture by first rendering the surface of an object with the existing texture and lighting and then converting the resulting render into its own texture. Also known as **Baking** or **Rendering-to-Texture**.

Texture clamping

A method of resolving a conflict between a texture's coordinates and the size of its body by anchoring the coordinates to a specific location on the image.

Texture dropping

An error in which a piece of geometry no longer displays its assigned texture.

Texture filtering

Any of several methods to prevent undesired graphical anomalies when textures are viewed from different angles or distances.

Texture layering

Merging textures one on top of another to gain a cumulative effect.

Texture mirroring

Pairing the reverse of a texture on one half of a symmetrical object with its nonreversed form on the other half thereby reducing the memory requirements for storing the texture necessary to cover the object.

Texture wrapping

The placement of textures around the surface of a 3D object.

TF

Trilinear texture filtering. A method of maintaining the visual quality of a texel whenever it's enlarged or made smaller by applying bilinear filtering to two different scales of a texture and averaging the results.

Theme

1. The message, often expressed as a moral, that a story imparts. See also **Moral**.
2. The overall context of a game. See also **High Concept**.
3. The subject-matter of a game.
4. A reoccurring, often abstract element within a game or story.

Theorycrafting

The act of speculating on the effectiveness of different strategies, often by evaluating the formulas used within a game.

Third party

1. A party that creates software designed for use on a system or device that another party produces. ♪

2. A party that is not a direct member of an agreement or contract but may be affected by it. ♪

Thread

1. A path of implementation within a program that allows for a faster and more responsive execution by the processor when multiple threads are used. ▦

2. A continuing discussion posted in a forum. ♪

Threat list

A record, based on events during combat, that prioritizes the combatants on which an AI entity will focus. Also known as a **Hate List**. ▣ ▦

Three-act structure

The traditional structure of storytelling in stage and film in which the story is introduced, complicated, then resolved. ✠

Three-point lighting

A lighting method that utilizes a key light, a back light, and a fill light. ▚

Third-person camera

A camera that provides a view of a scene from behind the character, revealing the majority of its body, thereby allowing the player to see the area immediately occupied by his or her avatar. ▚

Tick

1. The smallest unit of time that a game recognizes per its programming. ▦

2. A specific number of nanoseconds as defined by different hardware standards. ▦

Ticking bomb

A technique of increasing suspense by clueing the audience in to a danger of which the hero is unaware. ✠ ▣

Ticking clock

An element that brings a sense of immediacy to a player, particularly when she or he is engaged in a race-type challenge. ▣

Tier

An iterative stage in the game development cycle in which new elements are added to the previous version of a game. 🔲

Tier design method

An iterative creation process in which components are added as scheduled to a functioning prototype then tested and refined before the next iteration. 🔲

Tile

1. A defined, repeating space in the game environment's XY plane that objects can be placed upon. ▮ ▰ 🔲

2. A piece that can be assembled next to another to create a game board. 🔲

3. A subdivided portion of a screen that is drawn individually. ▮

4. A block, used as a game piece, that has a value or symbol marked on one side which, when turned face down, does not indicate what that value or symbol is. 🔲

Tile rendered

A rendering process in which the area to be rendered is divided into smaller sections, each of which are individually rendered. ▮

Time boxing

An estimating of the man-hours required to complete a task by giving it the maximum amount of time that the task can be assigned without negatively affecting the project. ♪

Time-constrained model

A scheduling pattern that focuses on the actual time requirements of the tasks within the project, and the dependencies and division of ownership of those tasks. ♪

Time of performance

The listing within a contract of when work will begin and when it is due to be finished and delivered. ♪

Timeout

1. A function that if an anticipated input is not received the pending action is cancelled. ▰

2. An action a player can take within a timed activity that pauses the timer. 🔲

Timer

An object that keeps track of the passage of time either by counting up or down.

Timing diagram

A chart used in UML to illustrate the order in which the processes interact with one another. Also known as an **Event Diagram**, an **Event Scenario**, and a **Sequence Diagram**.

Timing issue

1. A problem or conflict arising from sequencing rules.

2. A conflict related to when a game is released in terms of seasonal fluctuations and competing products.

Title safe area

The area of an image that the vast majority of monitor and television screens do not crop and therefore is considered safe to place text in. See also **Action Safe Area**.

Title screen

A full-screen image that displays the software's title and often the logos of the companies that contributed to its development. See also **Splash Screen**.

TK

Telecine. The process of transferring film to video.

TOA

Terms of Agreement. The portion of a contract that lists each party's responsibilities to each other within that contract. In software, the TOA is often listed with the product and the user is responsible for either accepting it or not using the software.

Token

1. A piece used to represent something else.

2. A unit of text that has been categorized by the programming language based on its function.

Tool

Ancillary software used in the development of a product.

Top-down AI

An artificial intelligence technique in which the AI has been supplied with a desired end result and is tasked to find the most effective way of manipulating individual units to achieve it. ▪

Top-down camera

A camera that provides an overhead view of a scene. ▪

Top-down planning

Scheduling based on senior management's view of the project. See also **Bottom-up Planning.** ♪

Topshelf

1. A high-quality game intended to appeal to a large consumer base and named for the practice of putting highly desirable merchandise on shelves that are eye level with the consumer. Primarily used in the U.S. See also **AAA.** ♪

2. An adult product placed above the eye level of children. Primarily used in the U.K. ♪

Total conversion

A mod that is so different than the original game it was derived from that it is considered a new game in its own right. ♪

Total Party Kill (TPK)

The result of an encounter in which all allied characters are defeated and the encounter must be restarted. See also **Wipe.** ♪ ▣

Toy

A genre of video game that focuses on free-play over assigned objectives and competition. ♪

TPK

Total Party Kill. The result of an encounter in which all allied characters are defeated and the encounter must be restarted. See also **Wipe.** ♪ ▣

Trackability

The ability to determine the current and past responsibility of ownership for an issue or asset. ♪ ▪

Trademark

A symbol, image, or text that a party claims as exclusively representative of their product, service, or property. ♪

Tradeoff

A mechanic in which limited resources force a player to evaluate and decide between two beneficial options. 🎲

Tragedy of the commons

An illustration of the conflict between short-term self-interest and the long-term common good when dealing with limited resources. The example is of a common plot of land owned by several people. If everyone tries to collect all of the resources at the same time the land will become barren, whereas if they cooperate and take turns, the land can continue to renew its resources and feed everyone sufficiently. Also known as the **Commons Dilemma**. 🎲

Trailer

A noninteractive preview primarily composed of clips from the game and used to promote interest in it before it is released. ♪ 🖌

Trainer

An NPC that provides characters additional skills and abilities, often at a cost. 🎲

Transform

An early step in the rendering process in which the engine determines which objects will be drawn on screen. 🖌

Transition

1. The movement from one shot to the next. ✍
2. The internal change of a character from one state to another. ✍
3. The visual effect used when moving from one shot to the next. 🖌
4. The area of a model in which one distinct part connects to another distinct part. 🖌

Translate

To move an object from its origin. 🖌

Translucent map

A texture that allows different amounts of diffuse light to shine through parts of the model it is applied to based on the varying degrees of thickness throughout the model. Also known as a **Depth Map** and a **Translucent Shadow Map**. 🖌

Translucent shadow map

A texture that allows diffuse light to shine through parts of the model it is applied to based on the model's thickness at various coordinates. Also known as **Depth Map** and **Translucent Map**. ⬤

Transmedia

The use of multiple communication platforms to form a unique collaborative message which, as a whole, differs from the message delivered by any one channel. ♫

Transparency

1. The game's ability to allow a player to see the connection between their actions and the results of those actions. ⌨

2. A channel that allows a portion of a texture to be partially or completely invisible. See also **Alpha Channel**. ⬤

3. A clear sheet, often acetate, that an illustration can be applied to in traditional animation. ⬤

4. The degree to which a project's details are revealed to those not directly involved. ♪

Trap

1. A play made to entice an opponent into changing their strategy. ⌨

2. An avoidable encounter in which some punitive effect takes place if it is not avoided and, even if it is successfully defeated, the player is usually not rewarded as much as if he or she had not triggered it. ⌨

Trash

An AI enemy that yields little reward when destroyed but must be defeated before a more desirable target can be engaged. ⌨

Traveler's dilemma

An illustration of the paradoxical advantage of real-world intuitive decisions over proven mathematical directives in some situations. In the example, two travelers must independently value a lost item with each traveler receiving the lowest of the declared values as compensation but with a bonus given to the traveler who submitted the lower amount. Through experimentation, the better payoff is often shown to be achieved with intuitive choices than with choices based on mathematical predictions. ⌨

TRC

Technical Requirements Checklist. Sony's list of technical guidelines for third-party publications on their consoles. ♪

Treadmill

A section of a game in which a similar series of events constantly reoccur. See also **Grinding**. ▣

Treatment

A detailed, step-by-step description of a story or game that is often used during the pitch process. ✦ ▣

TRG

Technical Review Group. A collection of employees tasked with the peer-review of a product or process. ♪

Tri

Triangle. A polygon with exactly three edges. ▚

Triage

The prioritization of issues so that the most important ones are addressed first. ♪

Triangle (Tri)

A polygon with exactly three edges. ▚

Triangularity

An equal balance between three points which is achieved by having each point out-rank one opposing point and being outranked by another, as proposed by Crawford. See also **Rock-paper-scissors**. ▣

Trigger

1. A button on the controller that is squeezed. ♪
2. An action that causes a predetermined event to take place within a game. ▣ ◼

Trilinear texture filtering (TF)

A method of maintaining the visual quality of a texel whenever it is made larger or smaller by applying bilinear filtering to two different scales of a texture and averaging the results. ▚

Trim

The reduction of a surface's area by removing a portion of the surface's whole. ▚

Trump

A play that supersedes a previous play which, until then, was winning. 🖭

Tug of war

A transitive balancing mechanic in which each resource is ranked in a linear hierarchy that determines each resource's relative strength, such as the ranking of cards within a suit. 🖭

Turn-based game

1. A classification of video games in which player's actions take place outside the game world's time. See also **Real Time**. ♪

2. A classification of games in which each player is assigned a segment in which to take actions. ♪

Turn order

The rules that dictate the sequence in which the player can perform his or her actions. Also known as **Order of Execution**, **Play Sequence**, **Sequence of Play**, or **Turn Sequence**. 🖭

Turn sequence

The rules that dictate the sequence in which the player can perform his or her actions. Also known as **Order of Execution**, **Play Sequence**, **Sequence of Play**, or **Turn Order**. 🖭

Turning point

An event, most often unexpected, that causes the story to change direction. 🖋

Turtling

A strategy of committing all resources to defense until the player feels that her or his interests are sufficiently protected. 🖭

Tutorial

An early portion of the game that is designed to teach the controls, rules, and basic strategy of the game. 🖭 🖌 🖋

Tweak

A minor adjustment made to achieve a precise result. 🖭 ♪ 🖌 ▪

Tweening

An animation technique of creating one or more frames between two existing frames so that the transition between those frames flows smoothly. 🖌

Tweens

Inbetweens. Animation frames created to smooth the transition between keyframes.

Twink

A character that has been given higher level items, either from another player or another character he or she controls, as opposed to earning them. See also **Twinking**.

Twinking

A strategy in which a low-level character is equipped with high-level items the character has not earned thereby reducing the risks that character assumes. See also **Twink**.

Twitch-based games

A classification of video games in which fast reflexes and good hand-eye coordination are essential to success.

Tyranny of small decisions

A principle, espoused by Khan, that the more decisions a person is required to make, the harder it is for that person to achieve the optimal strategy.

UI

User Interface. The system by which the player gains information about the game's state and interacts with the game's environment.

UI design

User Interface design. The creation, layout, and integration of the system by which the player gains information about the game's state and interacts with the game's environment.

Umbra

The dense, inner part of a shadow.

UML

Unified Modeling Language. An artificial standardized language designed for the visualization of the architecture of an object-oriented software system, primarily through the use of diagrams.

Uncanny valley

A theory brought forth by Mori that if an artificial entity, such as a CGI model, becomes too close in appearance and mannerism to a human being it will elicit a repulsive reaction.

Unified Modeling Language (UML)

An artificial standardized language designed for the visualization of the architecture of an object-oriented software system, primarily through the use of diagrams.

Unified process

An iterative software development framework that focuses on a compartmentalized structure and continual testing and from which many other frameworks have been devised. Also known as the **Unified Software Development Process.**

Unified software development process

An iterative software development framework that focuses on a compartmentalized structure and continual testing and from which many other frameworks have been devised. Also known as the **Unified Process.**

Uninstaller

1. An independent program responsible for the removal of all components of the software that were previously installed.

2. A function of the operating system that performs the role of an independent uninstaller.

Unique Selling Points (USP)

The elements of a game that separate it from its competitors.

Unit

1. An entity that represents an individual force and which has its own attributes and behaviors. Often used to describe military-themed actors within a strategy game.

2. A single copy of a product.

Unit testing

A quality-assurance methodology where the components of a program are tested independently of the whole as each one is completed.

Unity

A design element that determines how well all of the objects in a scene support each other. 🎨

Unlockable

An attribute of a game's element that prevents it from being used or encountered until a specific requirement is met. 🎮 ♪

Usability

How easy and intuitive a product or feature is to use. 🎮

Use case scenario

A detailed example that documents how a user will interact with a system and which thereby assists the developer to implement design improvements. ▪

User-generated content

Game elements that have been created by the fan community. ♪ 🎮

User Interface (UI)

The system by which the player gains information about the game's state and interacts with the game's environment. 🎮 ▪ 🎨

User Interface design (UI design)

The creation, layout, and integration of the system by which the player gains information about the game's state and interacts with the game's environment. 🎮 ▪ 🎨

User story

A brief, user-focused description, used during the design process, that documents the need for an included feature and the benefits it would provide. 🎮 ▪ ♪

USP

Unique Selling Points. The elements of a game that separate it from its competitors. ♪

UV

An orientation standard for 2D images. 🎨

UV Map

A hidden 2D texture which contains the coordinates used for the proper placement of another, viewable texture onto the 3D object it is associated with. 🎨

V & V

Verification and Validation. A formalized process in which software is evaluated to ensure that it meets all requirements and expectations. ■ ♪

Validation

1. A process that determines if a product meets its designed standards. ♪

2. A process that approves an entered password or code as authentic. ♪

Valorization

1. The assignment of a score to an achievement. ▣

2. A comparative ranking of an outcome, such as "fail," "pass," or "perfect." ▣

Value

1. The inherent or perceived worth of a resource to a player. ▣

2. An attribute of a unit expressed numerically thereby allowing comparisons between various units' effectiveness. ▣

3. The current numerical assignment to a variable or constant. ■

4. An element of design that determines an image's relative darkness. Also known as **Brightness**. ▮

Valve design process

A decentralized iterative design process in which specialized members are cycled through a design group tasked with reviewing and culling the existing prototype. Also known as the **Cabal Development Model**. ♪ ▣

Vanilla

An unmodified version of the software. ♪

Vaporware

An announced software project that ultimately is never released to the public. ♪

Variable

A temporary or permanent placeholder for a value that may change throughout gameplay, such as a character's health or a player's score. See also **Constant**. ■

Variable budget

A modifiable limitation on the financial resources that a project can use, with the adjustments usually based on changes in costs. Also known as a **Flexible Budget**. ♪

Variable interval reward

A benefit that is available only after a period of time, which has not been previously disclosed to the participant and which the participant cannot deduce. See also **Fixed Interval Reward**.

Variable ratio reward

A benefit that is available only after having successfully repeated an action a number of times, which has not been previously disclosed to the participant and which the participant cannot deduce. See also **Fixed Ratio Reward**.

Variable sum game

A game that allows win-win scenarios and win-lose scenarios. See also **Positive Sum Game** and **Zero Sum Game**.

Variant

A game that is played by an alternative set of rules.

VCS

Version Control System. A procedure, often automated, that tracks all changes made to the files during the life of a project. Also known as a **Revision Control System**.

Vector

A dynamically alterable, indexed list of elements within the code that the program can reference. See also **Array**.

Vector graphics

An image that is defined by its mathematical expression thereby allowing it to be scaled without affecting its resolution. Also known as a **Vector Image**.

Vector image

An image that is defined by its mathematical expression thereby allowing it to be scaled without affecting its resolution. Also known as **Vector Graphics**.

Vehicular combat

A genre of video games in which the primary focus is on battles between weapon-mounted vehicles in an arena or race track setting.

Velocity

The speed at which an object is moving.

Velocity vector

The speed and direction in which an object is moving. ▨

Vendor

1. An NPC designed to allow players to buy and sell items. ▨
2. To buy or sell items to an NPC. ▨
3. A retail seller. ▨

Verb set

The list of actions an object is expected to be able to perform. ▨

Verification

1. An inspection process that is focused on meeting a defined standard. ♪
2. The review of a reported issue to determine if its listed status matches its actual status. ♪
3. A process that checks the content of a file for authenticity and integrity. ▨
4. A process that confirms a result. ♪
5. The process of reexamining all reported issues to determine if they have been resolved satisfactorily. ♪

Verification and Validation (V & V)

A formalized process in which software is evaluated to ensure that it meets all requirements and expectations. ▨ ♪

Versatile balancing

A method of balancing in which weaker resources are designed so that they can be more effectively utilized in multiple strategies than stronger ones can be. ▨

Version

1. A unique identity, often numerical, assigned to a build to differentiate it from previous builds of the same project. ♪ ▨
2. The unique identity assigned to a draft used to differentiate it from its earlier forms. ✐
3. A draft of a piece that is different than its finalized form. ✎ ✐

Version control

The maintenance of a project's files as they change over time. Also known as **Revision Control**. ♪ ▇

Version Control System (VCS)

A procedure, often automated, that tracks all changes made to the files during the life of a project. Also known as a **Revision Control System**. ♪ ▇

Vertex

Vertices (plural). The corner of a polygon formed at the point where two edges meet. ▝▐

Vertex shading

The application of lighting effects to the surface being lit by altering the attributes of its vertices. ▝▐

Veto

The right of a player to prevent another player's attempted action. ▨

VFX

Visual Effects. The visual elements, usually computer generated, that are added to a scene after the action has been recorded. ▝▐

Video buffer

A data storage area that temporarily holds rendering information before sending it to a display device. ▇ ▝▐

Video footage shooting games

A genre of laser video games in which actual aerial combat footage is interjected with sprite-based explosions when a target is hit. ♪

Video game

1. Entertainment software designed to be played on a gaming console, arcade machine, electronic device, or personal computer. ♪

2. A game played on a set that receives and displays video signals. ♪

View frustum

The portion of a 3D virtual environment that the screen displays at any particular time. Also known as the **Viewing Frustum**. ▝▐

View space

A 3D environment in which the object locations are given in relation to the camera. Also known as **Camera Space** or **Eye Space**. 🔲

Viewing frustum

The portion of a 3D virtual environment that the screen displays at any particular time. Also known as a **View Frustum**. 🔲

Virtual displacement mapping

A texture mapping technique that creates a greater sense of depth within the texture by altering the texture based on the angle at which it is used. Also known as **Offset Mapping** and **Parallax Mapping**. 🔲

Virtual memory

The use of disk storage space as additional memory. 🔲

Visibility

An attribute of each of the components within a class that determines if that component can be seen and used by another class. 🔲

Visible Surface Determination (VSD)

Any of the numerous processes used for determining which faces of a 3D object are occluded and therefore do not need to be rendered. Also known as **Hidden Surface Removal**. 🔲

Vision doc

1. A description of the project, its expected budget, team composition, and company background that is often used as part of the pitch process. Also known as a **Concept Doc** or **Proposal Doc**. 🎵

2. A description of the project at its earliest stages that is used in internal communications. Also known as a **Concept Doc** or **Proposal Doc**. 🎵 🔲

3. Any summary of the project that emphasizes its viability and is distributed to potential investors or publishers to increase their interest. Also known as a **Proposal Doc** or **Vision Doc**. 🎵 🔲

Vision statement

A declaration of an organization's future expectations as it relates to their anticipated success. 🎵

Visual Effects (VFX)

The visual elements, usually computer generated, that are added to a scene after the action has been recorded.

Visual narrative

The use of environments, objects, and level design to craft a story thereby removing or reducing the need for expository dialogue or text.

Visualization

1. The ability to envision something without having first seen it, often utilized during the creation process.

2. A chart or other graphical representation used to illustrate abstract data and processes.

V.O.

Voice Over. Recorded dialogue that, while it is being played, is separate from the action occurring on screen.

Voice

1. The unique perspective and style the author uses.

2. The unique perspective and style with which a character within a story speaks.

Voice acting

The performance of actors whose delivery is recorded for use by in-game characters.

Voice Over (V.O.)

Recorded dialogue that, while it is being played, is separate from the action occurring on screen.

Volume light

A light source whose light permeates throughout a predefined area only.

Volumetric fog

The creation of cloud-like effects by placing a shader within a room or other container.

Volunteer's dilemma

An illustration of the reluctance of one person to incur the cost of an action when others are still capable of making the same action. The example given is of a power outage in which none of the residents want to place an expensive phone call to have the power turned back on and as a result the town continues in darkness. 🖳

Voxel

Volumetric Pixel. A cube shaped representation of solid matter that serves as a basic unit for volumetric modeling and, when combined with other voxels, gives them their 3D appearance. 📷▮

Voxel sculpting

A modeling method in which cube-shaped elements are used to form the geometry of an object thereby allowing divisions, merging, deforming, and volume building in an intuitive manner. 📷▮

VSD

Visible Surface Determination. Any of the numerous processes used for determining which faces of a 3D object are occluded and therefore do not need to be rendered. Also known as **Hidden Surface Removal**. 📷▮

Wagon wheel effect

A temporal aliasing effect commonly seen on wheels in which, when viewed at a certain speed creates the illusion that the wheels are rotating backward. See also **Temporal Aliasing**. 📷▮

Walk cycle

A loop of animation designed to create the impression that a character is walking. See also **Animation Cycle**. ♪ 📷▮

Walkthrough

A publication that provides a step-by-step demonstration of either the critical or optimal path through a game. ♪

Wall walking

A method of traveling through an area by moving the character forward along a wall or other barrier and relying on the physics of the game to dictate the character's degree of access to the environment. Often used by players as a means of entering an area that the designers intended to be inaccessible from that location. 🖳

Wargame

1. A subgenre of strategy games in which historical or potential military conflicts are presented in a way that encourages the use of strategies and tactics that

correlate closely to those used in militaristic encounters. Also known as a **Military Simulation.** ♪

2. A table-top game in which military battles are played out, often with miniatures. See also **Kreigsspeil.** ♪

Warranty

A contractual promise that guarantees a product's performance. ♪

Waterfall method

A design method that once each stage is completed and deemed successful it immediately continues onto the next stage without reexamining the earlier stages for any changes to their degree of success. Also known as the **Cascade Method.** ▣

WAU

Weekly Active Users. The number of unique end users that access a site or application within seven continuous days, particularly in reference to social media. ♪

Wave

A surge of enemy units. ▣

WBS

Work Breakdown System or *Work Breakdown Structure.* The division of a task into its most basic components. ♪

WBS sheet

A listing of all of the basic components for all tasks needed on a project to facilitate the scheduling, budgeting, and delegation of responsibilities within that project. ♪

Weekly Active Users (WAU)

The number of unique end users that access a site or application within seven continuous days, particularly in reference to social media. ♪ ▣

Weight

1. An assigned value to a bone or joint that determines how much of an affect it has on the geometry. ▮

2. An assigned value to an attribute that determines how much of an affect a routine will have on it. ▄

Whitebox testing

An evaluative process in which the tester is aware of the intended functionality and outcome of the product. ♪ ▦

Wholesale

The sale of product at a volume discount, usually with the intention that the purchaser will then be retailing that product to consumers. ♪

Wild sounds

A recording of background noise that does not need to be synched to the action within a scene. ♣

Will Not Fix (WNF)

A designation assigned to a reported issue that states no attempts will be made to correct it. ♪

Win condition

A game state that when reached the player reaching it wins the game. ▣

Window dressing

Elements added to a product to make it appear more desirable without adding any actual value to it. See also **Chrome.** ♪ ▣

WIP

Work In Progress. A work whose quality is not yet up to release standards. ♪ ▮

Wipe

1. The destruction of all of a player's forces. See also **TPK.** ♪ ▣

2. The removal of all code and other software remnants from a system. See also **Clean.** ♪ ▦

3. The removal of a player's characters and advancements from the server on which they are stored. ♪ ▦

Wireframe

A method of visualizing solid 3D objects in a see-through manner by using lines and perspective to illustrate the size and shape of the object. ▮

WNF

Will Not Fix. A designation assigned to a reported issue that states no attempts will be made to correct it. ♪

Work Breakdown Structure (WBS)

The division of a task into its most basic components. Also known as **Work Breakdown System**. ♪

Work Breakdown System (WBS)

The division of a task into its most basic components. Also known as **Work Breakdown Structure**. ♪

Work for hire

A negotiated, legal designation that the rights to the works created belong to the contracting party instead of their creator. ♪

Work in Progress (WIP)

A work whose quality is not yet up to release standards. ♪ 🕯

World design

The development of the environment in which the game's events take place and the creation of any relevant backstory. ⌨ ◣

World space

A 3D environment in which object locations are given in relation to an arbitrary origin spot. 🕯

World update module

The section of code that adjusts the current state of the game's environment to account for the player's actions. ▨

Worse is better

A design approach, described by Gabriel, that ranks simplicity higher than correctness, consistency, and completeness. Also known as **New Jersey Style**. ▨ ♪

Write combining

A technique of combining and storing data in a temporary memory buffer so that the data can be quickly accessed as a burst when needed instead of being built from scratch at that time. ▨

WSAD

An input scheme using the W, S, A, and D keys on the keyboard to control movement. ⌨

WYSIWYG (*"Wiziwig"*)

What You See Is What You Get. A feature in which objects' real-time display is nearly identical to how they will render.

XGD

Extreme Game Development. An agile design process, proposed by Demachy, in which regularly interspersed milestones serve as iterative cycles and the design team adjusts its project after each milestone based on the producer's feedback.

XML

Extensible Markup Language. An open standard for documentation encoding that allows stored text to be parsed by a program yet edited separately from the program's code.

XP

Experience Points. The points awarded a player that measure her or his progression in developing their character and are used to determine when additional benefits are unlocked.

XP debt

The amount of experience points that a character is penalized and must be re-earned before they can gain any new experience points, usually within an MMORPG due to death.

XP method

Extreme Programming method. A rapid-prototyping software development methodology in which the focus is on rapid cycling through the coding and testing phases with features added on an as-needed basis. Also known as **Code-fix Methodology**.

XP penalty

A negative amount of experience points applied to a character upon their death, most often used in MMORPGs.

XYZ coordinates

A method of measuring 3D space by assigning positive and negative numerical values to each axis. Also known as **Cartesian Coordinates**.

YAGNI

You Ain't Gonna Need It. A principle in extreme programming that functionality should only be added on an as-needed basis.

Z-buffer

A data storage area that holds information on each pixel's depth within a scene. Also known as a **Depth Buffer.** ■ ♪

Z-fail

A technique in lighting in which the rendering process evaluates the surfaces lying outside of the shadow's volume to determine which pixels are affected. Also known as **Carmack's Reverse** or **Depth Fail.** ▉

Z-fighting

A conflict between two objects whose surfaces occupy nearly the same space, resulting in a flickering alternation between the objects' surfaces during the rendering process. ▉

Z-pass

A technique in lighting in which the rendering process evaluates the surfaces lying inside of the shadow's volume to determine which pixels are affected. Also known as **Depth Pass.** ▉

Zerg rush

A strategy in which a player sends out an early, all-or-nothing attack on an opponent, usually with numerous inexpensive units. Named after a race in *Starcraft* for which this strategy was effective. ▣

Zero sum game

A game in which every gain or win must, by its nature, be offset by an equal loss to an opponent and therefore results in only one ultimate winner at the game's conclusion. See also **Positive Sum Game** and **Variable Sum Game.** ▣

Zone

1. A level of a game that is intended to be experienced as a subsection of a larger area. ▣

2. The entrance or exit to a level, particularly one that requires a pause in order for the area's new elements to be loaded. ▣

Zone of control

A mechanic, often included in wargames, in which a unit's presence prevents an opponent's units from entering the surrounding area. ▣

Zoning

The act of moving from one zone to another. ▣

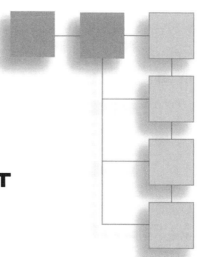

Listing of Words and Terminology by Subject Matter

Art
General
Categories
Animation

Cinematic

Motion graphics

Render

Sculpting

Texture

Concepts
Ambiance

Attenuation

Balance

Brightness

Color

Crop

Eye candy

Flicker fusion threshold

Focus

Gamma

Grid

Highlight

Hue

Image Quality (IQ)

Intensity

Interpolation

Mood

Negative space

Pulling focus

Ramping

Reflection

Resolution

Saturation

Creations

Asset

Camera-ready artwork

Concept art

Decal

Demo reel

Garbage matte

Icon

Loading screen

Logo

Map

Matte

Model

Motion graphics (mograph)

Object

Placeholder

Portfolio

Proxy

Scene

Screen capture

Screenshot

Title screen

Work in Progress (WIP)

Documentation

Camera-ready artwork

Creative design doc

Digital dailies

Mock-up

Model sheet

Storyboard

Target render

Principles

Aesthetics

Contrast

Implied line

Line

Movement

Scale

Shape

Space

Unity

Principles (Color Theories)

CMYK

Color depth

Four-color process

RGB

Principles (Shapes)

Arc

Contour

Curvature

Freeform surface

Inflection

Ogee

Ovoid

Parametric surface

Polycurve

Polyhedral

Ruled surface

Saddle point

Spun surface

Tangent

Style (Dimensionality)

2D

2.5D

3D

Parallax scrolling

Pseudo-3D

Tasks

Bevel

Bind

Chamfer

Clip

Clipping

Emboss

Engrave

Extrusion

Filleting

Framing

Highlight

Lathe

Loft

Merge

Revolve

Rounding

Scale

Transform

Translate

Trim

Tweak

Tools

Codec

Level editor

Mask

Material system

Terrain editor

Animation

Components

Acceleration

Actor

Animation conversion

Conversion

Deceleration

Easing equation

Elastic equation

Gravity

Model sheet

Particles

Rigid body

Soft body

Transparency

Creations

Animatic

Animation cycle

Animation set

Cinematic

Dump

Emote

Fidget

Frame dump

Frame rate

Hot spot

Idle animation

Inbetweens (Tweens)

Key

Mayamatic

Rigging

Scene graph

Screen splatter

Signature move

Walk cycle

Methodologies

Blending

Dynamic motion synthesis

Frame animation

Human motion engine

Keyframe animation

Kinetics

Morphing

Page flipping

Procedural animation

Ragdoll physics

Skeletal animation

Tagged animation

Rigging

Child

Constraint

Cyclic Coordinate Descent (CCD)

Parent

Skeletal animation

Skinned skeleton

Skinning

Weight

Techniques

Animation baking

Animation blending

Explicit animation

Forward Kinematics (FK)

Implicit animation

Inverse Kinetics (IK)

Keying

Simulation baking

Tweening

Cinematics

Components

Action safe area

Actor

Aspect Ratio

Camera

Compositing

Compression

Effects (F/X)

Frames Per Second (FPS)

Garbage matte

Letterbox

Matte

Overscan

Prop

Resolution

Scan data

Special effect

Stroboscopic effects

Title safe area

Visual Effects (VFX)

Visual Narrative

Creations

Clip

Cut-scene

End sequence

Full Motion Video (FMV)

Interactive cut-scene

Montage

Quick Time Event (QTE)

Real-time sequence

Scene

Methodologies

Active optical marker

Blue screen

Cheating

Computer-Generated Image (CGI)

Facial capture

Fly through

Green screen

Motion capture (Mo-cap)

Optical markers

Passive optical marker

Performance capture

Practical

Telecine (TK)

Techniques

Blocking

Chromo keying

Color keying

Dump

Establishing shot

Fade in

Fade out

Frame dump

Keying

Lossless

Lossy

Mise en scene

Motion blur

Pacing

Pull

Pulling focus

Scrubbing

Segue

Transition

Digital

Components

Anchor point

Bézier curve

Control point

Control vertex

Edit point

Handle

Isoline

Isoparm

Knots

Lattice

Layer

Pixel

Rail

Tetrahedron (Tet)

Concepts

Alpha channel

Bit depth

Bitmap

Computer-Generated Image (CGI)

Channel

Curvature continuity

Curve on Surface (COS)

Faceted

G0 continuity

G1 continuity

G2 continuity

Gamma

Geometric

Organic

Polysurface

Positional continuity

Raster

Rubber banding

Sampling

Sprite

Tangency continuity

Tessellation

Vector graphics

Vector image

Lighting and Shading

Characteristics

Contrast

Intensity

Opacity

Radiosity

Self-shadowing

Components

Barn doors

Hot spot

Light spill

Light trespass

Occlusion

Penumbra

Umbra

Concepts

Color bleeding

Color temperature

Colored lighting

Phong

Pulling focus

Shadow volume

Effects

Ambient light

Area light

Backlight

Bloom

Colored lighting

Deferred rendering

Diffuse lighting

Directional light

Dynamic lighting

Emissive lighting

Fill light

Fresnel effect

Hair light

Highlight

Key light

Kicker light

Lens flare

Point light

Rim light

Specular light

Spotlight

Volume light

Methodologies

Baking

Cel shading

Flat shading

Gouraud shading

Pixel shading

Real-time shading

Vertex shading

Techniques

Bidirectional Reflectance Distribution Function (BRDF)

Bump mapping

Diffuse light mapping

Forward rendering

Forward shadow mapping

Percentage closer filtering shadow mapping

Projective shadow

Ray casting

Ray tracing

Rendering-to-texture

Screen space blurred shadow mapping

Shadow map

Specular light mapping

Subsurface light scattering

Three-point lighting

Modeling

Components

Armature

B-spline

Bounding box

Edge

Face

Geometry

Gibs

Hull

Map

Mesh

N-gon

Naked edge

Non-Uniform Rational B-Spline (NURBS)

Normal

NURBS

Patch

Polygon (Poly)

Primitive

Quad

Scan data

Shell

Spline

Tag

Tetrahedron (Tet)

Texture

Triangle (Tri)

Vertex

Voxel

Wireframe

Concepts

Camera

Cartesian coordinates

Child

Destructible terrain

Edge

Environment

Euler angles

Gimbal-lock

High-Order Surface (HOS)

Node

Parent

Particles

Perspective correction

Placeholder

Polygon (Poly)

Predefined models

Proxy

Quaternion

Right-hand rule

Rigid body

Scene

Scene graph

Soft body

Solid model

Tessellation

Uncanny valley

UV map

XYZ coordinates

Methodologies

Box modeling

Edge modeling

Extrusion modeling

N-patching

NURBS modeling

Patch modeling

Polygonal modeling

Primitive modeling

Sculpting

Subdivision modeling (Sub-D modeling)

Tetrahedral modeling

Voxel sculpting

Techniques

Continuous LOD

Discrete LOD

Dynamic Level of Detail (DLOD)

Level of Detail (LOD)

Limb slicing

Rendering

Components

Camera

Depth buffer

Pixel fog

Radial fog

Rotated grid

Shader

Stencil Buffer

Tile

Video Buffer

Volumetric fog

Components (Cameras)

Camera space

Field of view

Fly through

Focus

Frustum

Frustum culling

Notional camera

Perspective

Point of View (POV)

View frustum

View space

Viewing frustum

Components (Space and Planes)

Clip space

Clipping plane

Eye space

Far plane

Homogeneous clip space

Light space

Near plane

Normalized device space

Object space

Screen space

Tangent space

World space

Concepts

Antialiasing

Compression

Depth complexity

Draw

Draw distance

Frame rate

Frame rate locking

Interlaced scan

Interpolation

Occlusion

Overdraw

Pass

Pipeline

Progressive scan

Reflection

Refrast

Refresh

Render budget

Resolution

Scanline rendering

Shading language

Target render

Tile rendered

Errors

Aliasing

Artifact

Banding

Bow wash

Clipping

Freeze

Ghost

Jaggies

Judder

Lock up

Moiré pattern

Pixelation

Temporal aliasing

Wagon wheel effect

Z-fighting

Methods

Nearest neighbor method

Ordered Grid Super Sampling (OGSS)

Point sampling

Sampling

Supersampling

Visible Surface Determination (VSD)

Principles

WYSIWYG (*Wiziwig*)

Process

Backface culling

Binary space partitioning

Cel shading

Culling

Deferred rendering

Depth cueing

Forward rendering

Hardware Transform and Lighting
    (Hardware T & L)

Hidden surface removal

Multipass

Multisampling

Occlusion culling

Painter's algorithm

Palette swap

Parallel projection

Perspective projection

Techniques
Blit (BLT)

Bullet time

Carmack's reverse

Depth fail

Depth pass

Rendering-to-texture

Z-fail

Z-pass

Techniques (Camera Views)
Context-sensitive camera

First-Person camera (FP camera)

Isometric view

Orthographic

Over-the-shoulder camera
    (OTS camera)

Perspective

Third-person camera

Top-down camera

Texturing
Components
Map

Reflection

Seamless texture

Skinning

Stitch line

Texel

Concepts
High Dynamic Range (HDR)

Skinning

Transparency

Errors
Hall of mirrors

Pixel popping

Pixelation

Shimmering

Tearing

Texture dropping

Methodologies
Bump mapping

Cubic environmental map

Decal

Depth map

Displacement mapping

Gloss mapping

Height map

MIP mapping

Normal mapping

Offset mapping

Parallax mapping

Projective texture

Reflection map

Skybox

Spherical environmental mapping

Translucent map

Translucent shadow map

Virtual displacement mapping

Techniques

Baking

Billboarding

Blending

Multitexturing

Rendering-to-texture

Sculpting

Texture baking

Texture clamping

Texture layering

Texture mirroring

Texture wrapping

Techniques (Filters and Sampling)

Anisotropic texture filter (AF)

Bilinear texture filtering (BF)

Linear texture filter

Multisampling

Nearest neighbor method

Point sampling

Texture filtering

Trilinear texture filtering (TF)

GAME DESIGN
General

Components

Chrome

Conditional dialogue

Polish

Risk

Strategy

Tactics

Theme

Window dressing

Concepts

Abstraction

Accessibility

Aesthetics

Affordance

Compatibility

Concept

Conceptualization

Convergence

Design scalability

Encapsulation

Granularity

Heuristic

Knowledge

Modularity

Natural mapping

Process

Synchronization (Sync)

Theme

Usability

Documentation

Architecture

Bible

Bio

Canon

Concept doc

Construction chart

Creative design doc

Design document

Design requirements

Draft

Feature list

Game bible

Game proposal

Logline

Proposal doc

Script

Style guide

Synopsis

Technical design doc

Technical specifications

Treatment

Vision doc

Principles

Comes Out in the Wash (COW)

CYA

Ergonomics

Form follows function

Future compatible

KISS

Overbuilding

Planned obsolescence

Satisficing

Process

Brainstorming

Concept-Knowledge theory (C-K theory)

Forward engineering

Gendanken experiment

High concept

Initial concept

Iteration

Iterative design

Mind mapping

Pass

Premise

Proof of concept

Reverse engineering

User story

Visualization

Techniques

Adaptive difficulty adjustment

Asymmetric game

Asymmetrical map

Asymmetrical objectives

Base stats

Buff

Cap

Dynamic difficulty adjustment

Hard cap

Item level

Negative feedback loop

Nerf

Positive feedback loop

Self-balancing

Soft cap

Symmetrical game

XP debt

Game Balance

Concepts

Absolute superiority

Compensating factor

Golden rule of balance

"I win" button

Intransitive interrelationship

Marginal superiority

Probability curve

Rule as Intended (RAI)

Rule as Written (RAW)

Snowballing

Methodologies

Attribute balancing

Compensative balancing

Component balancing

Strategic balancing

Supportive balancing

Synergetic balancing

Temporal balancing

Versatile balancing

Techniques

Rock-paper-scissors

Scale

Triangularity

Tug of war

Techniques (Resource Balancing)

AI cheat

Back loaded

Community pool

Draft

Draw

Front loaded

Games

Components (Physical)
Bit

Chip

Die (d)

Hex

Miniature (Mini)

Obstacle

Resource

Table

Tile

Timer

Token

Components (Virtual)
Entity

Environment

Fixed device

Fixed object

Gold

Interface

Load screen

Loot

Mode

Node

Paper doll

Player

Splash screen

Story

Tutorial

Zone

Entities (General)
Antagonist

Base

Gamemaster

Non-Player Character (NPC)

Party

Patrol

Player Character (PC)

Predator

Prey

Protagonist

Runner

Unit

Entities (Non-Player Characters)
Actor

AI

AI companion

Boss

Bot

Chatterbot

Creep

Dummy

Faction

Guardian

Lieutenant

Mini-boss

Minion

MOB

Pet

Quest ender

Quest giver

Subfaction

Trainer

Trash

Vendor

Entities (Player Characters)

Alt

Avatar

Hero

Main

Tabula rasa

Features

Alternate ending

Cheat code

Destructible terrain

Freerunning

Ghost

Gibs

Parkour (PK)

Self-shadowing

Skill showcase

Strategic map

Unlockable

User-generated content

Features (Balance)

Difficulty level

Dynamic difficulty adjustment

XP debt

XP penalty

Features (User Interface)

Auto aim

Auto follow

Auto run

Autoattack

Autocast

Autoloot

Automap

Automatic mode cancellation

Autosave

Heads-Up Display (HUD)

Hotkey

Inset map

Mini-map

Save anywhere

Save point

Slot

Socket

Features (World Design)

Bonus stage

Open world

Persistent world

Unlockable

Modes

Attract mode

Campaign

Capture the Flag (CTF)

Co-op mode

Deathmatch

Demo mode

Face-to-Face (FTF)

Free For All (FFA)

Horde mode

Hot seat

King of the hill

Multiplayer

New game plus

Over the Board (OTB)

Play by Email (PBEM)

Play by Web (PBW)

Player versus Environment (PvE)

Player versus Player (PvP)

Sandbox

Single player

Split screen

Story mode

Segments

Campaign

Critical point of loss

End Sequence

Puzzle

State

Abandoned

Advantage

Book win

Dead draw

Deadlock

Draw

End game

Game view

Lock

Lock-on victory

Lose condition

·Loss condition

Maxed out

Objective

Play time

Pyrrhic victory

Setup

Submission

Win condition

Systems

Artificial Intelligence (AI)

Camera system

Character creation

Character generation

Chat

Combat system

Consider (Con)

Crafting

Economy

Elo

Experience (XP)

Game configuration system

Handicapping System

Inventory

Item mall

Lobby

Matchmaking

Queue

Resource management

Rule system

Save game system

Sequence

Tutorial

User Interface (UI)

Systems (Bidding)

All-pay auction

Auction

Draft

Dutch auction

Snake draft

Types

2D

2.5D

3D

Agon

Alea

Alternating game

Collectable game

Finite game

Freerunning

Grand strategic scale

Ilinx

Linear

Ludology

Ludus

Mimicry

Multiplayer

Murder sim

Nonlinear

Operational scale

Paidea

Parkour (PK)

Player versus Environment (PvE)

Player versus Player (PvP)

Rock-paper-scissors

Sandbox

Serious game

Simulation (Sim)

Simultaneous game

Single player

Strategic scale

Tactical scale

Twitch-based games

Game Construction

Concepts

Burden of knowledge

Cost curve

Difficulty curve

Difficulty independence

Directness of conflict

Dynamic scalability

Emergent gameplay

Emergent storytelling

Fun button

Fun factor

Gameplay

Immersive gameplay

Learning curve

Pacing

Pillar

Play-life

Player acknowledgement

Quantification

Transparency

Valorization

Design Responsibilities

Content design

Level design

Narrative design

Player advocacy

System design

User Interface design (UI design)

World design

Framework

Balance

Conditions

Conflict

Constitutive rules

Core gameplay

Dynamics

Emergence

Feature

Game design

Game state

Game theory

Gameplay

Genre

Housekeeping

Implied rules

Mechanics

Metagame

Negotiable consequence

Operational rules

Rules

Scope

State

Tier

Value

Game Theory

Assurance game

Cake-cutting dilemma

Centipede game

Chicken game

Commons dilemma

Deadlock game

Divide and choose

Fair division problem

Hawk dove game

Imperfect information

Lottery-based decision making

Nash equilibrium

Non-parametric decision

Parametric decision

Perfect information

Positive sum game

Prisoner's dilemma

Privileged information

Stag hunt

Tragedy of the commons

Traveler's dilemma

Variable sum game

Volunteer's dilemma

Zero sum game

Level/World Design (Concepts)

Background (b.g.)

Conditional dialogue

Event

Game time

Gamemaster

Instance

Mirror match

Real-time sequence

Script

Sequence

Theme

Ticking clock

Tile

Wave

Level/World Design (Content)

Camera

Clip

Control point

Easter egg

End sequence

Flight path

Gate

Ingredient

Key

Level

Lock

Mission

Objective

Obstacle

Occluder

Placeholder

Port

Power up

Prop

Quest

Quest chain

Reagent

Ride path

Scope

Spawn point

Trigger

Tutorial

User-generated content

Zone

Level/World Design (Principles)

Backtracking

Bread-crumbing

Chekhov's gun

Compression

Experiential density

Funneling

Insurmountable obstacle

Line of Sight (LOS)

On rails

Populate

Ticking bomb

Unlockable

Visual narrative

Mechanics

Aggro

Chance

Consider

Contingency

Core mechanic

Despawn

Divide and choose

Downtime

Faction

Faction points

Fumble

Hit points

Honor system

House rules

Intensity

Kingmaker

Lottery-based decision making

Ordering

Pseudo-Random Number Generator (PRNG)

Random Number Generator (RNG)

Real time

Tag

Tradeoff

Mechanics (Ability)

Action-response mechanic

Active ability

Channeling

Clearcast

Cooldown

Disruption

Duration

Force multiplier

Freecast

Interrupt

Passive ability

Power up

Resurrection sickness

Silence

Skill

Summoning sickness

Trump

Mechanics (Character Advancement)

Base stats

Build

Experience Points (XP)

Level cap

Node tree

Node web

Reroll

Skill point

Skill tree

Skill web

Tech tree

Tech web

Mechanics (Combat)

Aggro

Area of Effect (AoE)

Buff

Burst damage

Chain

Close combat

Combo

Critical hit (Crit)

Crowd Control (CC)

Damage

Damage avoidance

Damage mitigation

Damage Over Time (DOT)

Damage Per Second (DPS)

Debuff

Direct damage

Direct heal

Enrage

Finishing move

Fog of war

Ganking

Heal over time

Juggle

Line

Line of Sight (LOS)

Melee

Ranged combat

Rate of fire

Snowballing

Splash damage

Stun lock

Zone of control

Mechanics (Inventory)

Bind on Equip (BoE)

Bind on Pickup (BoP)

Bind on Use (BoU)

Ingredient

Item decay

Recipe

Mechanics (Progression)

Branching story

Checkpoint

Delay

Fork

Gating

Grinding

Pass

Portal

Teleport

Timeout

Treadmill

Mechanics (Resource)

Bidding

Draft

Drain

Draw

Farming

Power up

Sink

Stack

Methodologies

Agile software development

Behavioral game design

Cabal development model

Cascade method

Clone and tweak

Design for cause

Design for effect

Evolutionary prototyping

Incremental accretive design

Interactive prototype

Linear design

Linear level design

MDA

Modular design

Nonlinear

Rapid prototyping

Sandbox design method

Testbed design method

Tier design method

Tweak

Valve design process

Waterfall method

Techniques

Bread-crumbing

Conditional dialogue

Critical objective

Critical path

Feedback

Function

Hook

Individual objectives

Minimax matrix

Order of execution

Play sequence

Play session

Player procedures

Reinforcer

Relationship management

Replayability

Resource

Resource curve

Risk

Sequence of play

Solvability

Stack

Structured conflict

System procedures

Ticking clock

Trap

Turn order

Turn sequence

Tyranny of small decisions

Value

Variant

Gameplay
Activity
Action

Candidate move

Candidate play

Encounter

Event

Load time

Play

Ply

Proc

Random encounter

Sequence

Errors
Exploit

Feature creep

Overengineered

Snowballing

Software bloat

Timing issue

Wall walking

Strategies (Components)
Attack resources

Cost

Dynamic play

Fork

Metagame

Reward

Risk

Switching cost

Tactics

Theorycrafting

Strategies (Methodologies)

Backwards induction

Bluff

Book win

Cheating

Degenerate strategy

Dominant strategy

Exploit

Gambit

Griefing

Metagaming

Min-maxing

Minimax

Mixed strategy

Near dominant strategy

Non-credible threat

Nuclear

Optimal strategy

Pure strategy

Push

Reactive strategy

Risk aversion

Simplification

Subversive play

Tactics

Backdoor

Backtracking

Camping

Corpse camping

Farming

Focus

Kamikaze

Kill on Sight (KOS)

Kill Stealing (KS)

Kiting

Leashing

Leeching

Naked mage syndrome

Peeling

Point squeezing

Poison pill

Power leveling

Prophylaxis

Pull

Save scumming

Spamming

Strafing

Suicide cheat

Team killing

Trap

Turtling

Twinking

Zerg rush

Player

Abilities

Information reduction

Number crunching

Numerical reasoning

Pattern recognition

Player intentionality

Player interaction pattern

Sequential reasoning

Social reasoning

Spatial reasoning

Suspension of disbelief

Activities
Action

Anticipation of decision

Bargaining

Block

Blow

Bunny hopping

Capture

Casting

Channeling

Corpse run

Crawl

Crowd Control (CC)

Disband

Dynamic play

Fatality

Frag

Hit

Interrupt

Kick

Killing blow

Move

Multiboxing

Ninja looting

Patrol

Play

Ply

Punch

Say

Silence

Tag

Teleport

Vendor

Veto

Zoning

Behavior Theory
Flow

Flow model

Fun

Griefing

Operant conditioning

Play

Decisions
Blind decision

Dilemma

False dilemma

Frequency of decision

Hobson's choice

Meaningless decision

Meier's maxim

Micromanagement

Moral decision

Morton's Fork

Negotiable consequence

Obvious decision

Option

Objectives

Achievement

Advancement

Collection play

Completion achievements

Fed-Ex quest

Goal

Level

Measurement achievements

Mission

Objective

Progression

Quest

Reward

Score

Side quest

Policies

Naming policy

Need before greed

Play nice rules

Psychology

Avoidance reward

Behavioral contrast

Closure

Cognitive immersion

Emotional immersion

Eustress

Extinction

Fixed interval reward

Fixed ratio reward

Fun

Narrative immersion

Reinforcer

Reward

Sensory-motoric immersion

Spatial immersion

Strategic immersion

Stressor

Tactical immersion

Variable interval reward

Variable ratio reward

Socialization

Clan

Grand coalition

Party

Pickup Group (PuG)

States

AFK

Dead

Link Dead (LD)

Out of Character (OOC)

Paralysis by analysis

Permadeath

Rage quit

Respawn

Total Party Kill (TPK)

Wipe

Types

Carebear

Cookie cutter

Daily Active Users (DAU)

Dictator

Free rider

Fringe gamer

Griefing

Kingmaker

Leaver

Monthly Active Users (MAU)

Newbie

Noob

Player Killing (PK)

Power gamer

Rule lawyer

Team killing

Twink

Weekly Active Users (WAU)

User Interface

Components

Button

Check box

Command Line Interface (CLI)

Context menu

Directional pad (D-Pad)

Drop-down list

Field

Graphical User Interface (GUI)

Heads-Up Display (HUD)

Inset map

List box

Loading bar

Loading screen

Main menu

Map

Menu

Menu bar

Mini-map

Pop-up

Progression bar

Radio button

Reticle

Shell

Strategic map

Tab

Text

Text box

Title screen

Trigger

Concepts

Bind

Game configuration system

Menu system

Natural language interface

Shield

Spamming

Principles

Affordance

Feedback

Functional fixedness

Haptic

Natural mapping

Techniques

Button mashing

Context-sensitive menu

Magnetism

Spamming

WSAD

PRODUCTION
General

Agencies and Standards

AFTRA

ATSC

DTMB

DVB

Entertainment Merchants Association (EMA)

Entertainment Software Rating Board (ESRB)

ISDB

Lotcheck

NTSC

PAL

Pan European Game Information (PEGI)

SAG

Technical Certification Requirements (TCR)

Technical Requirements Checklist (TRC)

Concept

Censorship

Deliverable

Note

Post

Prototype

Stock Keeping Unit (SKU)

Unit

Documentation

Build notes

Component-based development

Cover letter

Daily delta report

Database Manager Report (DMR)

Essence statement

Gantt chart

PERT chart

Product plan

Profit and Loss statement (P & L statement)

Regression list

Request For Proposal (RFP)

Research proposal

Risk mitigation plan

SKU plan

WBS sheet

Documentation (Marketing)

Executive summary

Originating document

Protection and Security

Authentication

CD key

Code

Copy protection

Crack

Key

Key code

Keygen

Keylogging

Modchip

Modification (Mod)

Phishing

Piracy

Validation

Verification

Roles (Publishers/Developers)

Actor

Animator

Brand manager

Business Development executive (Biz Dev)

Code Release Group (CRG)

Creative director

Customer support

Developer

Distributor

Focus group

Independent contractor

Internship

Lead

Lead architect

Modeler

Moderator (Mod)

Playtester

Producer

Programmer

Project manager

Publisher

Quality Assurance (QA)

Software designer

Software planner

Sound designer

Steering committee

Surgical team

Technical Review Group (TRG)

Technical support (Tech support)

Business

Distribution

Black Friday

Channel

Day and date

Delivery method

Gutted

Loss leader

Manufacturer's Suggested Retail Price (MSRP)

Point of Purchase (POP)

Returns

Sell ins

Sell throughs

Ship date

Sim

Suggested Retail Price (SRP)

Timing issue

Distribution (Methods)

Business to Business (B2B)

Business to Customer (B2C)

Free to Play (F2P)

Freemium

Gray market

Micro transactions

Original Equipment Manufacturer (OEM)

Preorder

Subscription based

Wholesale

Financing

Ancillary revenues

Budget

Capital costs

Contingency planning

Contingency reserve funds

Cost

Cost of Goods (COG)

Cost Per Unit (CPU)

Departmental budget

Financial modeling

Fixed budget

Fixed costs

Flexible budget

Formal budget

Functional budget

Manufacturer's Suggested Retail Price (MSRP)

Marketing Development Funds (MDF)

Number crunching

Overhead

Perceived value

Price point

Profit and Loss statement (P & L statement)

Return on Investment (ROI)

Returns

Sell ins

Sell throughs

Static budget

Suggested Retail Price (SRP)

Variable budget

Management

80/20 rule

Assigning

Client

Contract

End user

Mission statement

Paralysis by analysis

Pareto principle

Project triangle

Sign off

Startup

Third party

Vision statement

Management (Team)

Brooks' law

Flow

In-house

Internship

Job requirements

Learning curve

Man-hours

Micromanagement

Note

Outsourcing

Performance review

Pipeline

Quality of Life (QOL)

Tag

Task rejection

Tool

Transparency

Version

Version control

Version Control System (VCS)

Manufacturing

Burning

Glass master

Gold

Gold master

Gone gold

Green disc

Laser Beam Recorder (LBR)

Metal family

Metal father

Metal mother

Metal son

Metallization

Original Equipment Manufacturer (OEM)

Stamper

Product Development

Ancillary revenues

Design spec

Feasibility

Implementation risk

Market risk

Market share

Pre-production plan

Product research

Production plan

Project plan

Review

Risk analysis

Spec

Unique Selling Points (USP)

Deliverables

Content Delivery and Storage

Cartridge

Downloadable Content (DLC)

Flash

Social media

Transmedia

External

Box and docs

Cheat sheet

Crib sheet

Manual

Reference sheet

Sell sheet

Strategy guide

Walkthrough

Work in Progress (WIP)

Internal

Corporate CD/DVD

Credits list

Digital dailies

Engine proof

Mock-up

One off

Proof

Proof of concept

Proof of technology

Proposal doc

Prototype

Storyboard

Super storyboard

Software

Build

Code release candidate

Critical patch

Final candidate

Hotpatch

Interactive prototype

Patch

Point release

Release Candidate (RC)

Shadow patch

Submission

Version

Development

Methodologies

Brainstorming

Critical path methodology

Front-loaded development model

Hard architecture

Iterative design

Reverse engineering

Scrum

Soft architecture

Software factory

Phases

Aftermarket

Alpha

Beta

Closed beta

Code release

Crunch time

Downtime

First Playable Prototype (FPP)

Gamma

Gone gold

Green light

Launch

Localization

Manufacturer testing

Open beta

Paper launch

Patch

Pitch

Platform transition

Post-production

Post-release

Pre-production

Quality Assurance (QA)

Release Candidate (RC)

Request For Proposal (RFP)

Requirement analysis

Technical review

Termination

Testing

Phases (Agile)

Adapt stage

Envision stage

Explore stage

Finalize stage

Speculate stage

Scheduling

Bottom-up estimating

Bottom-up planning

Contingency planning

Extremely flexible project planning
   formula

Fast tracking

Fixed deadline

Front-loaded development model

Milestone

PERT analysis formula

Resource-constrained model

Time boxing

Time-constrained model

Top-down planning

Status
Fail

Freeze

Fuzzy milestone

Gone gold

Green light

Launch

Lock

Pass

Targets
Build

Code release

Day and date

Interactive prototype

Launch

Milestone

Release candidate (RC)

Submission

Tasks
Casting

Code Release Checklist (CRC)

Deployment design

New Product Development (NPD)

Postmortem

Quality Assurance (QA)

Requirement capture

Revision control

Technical review

Testing

Work Breakdown Structure (WBS)

Work Breakdown System (WBS)

Tools
Auto-patcher

Big file system

Bug tracking

Build number

Engine

Installer

Revision control system

Software Development Kit (SDK)

Source code management

Uninstaller

Legal
Concepts
Copyright

Digital Rights Management (DRM)

First-sale doctrine

Gray market

Patent

Piracy

Right of first sale

Section 86

Section 131

Soft fraud

Trademark

Contract Law

Acceptance

Advance

Agent

Ancillary rights

Assignment

Back loaded

Bid

Boiler plate

Breach of contract

Cancellation

Choice of law clauses

Completion date

Conditions

Cross-collateralization

Earn out

Exercise

Exhaustion rule

Front loaded

Intellectual Property (IP)

Kill fee

Letter of Intent (LOI)

Milestone

Offer

Option

Place of performance

Proprietary

Recoupable

Remedy

Right of first refusal

Royalties

Termination

Time of performance

TOA

Warranty

Contract Law (Employment)

Bonus

Independent contractor

Non-compete agreement

Non-Disclosure Agreement (NDA)

Termination

Work for hire

Licensing

Affiliate label deal

Click-through agreement

Clickwrap agreement

End User License Agreement (EULA)

License

Licensee

Licensing

Licensor

Public domain

Marketing

Information

Essence statement

Key promise

Manufacturer's Suggested Retail Price (MSRP)

Play-life

Product description

Ship date

Suggested Retail Price (SRP)

System requirements

Target market

Unique Selling Points (USP)

Materials

Box and docs

Feature list

Lead time

Mock-up

One off

Preview

Proof

Review

Sell sheet

Strategy guide

System requirements

Promotion

Ad shots

Boiler plate

Box art

Box shots

Brand

Buzz

Convention (Con)

Corporate CD/DVD

Cover art

Crossover

Demo

Editors' day

Feelie

Original Equipment Manufacturer (OEM)

Packaging

Polish

Preview

Product placement

Public Relations (PR)

Q & A

Q & A doc

Review

Sell sheet

Sizzle

Swag

Trailer

Research

Base

Competitive analysis

Consumer research

Demographic (Demo)

Feedback

Focus group

Forum

Install base

Market research

Software Classifications

Development Method

Clone

Compilation

Derivative work

Episodic game

Expansion

Homebrewed

Mod

Sequel

Spiritual successor

Genre (Games)

Action

Action-adventure

Adventure

Arcade-style game

Beat 'em up

Beer & pretzel game

Casual game

Casual Multiplayer Online game
(CMO game)

Cross-genre

CRPG

Dungeon crawl

Eurogame

Fighting game

First-Person Shooter (FPS)

Gambling games

God-game

Hidden object game

Historical simulation

Kriegsspiel

Laser game

Limited-decision animated stories

Massively Multiplayer Online Social
Game (MMOSG)

Military simulation

Multiplayer Online Battle Arena
(MOBA)

Multiple-User Dungeon (MUD)

On-rails shooter

Puzzle

Rail shooter

Real-Time Strategy (RTS)

Rhythm game

Role-Playing Game (RPG)

Sports management sim

Sports sim

Strategy game

Text-based games

Vehicular combat

Video footage shooting games

Wargame

Legal

Abandonware

Creative Commons

Freeware

Open source

Shareware

Platform (Game)

Browser-based

Computer game

Console game

Location-Based Entertainment (LBE)

Miniature game

Mobile games

Parlor games

Social game

Video game

Purpose

Application (App)

Demo

Edutainment

Infotainment

Launch title

Middleware

Multiple-User Domain (MUD)

Quality

AAA

Arcade perfect

Crippleware

Killer app

Low budget

Shovelware

Topshelf

Vanilla

Vaporware

Testing and Evaluation

Bug (Attributes)

Reproducibility

Severity

State

Trackability

Bug (Statuses)

Closed

Dupe

NAB

Open

Will Not Fix (WNF)

Methods

Ad hoc testing

Automated testing

Blackbox testing

Blind testing

Boundary testing

Defect pooling

Defect seeding

Development testing

Focus group

Manufacturer testing

Negative testing

Play-through

Positive testing

Regression testing

Scripted testing

Smoke test

Soak test

Stress test

Testing to fail

Testing to pass

Unit testing

Verification

Whitebox testing

Phases

Alpha

Beta

Closed beta

Compatibility

Compliance testing

Configuration testing

Creative design review

Gamma

Master verification

Open beta

Public beta

Review

Technical review

Verification and Validation (V & V)

Tools

Benchmark

Code Release Checklist (CRC)

Milestone Acceptance Tests (MATs)

Regression list

Test harness

Test plan

Testing plan

Triage

PROGRAMMING
General
Components

Algorithm

Array

Attribute

Behavior

Bit

Child

Class

Command Line Interface (CLI)

Comment statement

Constant

Data

Datum

Error Code

Fork

Function

Graphical User Interface (GUI)

Hard copy

Header file

Library

Line

Log

Modifier

Node

Object

Object code

Operator

Parent

Pass

Prefab

Process

Runtime sequence

Script

Sequence

Source code

Table

Thread

Tick

Token

Trigger

Variable

Vector

Components (Modules)

Artificial Intelligence (AI)

Catch statement

Collision detection

Collision reaction

Draw

Exception handling

Housekeeping

Player input module

Player restriction module

Player update module

Prediction code

Pseudo-Random Number Generator (PRNG)

Random Number Generator (RNG)

Rule system

Save game system

World update module

Components (System Design)

Application Programming Interface (API)

Artifact

Design pattern

Engine

Finite state machine

Hardware

High-level software design

Pipeline

Shell

Software

Software architecture

Concepts

Acceleration

ACID

Agency

Assigning

Attenuation

Bang

Boolean

Bounding box

Build time

Clean

Collision

Comment out

Compression

Control scheme

Conversion

Critical patch

Data compression

Debug

Deceleration

Delimited

Dependency

Encryption

Event

Exception

Executable (EXE)

Feedback

Flash

Granularity

Heuristic

Instance

Iteration

Lossless

Lossy

Multiplicity

Operation

Order of execution

Ordering

Overhead

Parse

Patch

Populate

Port

Probability curve

Procedural generation

Protocol

Pseudo code

Punch

Ramping

Real time

Refresh

Rounding

Sampling

State

Synchronization (Sync)

System Design

Timeout

Velocity

Velocity vector

Weight

Wipe

Concepts (Relationships)

Aggregation relationship

Association

Composition relationship

Generalization relationship

"Has a" relationship

"Is a kind of" relationship

"Is a" relationship

"Owns a" relationship

Realization relationship

Role name

Documentation

Activity diagram

Architecture document

Behavior diagram

Component diagram

Dynamic behavior diagram

Event diagram

Event scenarios

Flowchart

Hard copy

Implementation requirements

Interface requirements

Log

Module documentation

Object diagram

Package diagram

Performance requirements

Regression list

Requirement analysis

Sequence diagram

Static structure diagram

Structure diagram

Technical design doc

Technical specifications

Timing diagram

Use case scenario

User story

Verb set

Errors

Bottleneck

Bug

Crash

Deadlock

Downtime

Freeze

Infinite loop

Lock

Logic error

Race condition

Syntax error

Languages

Assembly

Extensible Markup Language (XML)

Script

Shading language

Unified Modeling Language (UML)

Methodologies

Boiler plate

Code-fix methodology

Cowboy coding

Extreme Game Development (XGD)

Extreme Programming method
  (XP method)

MIT approach

New Jersey style

Pair programming

Principle of Good Enough (POGE)

The Right Thing

Tweak

Unified process

Unified software development process

Worse is better

Methodologies (Software Models)

Analysis model

Class diagram model

Component-based development

Dynamic modeling

Static modeling

Unified Modeling Language (UML)

Principles

Atomicity

Brook's Law

Comes Out in the Wash (COW)

Compatibility

Consistency

Durability

Garbage in, garbage out

Information hiding

Isolation

KISS

Loose coupling

Maintainability

Normalization

Object oriented

Open/closed

Portability

Quantization

Reproducibility

Reusability

Robustness

RTFM

YAGNI

Principles (System Design)

Abstraction

Closed architecture

Design scalability

Emulation

Encapsulation

Failover

Hardware abstraction

High availability

Modularity

Navigability

Open architecture

Trackability

Techniques

Automatic mode cancellation

Branch predicting

Camel casing

Checksum

Cyclic Redundancy Check (CRC)

Easing equation

Elastic equation

Error Checking and Correcting (ECC)

Frame rate locking

Inheritance

Interpolation

Naming convention

Number crunching

Object manager

Parallel streaming

Polymorphism

Prefetch

Quantification

Refactoring

Seeding

Shield

Write combining

Techniques (Software Design Patterns)

Chain of responsibility pattern

Command pattern

Composite pattern

Decorator pattern

Façade pattern

Factory method pattern

Flyweight pattern

Mediator pattern

Singleton pattern

Spatial index pattern

State pattern

Strategy pattern

Template method pattern

Testing (Code)

Benchmark

Integration testing

Method level testing

Object level testing

System testing

Tools

Compiler

Development Kit (Dev Kit)

Implementation requirements

Installer

Link editor

Linker

Performance analyzer

Profiler

Software Development Kit (SDK)

Structural modeling

Uninstaller

Artificial Intelligence

Elements

AI companion

Bot

Cone of vision

Dynamic bot

Emergent behavior

Predator

Prey

Static bot

Methodologies

A*

Adaptive AI

Adversary search

Alpha-beta pruning

Bayesian learning methods

Breadth-first search

Depth-first search

Fuzzy logic

Game tree

Genetic programming

Iterative depth

Minimax

Neural network

State space search

Strategy pattern

Tasks

Candidate move

Candidate play

Enrage

Object tracking

Obstacle avoidance

Pathfinding

Pathing

Patrol

Ply

Ragdoll physics

Techniques

Aggro

AI cheat

Bottom-up AI

Chase algorithm

Deterministic algorithm

Evasion algorithm

Finite state machine

Goal-Oriented Action Planning (GOAP)

Hate list

Leashing

Nodal pathing

Pattern list

Rubber banding

Threat list

Top-down AI

Hardware

Architecture

Application-Specific Integrated Circuit (ASIC)

Buffer

Cache

Central Processing Unit (CPU)

Channel

Chip

Graphical Processing Unit (GPU)

Hardware acceleration

Memory card

PC

Physics Processing Unit (PPU)

Port

Server

Stencil buffer

Video buffer

Z-buffer

Components (Interface)

Button

Controller

D-pad

DirectX

Driver

Firmware

Registry

Socket

Components (Topography)

Client

Dedicated server

Host

Network

Network Operating Center (NOC)

Peer-to-peer

Concepts

Bandwidth

Bind

Chipped

Directory (Dir)

Frame rate

Jailbreaking

Key

Lag

Memory consumption

Next gen

Packet

Page file

Pipeline

Platform

Tick

Virtual memory

Errors (Hardware Related)

Blue Screen of Death (BSOD)

Bottleneck

Crash

Lag

Latency

Lock up

Memory leak

Packet loss

Rubber banding

Tasks

Call

Call stack

Flash

Hardware Transform and Lighting (Hardware T & L)

Information transmission

Kernel

Loader

Soft modem

Stack

Startup

SOUND

Characteristics

Delay

Intensity

Monaural (Mono)

Pitch

Reflection

Stereophonic (Stereo)

Concepts

Attenuation

Channel

Chorus

Clipping

Data compression

Doppler effect

Dynamic Range Compression (DRC)

Dynamic sound

Fade in

Fade out

Feedback

Normalization

Occlusion

Placeholder

Polyphony

Ramping

Documentation

Edit Decision List (EDL)

Music

Adaptive music

Algorithmic music

Ambient music

Chase music

Exploration music

Interactive music

Musical sting

Note

Original music

Pitch

Score

Recording

Audio Capture

Bark

Clip

Closed caption

Compression

Dead room

Dialogue

Dry audio

Dubbing

Foley

Hard room

Line

Pickup session

Real-time speech

Room tone

Sampling

Synchronization (Sync)

Voice acting

Voice Over (V.O.)

Wild sounds

Tools

Codec

Digital Audio Tape (DAT)

Sequencer

WRITING
General

Creations

Ad copy

Back matter

Biography (Bio)

Character brief

Closed caption

Crawl

Demo script

Draft

Essence statement

Flavor text

Front matter

Logline

Manual

Preview

Review

Script

Slug line

Speculation (Spec)

Story

Subtitles

Synopsis

Text

Treatment

Layout and Editing

Boiler plate

Castoff

Font

Icon

Localization

Style guide

Storytelling

Character

Antagonist

Archetype

Guardian

Hero

Protagonist

Shadow character

Silent protagonist

Stereotype

Tabula rasa

Components

Background (b.g.)

Biography (Bio)

Dialogue

Encounter

Establishing shot

High concept

Hook

Moral

Narrative

Plot

Premise

Scene

Sequence

Setting

Theme

Concepts

Action

Adventure

Allusion

Canon

Conflict

Continuity

Contrast

Dramatic tension

End sequence

Exposition

Flashback

Flashforward

Foreshadowing

Fourth wall

Framing

MacGuffin

McGuffin

Montage

Mood

Motif

Pacing

Personification

Perspective

Plant

Point of View (POV)

Segue

Subtext

Symbolism

Tension

Transition

Voice

Dialogue

Bark

Branching dialogue

Conditional dialogue

Distracter

Exposition

Line

Subtext

Errors

Deus ex machina

On the nose

Talking heads

Plot

Arc

B storyline

Backstory

Character arc

Climax

Denouement

Dynamic plot

Inciting incident

Interactive plot

Moral decision

Obstacle

Plot coupon

Subplot

Ticking bomb

Turning point

Principles

80% stereotype rule

Bechdel test

Chekhov's gun

Fanservice

Narrative Design

Personalization

Suspension of disbelief

Techniques

Alternate ending

Branching story

Bread-crumbing

Linear

Nonlinear

On rails

Visual narrative

World design

Techniques (Structures)

Act structure

Actants layer

Braided plot structure

Branching narrative structure

Character-level narrative structure

Directed network narrative structure

Discourse level

Dynamic labyrinth narrative structure

Emergent storytelling

Event layer

Exploratorium structure

Exploratory narrative structure

Falling action

Fractal structure

Framing Narrative

Generative substrate

Hero's journey

Hidden story structure

Hub and spoke narrative structure

Hyperstory

Modular narrative structure

Modulated narrative structure

Narrative layer

Nodal narrative structure

Object-oriented narrative structure

Open narrative structure

Parallel narrative structure

Performance level

Point of no return

Refusal of the call

Reveal

Rhizome structural model

Rising action

Simulation level

Structural substrate

Three-act structure

APPENDIX A

PERSONS LISTED WITHIN ENTRIES

Adams, Ernest—Game designer, author, founder of the International Game Developer's Association. Best known for his book *Fundamentals of Game Design* and his many published articles.

Bechdel, Alison—American cartoonist and author best known for her strip *Dykes to Watch out For*.

Birdwell, Ken—American software developer and animation specialist best known for his description of the Cabal process used in the game *Half-Life*.

Björk, Staffan—Swedish educator and researcher best known for his coauthorship of *Patterns in Game Design*.

Brook, Fred—American computer scientist and educator best known for coining the phrase "computer architecture" and whose works include *The Mythical Man-Moth* and *No Silver Bullet: Essence and Accidents of Software Engineering*.

Caillois, Roger (1913–1978)—French philosopher, editor, and author of *Les Jeux et les Hommes* (*"Man, Play, and Games"*).

Campbell, Joseph (1904–1987)—American mythologist, educator, and author well known for his works *The Hero with a Thousand Faces* and *The Masks of God*.

Carmack, John—American programmer best known for his advancements in computer graphics and his work in games such as *Doom* and *Quake*.

Chekhov, Anton (1860–1904)—Russian playwright and author known for his influence in literature with many of his works, such as *The Seagull* and *The Cherry Orchard*, considered masterpieces.

Crawford, Chris—American game designer and founder of the Game Developers Conference. Best known for his game *Balance of Power* and his books *The Art of Computer Game Design*, *Chris Crawford on Game Design*, and *Chris Crawford on Interactive Storytelling*.

Csíkszentmihályi, Mihaly—Hungarian psychologist, educator, and author best known for his studies and observations on human happiness and whose work includes *Flow: The Psychology of Optimal Experience*.

Demachy, Thomas—Programmer and production manager known for his promotion of the Extreme Game Development methodology.

Elo, Arpad (1903–1992)—Hungarian-born physicist, educator, and chess master known for creating the ranking system that bears his name and which has been modified for use in a variety of competitive sports and games.

Emrich, Alan—American game journalist, author, educator, and designer who served as an editor for *Computer Gaming World* and is known for his extensive work in strategy games.

Gabriel, Richard P.—American programmer and author known for popularizing the Worst Is Better methodology of programming. His works include *Lisp: Good News, Bad News, How to Win Big*, and *Patterns of Software: Tales From the Software Community*.

Gantt, Henry (1861–1919)—American management consultant and author best known for his development of easy-to-follow bar charts for project management, which now carry his name.

Holopainen, Jussi—Researcher and educator best known for his coauthorship of *Patterns in Game Design*.

Hunicke, Robin—Game designer and producer best known for her research into formal game design and the co-creation of the MDA framework.

Irish, Dan—Producer and author whose works include *The Game Producer's Handbook*.

Juran, Joseph M. (1904–2008)—Business manager and author best known for his works *Quality Control Handbook* and *Managerial Breakthrough*.

Khan, Alfred E. (1917–2010)—American economist and educator best known for his work in deregulation and his essay "The Tyranny of Small Decisions."

LeBlanc, Marc—Game designer best known for his research into formal game design and the co-creation of the MDA framework.

Lindley, Craig A.—Educator, researcher, and author whose work includes *Story and Narrative Structures in Computer Games.*

Meier, Sid—Canadian game designer and programmer best known for his games *Civilization, Alpha Centauri, Pirates!,* and *Railroad Tycoon.*

Mori, Masahiro—Japanese robotic engineer and author whose work includes *Bukimi No Tani* (*"The Uncanny Valley."*)

Morris, David—British author and game designer who is best known for his fantasy novels, RPG games, and coauthoring *Game Architecture and Design.*

Nash, John—American economist and mathematics pioneer whose work in game theory lead to his winning of the 1994 Nobel Memorial Prize in Economic Sciences with other game theorists.

Pareto, Vilfredo (1948–1923)—Italian economist, philosopher, and educator best known for his research into the distribution of wealth and income. His works include *Trattato di sociologia generale* (*The Mind and Society*) and *Manuele di economia politica* (*Manual of Political Economy*).

Rollings, Andrew—Software designer and coauthor of *Game Architecture and Design,* and *Andrew Rollings and Ernest Adams on Game Design.*

Ryan, Marie-Laure—Educator and author best known for her work on narration and its use in virtual reality. Her work includes *Narrative as Virtual Reality: Immersion and Interactivity in Literature and Electronic Media.*

Salen, Katie—Educator and author whose works includes coauthoring *Rules of Play* and co-editor of *The Game Design Reader: A Rules of Play Anthology.*

Searle, John—American educator and philosopher whose work includes the paper "How to Derive 'Ought' from 'Is.'"

Simon, Herbert (1916–2001)—Nobel Prize–winning American educator, economist, and psychologist best known for pioneering the field of artificial intelligence, his research into economic decision making, and his vast contributions to other scientific fields.

Skinner, B.F. (1904–1990)—Prominent American psychologist, inventor, and author best known for his pioneering work in behaviorism.

Von Resiswitz, Georg (1764–1828)—Prussian military officer and knight who developed war-gaming (*Kriegalspeil*) as a training exercise for the officers of the Prussian Army.

Zimmerman, Eric—Game designer, educator, and author whose works include coauthoring *Rules of Play* and co-editor of *The Game Design Reader: A Rules of Play Anthology*.

Zubek, Robert—Software engineer best known for his research in formal game design and the co-creation of the MDA framework.

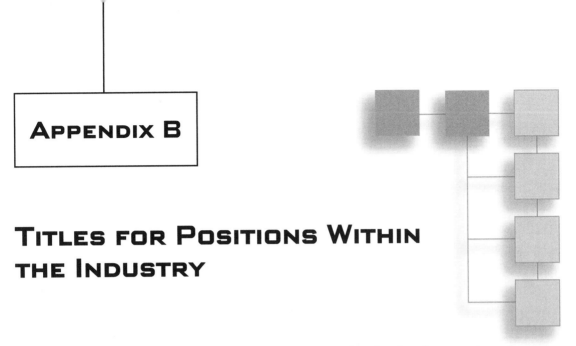

APPENDIX B

TITLES FOR POSITIONS WITHIN THE INDUSTRY

The game industry has not yet settled on standardized titles for positions in video game development. Each company, and even each project within a company, may refer to the same role by a different title or may use a particular title to describe several different roles. Some studios are well known for creating unique, often tongue-in-cheek titles for their positions. For these reasons, the following listings should serve only as a general guideline and be accepted with the understanding that the actual descriptions may vary greatly in the real world; questions about a specific title and its role are often best answered by the company that created the position.

It should also be noted that many terms are used interchangeably within various positions, creating a "mix-and-match" type of title. Among these terms are qualifiers, words that are designed to describe the holder's experience or leadership responsibilities. Because nearly any title can have these qualifiers added to them, they appear in a separate list.

QUALIFIERS

Assistant

A position in which one individual supports another, more senior member by performing some of their tasks without taking on their level of responsibility.

Chief

A leadership position in which the individual is assigned primary responsibility for a department or division.

Floor Lead

A position in which the team member assumes responsibility for the day-to-day performance of the team.

Freelance

A position in which the individual provides work as an independent contractor and works outside the standard team environment.

Intern

A position in which the individual is employed primarily to receive training in their field.

Junior

A journeyman position in which the team member generally has less experience than other members of the team.

Lead

A position in which a team member is given oversight of the team and is responsible for their performance.

Manager

A supervisory position in which the individual has oversight of a team or process without necessarily being personally responsible for performing any of the teams' work.

Principal

A position in which the individual has oversight of the team and is responsible for their performance.

Senior

A position in which the team member has notable experience in his or her area of expertise.

Supervisor

A managerial position in which the individual has oversight of a team or process without necessarily being personally responsible for performing any of the teams' work.

TITLES AND RESPONSIBILITIES

Note: The term engineer is often used as a synonym for programmer. For clarity, the *Game Developer's Dictionary* prefers the use of "programmer" when referring to a person who writes code. In cases where engineer is used in the title, it will refer either to a non-programming engineer, or a programmer with additional engineering responsibilities. Consult the description to best determine usage.

2D Animator

Poses, renders, and loops objects to create the sense of movement within a 2D environment.

2D Artist

Creates 2D visual assets for a project.

2D Programmer

Creates the software code for an application that runs in a 2D environment.

3D Animator

Poses, renders, loops, and often rigs 3D models to create the sense of movement within a 3D environment.

3D Artist

Creates 3D visual assets for a project.

3D Programmer

Creates the software code for an application that runs in a 3D environment.

Accountant

Maintains and audits financial records.

AI Designer

Creates and implements the scripts that determine NPC interactions.

AI Programmer

Creates the software code that determines NPC interactions.

Animation Programmer

Develops and supports the software code for an animation system and its interface.

Animator

Poses, renders, and loops objects to create the sense of movement within the environment.

Application Tester

Evaluates software, often specific to the mobile platform market, for quality issues.

Art Director

Sets and verifies the standards of the art created by a team.

Art Tools Programmer

Creates utility applications that assist the art team in creating their assets.

Artist

Creates the visual assets for a project.

Associate Producer

Supervises specified activities as assigned by the producer.

Audio Coordinator

Manages, catalogues, and coordinates the creation of sound assets for a project.

Audio Designer

Creates, records, mixes, and implements sounds into the game's environment.

Audio Director

Manages, catalogues, and coordinates the creation of sound assets for a project.

Audio Engineer

Creates, records, mixes, and implements sounds into the game's environment.

Back-end Web Designer

Creates the software code and structure for a server's data storage elements in an Internet-based system.

Beta Tester

Evaluates the software for quality issues at the later stages of development. Often an external volunteer.

Build Engineer

Constructs and maintains the system used for software builds to ensure accurate releases.

Build Tools Programmer

Creates utility applications that assist the team in compiling, deploying, and tracking new versions of the software being developed.

Business Coordinator

Manages the communications and processes between all departments within a business structure.

Business Development Manager

Investigates, identifies, and recommends potential products to be pursued for development.

Business Manager

Provides supervision, staffing, and organization for a department or collection of departments within a business.

Business Operations Manager

Supervises the daily procedures and activities performed within a company and coordinates them with necessary outside parties.

Camera Designer

Places and integrates the cameras within a video game.

Camera System Designer

Develops and maintains a coordinated organization of the cameras and how they react to changes in the game.

Campaign Designer

Creates the layout and structure for a series of independent but related scenarios within a game, and their effects on gameplay.

Casting Director

Researches, auditions, and recommends actors for specific parts within a project.

Casting Supervisor

Researches, auditions, and recommends actors for specific parts within a project.

Character Animator

Poses, renders, and loops PC and NPC models to create the sense of movement within the environment.

Character Artist

Creates the visual representation of PCs and NPCs within a project.

Character Rigger

Creates the system of movable joints for PC and NPC 3D models so that they can be animated.

Cinematic Animator

Poses, renders, and loops object models for their use within cinematics and trailers.

Cinematic Artist

Creates the visual assets for a project's cinematics and trailers.

Cinematic Designer

Conceptualizes and supervises the animation and framing of cut-scenes.

Cinematic Director

Oversees the creation of cut-scenes within a project.

Cinematic Producer

Coordinates the work flow for creating cinematics and trailers.

Cinematic Technical Artist

Creates the application and scripts used by artists to develop the assets for the game's cinematics.

Cinematic Trailer Director

Oversees the creation of trailers within a project.

Cinematic Trailer Writer

Creates the order and narrative of a project's trailer.

Cinematic Writer

Creates the narrative and dialogue within a cut-scene.

Client Programmer

Creates the software code necessary for client-server relationships with an emphasis on client-side performance.

Client-side Game Programmer

Creates the software code necessary for client-server relationships with an emphasis on client-side performance.

Code Release Group Tester

Evaluates the current submitted build against the minimum standards the company has for publication.

Combat Designer

Creates the system, structure, formulas, and mechanics for conflict resolution within the game.

Community Manager

Supervises communications with the external fan base for a project.

Community Website Manager

Supervises communications with the external fan base at the project's official website.

Compatibility Analyst

Evaluates and benchmarks the performance of builds on various platforms and configurations.

Compatibility Lab SDET (Software Development Engineer in Test)

Creates the software systems used within QA to test the games' compatibility with various hardware configurations.

Compatibility Tester

Evaluates and benchmarks the performance of builds on various platforms and configurations.

Compliance Tester

Evaluates the current submitted build to guarantee fulfillment of the standards set by an outside party, such as a licensor.

Composer

Authors the music that is to be included within a project.

Concept Artist

Creates the initial visual representation of the persons, places, and objects that are to be included within a project, often by means of traditional media.

Configuration Lab SDET (Software Development Engineer in Test)

Creates the software systems used within QA to test the games' compatibility with various hardware configurations.

Consumer Products Engineer Manager

Recommends and supervises the overall development of new products, services, and technologies.

Content Designer

Creates and integrates the specified elements within the environment in which the game takes place.

Core System Software Programmer

Provides software code that focuses on the performance and functionality of the game engine and its connection to the hardware.

Corporate Affairs Attorney

Provides legal council with specialization in areas such as financing, intellectual property, acquisitions, employment, and other such business-related matters.

Creative Director

Responsible for the overall direction and vision of a project or set of projects. May or may not be the same as the Lead Designer.

Customer Support Representative

Provides assistance to end users through a variety of means, such as phone, email, online forum, or in-game tickets.

Data Archivist

Preserves and maintains the digital files created within a team or company.

Database Administrator

Organizes and maintains all records within a system that supports a project, company, or their consumers.

Database Manager

Organizes and maintains all records within a system that supports a project, company, or their consumers.

Design Director

Creates the basic framework for games and evaluates them throughout the production cycle both in terms of design and production requirements. Often supervises multiple games at the same time.

Designer

Creates and balances any of the various systems or subsystems within a game.

Development Director

Develops and supervises the strategy for acquiring, creating, and distributing new products.

Development Manager

Supervises members of the development team to ensure compliance with milestones and production goals.

Documentation Designer

Creates and maintains the technical documents generated for the team.

Editor, Print

Evaluates, arranges, and corrects documents prior to their publication.

Editor, Video

Combines and adjusts unprocessed video and related audio elements into a finished audio-video segment suitable for inclusion into the game.

Effects Artist

Creates the computer-generated particles and physics-based results within an animated segment.

Engine Programmer

Creates the software code that provides the core functionality of the hardware interface system.

Engine Tools Programmer

Creates the applications that allow additional access to elements of the game engine, often for other members of the team.

Engineer

Designs and adjusts the technical structure of hardware.

Environmental Artist

Creates the visual representation of the game's physical world.

Environmental Effect Artist

Creates the computer-generated particles and physics-based results within the game's physical world.

Executive Producer

Responsible for the overall production of a project or projects without direct daily team management. May be a studio-created position or a position assigned by the publisher.

Facial Rigger

Creates the facial expressions and lip synching of a 3D model.

Facilities Manager

Oversees the use, maintenance, and integration of a work environment and its equipment.

Finance Manager

Responsible for the supervision of the fiscal elements of a business through the development and analysis of budgets and appropriate business models.

Flash Artist

Creates the 2D art used within Adobe's multimedia software, *Flash*.

Flash Developer

Creates applications within Adobe's multimedia software, *Flash*, utilizing all elements of production, including animation, UI design, and scripting.

Flash Programmer

Provides the scripting and supporting code necessary for the utilization of Adobe's multimedia software, *Flash*, on a website or through an application.

Floor Lead

Supervises the minute-to-minute performance of an independent, local team.

Focus Group

A collection of potential consumers used to evaluate a product's appeal to the market.

Front-end Web Designer

Creates the software code and structure for the display of data on an Internet-based system.

FX Artist

Creates the computer-generated particles and physics-based results within an animated segment.

Game Designer

Creates the rules, systems, and themes of a game.

Game Developer

Any person or company that assumes responsibility for the creation of a game.

Game Development Engineer

Creates the software code for game systems, often with an emphasis on hardware architecture.

Game Master

Provides in-game customer support within an MMO environment, often as an NPC. May, but often does not, relate to a position that provides real-time challenges and events to the player population.

Game Producer

Manages the daily overall creation of the game with a focus on scheduling and budgetary concerns.

Game Tester

Evaluates the game and reports any errors or other issues.

Gameplay Designer

Devises the systems and adjusts the balance of play within the game with an emphasis on elements that have a substantive impact on the player's performance.

Gameplay Programmer

Creates the software code for the implementation of the game's systems and subsystems.

General Manager

Supervises all other managers and departments within an organization providing centralized planning and direction.

Generalist Programmer

Creates software code with the capability of utilizing their broadly applicable programming skills in a variety of areas.

Global Brand Manager

Creates and supervises the strategy for the promotion of intellectual properties and marks throughout all regions.

Graphics Artist

Creates the images used within the game or its print material. Usually limited to 2D art.

Graphics Coordinator

Implements and supervises the production process, pipeline, and distribution of visual assets, particularly those generated by computers.

Graphics Programmer

Creates the software code needed to render and affect the images that are to be displayed.

Group Manager

Supervises workers of a team that is usually permanent in duration.

Group Product Manager

Evaluates actual, potential, and competing products and their markets in order to increase the company's ability to attract more consumers.

Helpdesk

Provides technical assistance to users, either within the company or to a contracted party.

Hiring Manager

Responsible for the recruiting, interviewing, evaluating, and offering of employment to fill positions within a company.

Human Resources Director

Supervises the overall implementation of the recruiting, hiring, training, and evaluation of employees within a company.

Human Resources Manager

Supervises a specific area of human resources, such as the recruiting, hiring, training, and evaluation of employees within a company.

Illustrator

Creates artwork, primarily for reference or print.

In-Game Support Manager

Supervises the real-time customer support process within an online environment.

In-Game Support Representative

Provides customer support within an online environment, either through a virtual avatar or a ticketing system.

Information Technologies Manager

Supervises the allotment and maintenance of hardware and software within an organization.

Information Technologies Technician

Provides technical services for hardware- and software-related issues within an organization.

Install, Patch, and Distribution Producer

Supervises the processes and methods used to distribute the software to the consumer.

Install, Patch, and Distribution Programmer

Creates the software code used in the applications that distribute the software to the consumer.

IT Engineer

Creates the systems and builds the hardware necessary to meet the technological needs of an organization.

IT Manager

Supervises the use and maintenance of hardware and software within an organization.

Language Tester

Evaluates the game for translation issues.

Legal Counsel

Advises an organization as to what policies are within the law, what potential legal threats exist, and what recourses are available during disputes.

Level Designer

Constructs the layout of a map's physical environment with an emphasis on elements that create a challenge to player progression.

Linguistic Coordinator

Translates reports, contracts, communications, and other material from one language to another.

Linguistic Project Manager

Supervises the localization of a game to ensure that it is compliant with the target market's cultural and linguistic norms and standards.

Localization International Program Manager

Supervises the production of a region-specific version of the game.

Localization Producer

Manages the day-to-day production of a region-specific version of the game with a focus on scheduling and budgetary concerns.

Localization Project Manager

Supervises the production of a region-specific version of the game to ensure that it is compliant with the target market's cultural and linguistic norms and standards.

Localization Tester

Evaluates a game for linguistic and cultural issues related to the geographical market in which it will be released.

Manual Artist

Provides the illustrations and other images for the game's manuals and related materials.

Manual Editor

Supervises, evaluates, and corrects the writing and layout of the game's manual and related materials.

Manual Producer

Oversees the general scheduling and development of the manual and related materials.

Marketing Game Manager

Develops the strategies for marketing the game.

Marketing Representative

Provides communication, promotion, and support between the organization and potential resellers.

Marketing Traffic Manager

Supervises the creation and flow of marketing material to meet the time constrains of the project.

Master Verification Engineer

Evaluates the quality and condition of the master disks before reproduction.

Mechanics Designer

Creates the rules and reactions of a system within the game.

Mission Designer

Constructs the chronology, challenges, and objectives for the quests or missions within the game.

Motion Graphics Artist

Creates non-interactive art that transforms and moves over a scene or background.

Music Director

Coordinates the musicians during the creation of the music for use within a game.

Narrative Designer

Creates the story and plot of the game, with an emphasis on how it coalesces with gameplay.

Network Designer

Plans and implements the hardware and software needed for internal data communications within an organization.

Network Programmer

Creates the software code utilized in communications between systems on a network.

Network Tester

Evaluates the stability and synchronization of games when played through the Internet or a local area network.

Office Administrator

Coordinates and supports the activities of a team or collection of teams within a centralized location.

Online Producer

Supervises and coordinates the overall development of a project, its schedule, and its budget, with an emphasis on its online presence and gateways.

Online Programmer

Provides the software code for the online portion of a video game.

Online Technical Director

Determines the technical standards of a project, particularly one with a large online component.

Onsite Tester

Evaluates and reports issues and errors in the game from a centralized location.

Orchestra Contractor

Supervises and coordinates the performance of the musicians creating the score for a game.

Package Designer

Creates and lays out the visual elements of the product that are seen while it is displayed on a retail shelf.

Packaging Artist

Creates the visual elements of the product that are seen while it is displayed on the retail shelf.

Paralegal

Supports legal counsel by means of research and creating documents.

Physics Programmer

Creates the software code that simulates the physical reaction of objects and forces within the game's environment.

Playthrough Tester

Evaluates the user's experience while playing the game with an emphasis on the game's ability to be completed.

Porting Programmer

Adapts, adjusts, and rewrites an existing game's code so that it can be transferred from one platform to another.

Post-production Supervisor

Manages the editing and polishing of cinematics once they have been created.

PR Representative

Provides communications to the media and occasionally with the general public with the intent of building a favorable public image for a project.

Preproduction Producer

Supervises and coordinates the overall development of the project, its schedule, and its initial budget early in the project's lifecycle, before its full team has been assembled.

Print Designer

Utilizes typography and layout in the creation of printed material.

Producer

Supervises and coordinates the overall development of the project, its schedule, and its budget. Serves as a liaison between the development teams and upper management or investors.

Product Management Director

Evaluates market conditions, develops new product criteria, and manages production lines to ensure products meet market demands.

Product Manager

Supervises the production and distribution of a product or brand throughout its life cycle.

Production Director

Supervises the production and distribution of a product throughout its life cycle.

Production Illustrator

Creates concept art, storyboards, animatics, and other conceptual pieces for reference during the development of the game.

Production Programmer

Creates the software code for an application.

Programmer

Creates the software code for an application.

Project Manager

Responsible for the day-to-day progression of the overall project.

Prop Modeler

Creates the nonessential objects within the game, which are primarily used to assist the player's immersion in the scene.

Public Relations Representative

Provides communications to the general public and the media with the intent of building a favorable public image for a project.

Publisher

An organization responsible for the manufacturing, promotion, and distribution of a product.

QA Database Manager

Organizes and maintains the records of all reported issues for the project being tested.

QA Director

Manages the overall performance of the quality assurance department.

QA Manager

Creates the testing procedures and standards for a QA team or set of teams and oversees their performance.

QA Programmer

Provides software code for applications that can be used in the testing and evaluation of the game.

QA Supervisor

Manages the performance of a team or set of teams tasked with evaluating the game for errors and other issues.

QA Technical Programmer

Provides software code for applications that can be used in the testing and evaluation of the game.

QA Tester

Evaluates a game for errors and other issues.

Quest Designer

Creates the chronology and overall arcs of the missions within a game, particularly an RPG.

Real-time Graphics Programmer

Provides the software code for systems that have real-time effects within the game.

Recruiter

Identifies and contacts potential employees.

Release Engineer

Constructs and maintains the system used for creating, tracking, and distributing software builds to ensure accurate releases.

Render Wrangler

Maintains and monitors the progress of a system of computers used exclusively for rendering.

Rendering Programmer

Provides the software code for the rendering of the game's assets by the hardware.

Researcher and Analyst

Evaluates the current market conditions and opportunities that exist for the development of new projects.

RTM Validation Engineer

Evaluates the quality and condition of the master disks before reproduction.

Sales Representative

Communicates with potential buyers (resellers) and arranges for their purchase of the company's products.

Scripter

Creates instructions and data sets for use by the game engine to allow the adjusting of those elements without requiring the adjuster to have direct access to the software's code.

Server Programmer

Provides the software code needed by the server to host the game's online components.

Services Programmer

Provides the software code needed for network integration, compliance, and optimization.

Skeletal Animator

Poses, renders, and loops PC and NPC models through the use of an underlying rig to create the sense of movement within the environment.

Social Designer

Creates the systems of social interaction within an online environment.

Social Game Designer

Creates the rules, systems, and themes for social media games.

Social Games Programmer

Provides the software code for social media games.

Software Development Engineer (SDE)

Designs, codes, and implements the architecture and systems within a software application.

Software Development Engineer in Test (SDET)

Designs, codes, and implements software systems used within QA for the testing of games.

Software Engineer

Designs, codes, and implements the software systems within an application.

Software Test Engineer (STE)

Creates testing procedures, plans, and scripted tools for evaluating games.

Sound Designer

Records, collects, and constructs the audio elements used within a game.

Sound Editor

Implements and synchronizes the audio elements into a game.

Sound Producer

Supervises the recording, construction, and implementation of the dialogue, sound effects, and music within a game.

Story Editor

Supervises the overall progression of the story as it is developed.

Storyline Developer

Creates the narrative chronology of a game or its missions.

Studio Manager

Provides supervision, direction, and organization for the creative work within a studio.

SW Engineer

Designs, codes, and implements the software systems within an application.

System Administrator

Monitors, maintains, and upgrades a network's hardware, software, and services.

System Designer

Develops and adjusts the formulas, mechanics, and procedures used by a specific system or subsystem within the game.

Systems Programmer

Creates the software code for the various formulas, mechanics, and procedures used within the game.

Technical Animator

Creates and evaluates the results of procedural animation and its related pipelines.

Technical Artist

Creates the applications and scripts used by artists to develop the assets of a game.

Technical Director

Determines the technical standards of a project.

Technical Producer

Evaluates the technical needs of a project and develops the procedures and plans to meet those needs.

Technical Support Manager

Supervises the team responsible for providing end users with assistance for issues related to hardware or software.

Technical Support Programmer

Provides software code for applications that assist with hardware and software issues that end users may experience.

Technical Support Representative

Provides end users with assistance for issues related to hardware or software.

Technical User Interface Designer

Develops and implements the input and output elements used within the game.

Technology Programmer

Experiments with software code to discover new means for technological advancements in game development.

Test Manager

Creates the testing procedures and standards for a QA team or set of teams and oversees their performance.

Tester

Evaluates a game for errors and other issues.

Texture Artist

Creates, optimizes and maps textures to objects.

Tools Programmer

Creates the applications designed to assist others during the creation of a video game.

UI Programmer

Creates the software code that allows the user interface to be displayed and function properly.

User Experience Designers

Evaluates the user's experience with the product and provides solutions to improve that experience.

User Interface Artist

Creates the visual representation of the input and output elements used within the game.

User Interface Designer

Develops the input and output elements used within the game.

User Researcher

Evaluates players and player activity with an emphasis on improving the game's play-ability and desirability.

User Research Engineers

Evaluates players and player activity with an emphasis on improving the game's play-ability and desirability.

User Research Manager

Supervises research into the player's experience while playing the game.

UX Designer

Evaluates the user's experience with the product and provides solutions to improve that experience.

VFX Artist

Creates and incorporates nonmodeled computer-generated elements, such as particles into the game.

VFX Tools Programmer

Creates the software code for applications designed to assist others in the implementation of nonmodeled computer-generated elements, such as particles into the game.

Video Processing Supervisor

Manages the postproduction process for cinematics and trailers.

Visual Effects Artist

Creates and incorporates nonmodeled computer-generated elements, such as particles into the game.

VO Editor

Selects, applies, and synchronizes voice over recordings to the cinematics.

Voice Actor

Provides the vocal dialogue that is used as the character's voices during the game.

Voice Casting Director

Researches, auditions, and recommends voice actors for specific parts within a project.

Voice Director

Provides instructions to the actors in regard to their performance.

Web Back-end Developer

Creates the structure for a server's data storage elements in an Internet-based system.

Web Content Specialist

Acquires and places content related to the project or organization onto the organization's website.

Web Designer

Creates and lays out the images, text, and interfaces for a website.

Web Developer

Creates the infrastructure for an Internet-based system.

Web Front-end Developer

Creates the structure to display data on an Internet-based system.

Web Producer

Supervises and coordinates the overall development of a project's online communication strategy.

Web Quality Assurance Analyst

Evaluates the organization's website and online offerings for errors and other issues.

World Content Artist

Creates the visual representation of specified elements within the game's world.

World Content Designer

Develops and integrates the specified elements that populate the game's world.

World Designer

Creates the overall laws, background, and populous of the game world.

Worldwide Launch Executive

Manages and makes all decisions regarding the introduction of a product to the global market.

Worldwide Launch Manager

Supervises the process of introducing a product to the global market.

Writers

Provides the story and dialogue of a game.

Writing Director

Supervises the overall writing of the game's story and dialogue.

APPENDIX C

THE 100 MOST SIGNIFICANT GAMES

Producing a list of the games that have most impacted what we play today has a unique difficulty. Not only are there many more than a hundred games that deserve recognition, but the history of games as a whole has been poorly preserved. Games were often dismissed as "a waste of time" or "trivial" and, as a result, the exact origins of many pre-twentieth century games were never documented.

Any attempt to list the many firsts (e.g., first use of dice, first RPG, first 3D game, etc.), will always be an exercise in futility to some degree because of this lack of verifiable history. Therefore, for our list we looked at three elements. First, we looked at innovation. Which games added new elements? Then we considered the game's popularity and, lastly, the influence that it had over the games that came after it.

Our list contains what we believe to be the 100 games or series that have had the greatest influence over the games being made today. To ensure a game's influence can be fairly evaluated, the titles must have been released 10 years ago or longer. This accounts for the exclusion of what otherwise would be likely entries, such as *World of Warcraft* and *Portal*.

It should also be noted that this list includes not only video games but games of all types. For simplicity's sake (and to avoid having to draw too fine a line between different versions and releases) we categorized all like games within a series as a single entry; only in cases where the game significantly changes from its predecessors do we differentiate the game from its sequels. An added benefit of this is the list is composed of more than just *Mario*, *Ultima*, *Madden*, *Quake*, *Zelda*, and other games whose long list of innovation throughout their series would otherwise dominate these pages.

The games here are listed chronologically based on when they were first published, without any indication of their ranking. The date of their release to the public is listed in parentheses. A list of all variations, expansions, and sequels included in the evaluation is included within the brackets.

WEIQI (UNKNOWN, ESTIMATES RANGE FROM 2000 BC TO 300 BC)
[Baduk, Go]

There were many games played before Weiqi but there is little known about their rules. Most of these ancient games featured some element of luck, but this one diverged from them by focusing entirely on skill and strategic analysis. It also introduced some of the most basic concepts of gameplay: sacrificing resources, controlling territories, passing turns, and exerting influence over other pieces.

BACKGAMMON (CIRCA 600)
[Nard, Alea, Tables]

Originally a gambling game, it was sixth-century Rome (and later Asia) where the game took on its most familiar elements. It combined the luck of die rolling with the skill of strategic movement. The longest surviving roll-and-move style game, over time its strategic elements became more heavily emphasized and it evolved into the predominately skill-based game we know now.

CHESS (CIRCA 600)
[Chatrang, Shantranj, Queen's Chess]

By the fifteenth century, the modern European variant that is so well-recognized today took form, but even before then this game of Indian origin had already spread around the world. Utilizing a deterministic (entirely skill-based) system, it revolutionized the way games were played and despite being banned many times, it became the most respectable game in the Western world. It also became the second known commercially distributed PC game when *Microchess*, by Peter R. Jennings, hit the market in 1976.

SNAKES AND LADDERS (CIRCA 1200)
[Moksha Patam, Leela, Chutes and Ladders]

India's early game of religious education, designed to teach children the importance of moral behavior, became a family favorite in England of the late 1800s after its Hindu-based vices and virtues were changed to more closely match Victorian era values. Besides being one of the earliest (if not the earliest) children's board game, it also introduced a backward movement mechanic that has become popular in many race-to-the-end type games since.

PACHISI (CIRCA 1500)
[Ludo, Parcheesi, Jue de Petits Chevaux, Aggravation]

The exact origin of this game stretches back quite far, but the version that resembles what we know today seems to have formed some time in the fifteenth century. Suffering from an incomplete record, just as many other pre-nineteenth-century games do, it is hard to give it full credit for many of the influential mechanics it brought forth, but through its survival it has impacted nearly every game that has come by since. Perhaps most notable is its use of cooperative play, a rarity among classic board games, but now very popular in modern video games.

KREIGSSPEIL (1811)
[American Kreigsspeil, Strategos]

Originally designed as a military training exercise and only later adapted as a game, Kreigsspeil nevertheless featured many of the gaming concepts familiar to us today. The miniature-based table activity incorporated the use of a gamemaster to determine the legality of moves and the resolution of conflicts, and pioneered terrain-specific effects, combat systems, and asymmetrical win conditions. It would gain in popularity, not only as an educational tool for training officers but also as a hobby, and eventually evolved into what we now call tabletop miniature wargames.

POKER (CIRCA 1820)
[Straight Poker, Draw Poker, Stud Poker, community card poker variants]

Poker's exact history is often disputed, but the effect it has had on gameplay is undeniable. Simple in terms of its rules, the complexity contained in its strategies has been used to illustrate game theory, probability laws, and economic principles in classrooms for years. No other game has been as instrumental in exposing the mathematical framework of games to the public and its popularity has exposed players all over the world to the concepts of imperfect information, bidding strategies, risk/reward analysis, and player psychology.

MAHJONG (CIRCA 1860)
[Classical, Cantonese, Japanese, Western Classical, American, Korean, and other variants]

Despite stories to the contrary, there is little evidence of the game we recognize as Mahjong existing before the nineteenth century. It's also arguable as to how much impact the tile-based game affected set-matching card games and vice versa. Regardless, its worldwide popularity in the 1920s introduced the West to the concept of using tiles as game pieces and the idea of melding (i.e., a play made by combining pieces in a specific order).

PINBALL (1871)
[Pin games, mechanical pinball, electronic powered pinball, digital pinball]

Originally a mechanical game mostly of chance, pinball evolved into its modern form just before the 1950s. Though outlawed in many jurisdictions until as late as the 1970s, it brought the idea of electronic arcade games into the public's consciousness and without its influence it's hard to imagine a market for the video arcade machines that soon followed.

MONOPOLY (1903)
[The Landlord's Game, Finance, Monopoly Jr., and other variants]

Games designed to teach were not new, but in the early twentieth century Lizzie Magie created what is no doubt the most famous serious game ever made, even if its intention was obscured well before its popularity peaked. Designed to educate the public on the economics of landownership and promote a single tax system, *The Landlord's Game* was eventually modified and sold to Parker Brothers by Charles Darrow as *Monopoly* in 1935. It brought a new emphasis on graphics and stylization in the packaging of games, a change that would have as much of an impact on future game development as did its staple features: movement along a never-ending path and a last-man-standing win condition.

LITTLE WARS (1913)

H. G. Wells is well known for his fiction but it's his rulebook for a game he designed that has had a dramatic impact on the games we play today. Converting the miniature army men used in Kreigsspeil into actual game pieces, he laid out specific rules for movement, terrain, combat, and game resolution. Those easy-to-implement rules brought wargames to the masses, while the notes detailing his reasoning on them provide still-relevant insight into the game design process.

SCRABBLE (1948)
[Lexiko, Criss-Crosswords, Super Scrabble]

At a time when games were mostly considered to be little more than leisurely time-wasters absent any real social value, Alfred Mosher Butts released his game of spelling and successfully challenged that notion. Using frequency analysis to determine the game's balance, the game represents one of the first-known uses of a scientifically devised evaluation of the game itself within the design process.

TACTICS (1954)
[Tactics II]

Introducing elements such as combat tables, unit-specific stats, and zone of control, Charles S. Roberts's genre-defining game would go on to greater success when it was revised as *Tactics II* in 1958. Not only would it launch the wargame industry as such, but the resulting journals and magazines would provide a medium in which players and designers could discuss game elements. Much of today's game terminology first appeared in the pages of such publications.

RISK (1957)
[La Conquete du Monde, Risk 2010, and multiple other Risk versions]

The French game, *La Conquete du Monde*, took the concept of wargames and simplified the gameplay, moving it from a strategic sim to a more abstract world-domination style of game. In doing so, it became one of the most popular games of the twentieth century and inspired many similar games such as *Diplomacy* and *Axis and Allies*, which would add their own twist to the genre.

DIPLOMACY (1959)

Changing our perception on how games could be played, *Diplomacy* moved from outside mechanics like dice and cards and instead utilized social interaction to dictate gameplay. It also qualifies as one of the earliest real-time strategy games as turns are taken simultaneously by all players.

Spacewar! (1962)

When MIT students were tasked with creating a great demonstration on an early mini-computer, what they created was this game. While which game deserves to be called the first "computer game" can be argued, this offering, even if not granted that right, nevertheless has an impressive list of innovations all its own. It was the first to have a joystick, first to have a physics engine, and, in 1976, it became the first commercially distributed computer game.

Oregon Trail (1971)
[Oregon Trail 1st–5th edition, Oregon Trail II]

This game has been remade in so many versions that many who have been exposed to it as young students may fail to recognize just how old it is. Created for a Minnesota public school by three of its student teachers, this educational game became hugely popular with students. First available only through Minnesota's schools network, it would be seven years before the Minnesota Educational Computing Consortium would publish it. Its success and longevity has earned it a reputation of being one of the best, if not the best, example of educational software ever produced.

Pong (1972)
[Home Pong, Pong Doubles, other variations]

Undeniably inspired by Ralph Baer's early proof-of-concept demonstration, Atari's *Pong* first surfaced as an arcade hit. It was when it transitioned into a home game console, however, that it had its greatest influence as the first game to ever be ported. While the console version, *Home Pong*, did not beat Baer's Magnavox Odyssey to market as the first home video game platform, its remarkable success has led many historians to credit it with launching the video game industry.

Dungeons and Dragons (1974)
[AD&D 1st–4th edition]

It is not hard to see the impact that this game by Gary Gygax and Dave Arneson has had on the video game industry. Terms like PCs, NPCs, DM, Armor Class, Hit Points, Ability Stats, Alignment, Experience Points, and Encounters all originate from here, as do plenty of now-standard concepts and mechanics. It would be impossible to list everything that *D&D* has contributed to gaming, but nearly every mechanic of today's RPGs got their start here.

CHOOSE YOUR OWN ADVENTURE (1975)
[Adventures of You]

A major step in interactive fiction, this series of children's books, created by Edward Packard, allowed readers to move through the story by choosing their own paths with only one "winning" solution available. Other publishers joined in by adding stats and random results to their stories, but it was the emergence of personal computers that would eventually give this form of expression a home.

COLOSSAL CAVE ADVENTURE (1976)
[Colossal Cave, Adventure, Advent, and various modifications]

Known by a myriad of names as other publishers began to copy or clone the game, Don Wood's authorized adaptation of Will Crowther's cave exploration program is not only credited as the first adventure game, but first work of virtual interactive fiction. It would be a large influence on many of the early game pioneers as they created companies like Infocom and Sierra to make similar games.

BREAKOUT (1976)
[Super Breakout]

Expanding on the success of *Pong*, Atari popularized a new type of game. While others focused on increasing the realism in video games, the simple abstractness of *Breakout* would eventually lead to games such as *Tetris* and *Bejeweled*. Its impact extended beyond its direct influence on other games however. Two of the designers, Steve Jobs and Steve Wozniak, would use the experience as an inspiration for their next project, the Apple II.

MATTEL ELECTRONICS FOOTBALL (1976)
[Football II]

The second handheld electronic game, this release by Mattel skyrocketed in popularity. Nothing more than blips on a screen, the simple gameplay coupled with easy portability nevertheless captured the imagination of young gamers. It paved the way for not only the soon-to-emerge arcade explosion but the eventual handheld consoles of today.

DEMOLITION DERBY (1977)

One of the earliest auto racing arcade games, *Demolition Derby* was not the first racing game to come to the video arcade or even the first one with multiplayer. (Atari beats it to both of those distinctions with their *Gran Track 10* and *Indy 800* games, respectively.) It was, however, responsible for a major breakthrough when its creator, Jerry Lawson, introduced the first AI with evasion capabilities.

SPACE INVADERS (1978)
[Space Invaders Part II, Space Invaders II, Return of the Invaders, Super Space Invaders '91, Space Invaders DX, Space Invaders '95]

The blocky, monotonously marching aliens mentioned in the game's title are among the most recognized icons of classic gaming. It is undeniably the game that had the greatest impact in launching the video arcade industry and its port in 1980 to the Atari 2600 is considered by many to be the industry's first killer app. It pioneered concepts such as high scores, increasing difficulty, multiple lives, evade-and-shoot, and destructible terrain. It is often quoted by a generation of game designers as being one of their inspirations for their work.

ZORK (1979)
[Zork II, Zork III, Enchanter, Sorcerer, Spellcaster, Beyond Zork, Zork Zero, Zork: The Undiscovered Underground]

Looking for a project that captured and expanded on the spirit of *Colossal Cave Adventure*, which they had recently solved, a group of MIT students created what would go on to be the most influential interactive fiction game to date. Renowned at the time for its innovative puzzles, it would be a year later when distributed for home systems that it would demonstrate its technical muscles by pushing the practical boundaries of data storage further than what was thought possible. It also pioneered the idea of a hint book, the forerunner to the modern strategy guide.

AKALABETH: WORLD OF DOOM (1979)

Richard Garriott's first RPG not only helped launch the genre but its combination of overhead ASCI maps and first-person perspective dungeon crawling became a staple for early games. Even though the dungeons and monsters were wireframe, the game would serve as a template to future first-person designs as technology advanced. It is hard to imagine what RPGs would be like today if Lord British had not cut his teeth on this early milestone.

ASTEROIDS (1979)
[Asteroids Deluxe, Blasteroids, Asteroids Hyper 64]

The first videogame for which a copyright was filed (simultaneously with *Lunar Lander*), *Asteroids* built on the idea *Computer Space*, a game that Atari founder Nolan

Bushnell first adapted from *Spacewars!*. By scaling it back to a single-player game and improving on its physics with splintering asteroids, the game became the most popular and successful games of the '70s.

Mystery House (1980)

Graphical scenes were still an oddity at the time this Roberta and Ken Williams creation came about. The first graphical adventure game, its astonishing success led them to form Sierra On-Line, the company responsible for many of the most iconic adventure games of the '80s.

Pac-Man (1980)
[Ms. Pac-Man]

The dot-chomping icon of the 1980s helped launch not only the video game industry but, as fans clamored for a better chance of racking up the highest score at the local arcade, it popularized a new type of publication, the strategy guide. The game also introduced power-ups and can be considered the first hybrid video game (combining the then popular evasion-based games with the equally popular chase-based games). The biggest impact though, undeniably, is the introduction of mascots to video games. Not only is Pac-Man an immediately identifiable character, but the four villainous ghost each have, thanks to their individual AI, the slightest hint of personality.

Defender (1980)
[Stargate, Strike Force]

Created by pinball programmer, Eugene Jarvis, this early shoot 'em up introduced the arcade world to the concept of side-scrolling and it significantly upped the complexity of reflex-driven games by combining both a joystick and a series of buttons for the first time. Though many at the time thought such difficult games would be a turn off to consumers, the game became a commercial success and inspired other developers to explore adding greater challenges to their games.

Ultima (1980)
[Ultima II–IX, Worlds of Ultima: The Savage Empire, Ultima: Worlds of Adventure 2, Ultima Underworld: The Stygian Abyss, Ultima Underworld II: Labyrinth of Worlds]

Fresh off the success of *Akalabeth*, Richard Garriott created his iconic series, *Ultima*. A follow up to his earlier hobby-turned-commercial RPG, it created the standards for

RPGs with its player-driven stat allotment system, race- and class-based character variations, use of experience points, random combats, and (in later sequels) story-driven adventures. In 1992, *Ultima Underworld* would be the first truly 3D rendered game in video game history. The advancements the series is responsible for were not only limited to gameplay and technology though. Garriott had insisted that *Ultima II* be distributed in a box with a map and a manual, creating a standard for video game packaging that lasted nearly 20 years.

ROGUE (1980)
[Hack, NetHack]

Before graphics were standard on PC games, there was *Rogue*. Built on the simple premise of dungeon exploration, the player's movement drew in the map. The map, in this case, was made up of simple ASCI characters, as were the monsters and treasures. An earlier game entitled *Beneath Apple Manor* used a similar procedural generation system to create its dungeons; however, *Rogue* had a far greater impact as it moved through the early network of connected college computers than did the Apple II–only game.

DONKEY KONG (1981)
[Donkey Kong Junior, Donkey Kong 3]

A plumber versus an ape was the premise of what went on to become the most successful video game franchise ever. The first real platformer, it introduced not only iconic characters but the basic gameplay from which so many other games have evolved, namely the use of a jump, either to avoid obstacles or as a way to get to other areas in the environment. It was also the first to introduce a story, albeit a brief and simple one, into video arcade games.

WIZARDRY (1981)
[Wizardry II-VII, Wizardry 8]

The series, originally created by Andrew Greenberg and Robert Woodhead and then later advanced by pioneers such as D.W. Bradley and Brenda Brathwaite, introduced dungeon crawls to the general game-playing public. Competing against the recently released *Ultima* series, it created the first party-based video game, was the first to utilize advisory warnings on its packaging (for skill level), and brought the RPG concept to Japan where it became immensely popular. Nearly every computer and console RPG can trace its features back to the *Wizardry* and *Ultima* games.

ZAXXON (1982)
[Super Zaxxon, Zaxxon 3-D]

Sega's shooter was among the more popular video games of the '80s, but its innovation was in its use of an isometric view, a first for video games, pioneering a standard that would remain popular for 20 years.

PITFALL! (1982)
[Pitfall II: Lost Caverns, Super Pitfall]

David Crane's game introduced a new standard for sprites on home console systems and became one of the best-selling games of the decade. It was not only the forefather to the action-adventure game, it also helped propel third-party development as a valid distribution option by becoming Activision's first great hit.

POLE POSITION (1982)
[Pole Position II]

An early racing game by Namco, many of its features became the standard for racing games from then on, such as including a rearview mirror and the placement of the behind-the-car camera.

MARIO BROS. (1983)
[Super Mario Bros., Vs. Super Mario Bros., Super Mario Bros. Special, Super Mario Bros. 2, Super Mario Bros. 3, Super Mario World]

Shigeru Miyamoto followed up on his success with *Donkey Kong* by creating a brother for Mario and releasing this platformer with a two-player mode. While the first of the series added many of the elements now commonly associated to the brand, it was the sequel, *Super Mario Bros.*, that is best known for its impact on the genre. Adding scrolling, power-ups, destructible blocks, and hidden secrets; the game was a huge hit on the Nintendo Entertainment System. Its success helped the struggling video game industry to pull out from the death spiral that had been brought about by the abundance of poor-quality games being made at the time.

STAR WARS (1983)
[Empire Strikes Back]

It may not be much of a surprise, given Lucas's ability to successfully market his IP into other media, but this vector-based game that recreated the fighter combat scenes in *Star Wars* was among the most popular arcade games of its time and became the first successful movie crossover in the video game industry.

M.U.L.E. (1983)

Bringing economic simulation to video games, this Dan Bunten game defined what a multiplayer game could be. A forefather to both real-time strategy games and god games, it challenged players to compete and cooperate simultaneously. Not exceptionally successful from a commercial standpoint, it nevertheless became the inspiration for many future game designers.

KING'S QUEST (1984)
[King's Quest II–VII, King Quest: Mask of Eternity]

The *King's Quest* series, created by Roberta and Ken Williams, moved graphical adventures from the mostly static, simply illustrated scene to a fully immersive, fluidly animated world. While later sequels would revolutionize the genre by replacing the command parser with a point-and-click interface, even its earliest incarnations impacted the industry through the use of their unique brand of humor and storytelling style. Those warm, personal touches added as much, if not more, to the enjoyment of the game as any of its challenging puzzles did.

TETRIS (1984)
[Hatris, Welltris, Faces]

Perhaps no other game has created more drama and international intrigue than Alexey Pajitnov's puzzle game. Often cited as a case study due to the legal complications of licensing it, its greatest impact on the industry, however, was nothing short of ushering in casual games. It is arguably the world's most played video game and, in 1989, it became the Gameboy's killer app as it went on to become one of the best-selling video games of all time.

THE ANCIENT ART OF WAR (1984)
[The Ancient Art of War at Sea, The Ancient Art of War in the Skies]

One of forefathers to modern real-time strategy games, this tactical combat game provided players not only the opportunity to face various AI opponents, but was also among the first to allow players to create their own maps, formations, and missions. Its now-classic combat system helped solidify the rock-paper-scissors method of balancing that would remain popular with designers for years to come.

BALANCE OF POWER (1985)
[Balance of Power: The 1990 Edition, Balance of Power: 21st Century]

Chris Crawford's game helped pioneer serious gaming. Challenging players to handle the political brinksmanship inherent in being one of the world's superpowers, it took video games on another path, rewarding the player for exercising control over a dramatic escalation instead of encouraging their participation in it.

BARD'S TALE (1985)
[Bard's Tale II–III]

This game by Interplay's Michael Cranford helped set the expectation for computerized role-playing by adding an intuitive interface and colored images; two features that were lacking from earlier RPGs. The game's popularity was due in part to it having been designed with an audience unfamiliar with traditional role-playing in mind, something many of its earlier, more hardcore predecessors neglected to do. It also created a coherent, though limited, story by tying in the game's restricted environment (a technological constraint) to the plot.

GAUNTLET (1985)
[Gauntlet II, Gauntlet: The Deeper Dungeon]

Multiplayer games were not unusual by the mid-'80s, but Atari's four player co-op was. Partially inspired by Jack Palevich's earlier game, *Dandy,* it served as a forerunner to the dungeon-crawl, hack-and-slash style of gameplay that would be popular in the '90s. Its more immediate contributions, though, were its exposure of class-based adventuring to the arcade world, and defining a new standard for designing multiplayer arcade cabinets.

THE LEGEND OF ZELDA (1986)
[The Adventure of Link, A Link to the Past, Link's Awakening, The Ocarina of Time, Link's Awakening DX, Majora's Mask, Oracle of Season, Oracle of Ages]

Some games change everything; Zelda is one of them. Its influence over gameplay is so broad that its exact genre is often fiercely debated. Though it was the first console game to incorporate a save feature, Zelda's true genius is in its minimalism; it took elements from many of the early genres and simplified them, combining them together to create an easy-to-learn yet immensely enjoyable system of gameplay. Today, it's virtually impossible to find a game that is not somehow influenced by Zelda's early innovations.

DRAGON QUEST (1986)
[Dragon Quest II–VII, Dragon Warrior II–IV, Dragon Warrior VII]

Yuji Hori's game brought RPGs to a wide Japanese audience and, in doing so, set a standard for nearly all games that came after it. In Japan it became a merchandising phenomenon and, when it was released in North America several years later, it reinforced the growing popularity of Japanese-based fantasy games. Not only did the series introduce many to death penalties, overhead maps, monster collecting, turn-based battles, refined musical arrangements, and extensive storytelling, but it was also one of the earliest and, at the time, strongest examples of open world, nonlinear gameplay.

METROID (1986)
[Metroid II: Return of Samus, Super Metroid]

Metroid's creative open-ended gameplay and its then-unique password save system definitely had an influence on today's games, but it's the game's breaking of a social norm that has had the greatest impact. At the end of the game, the heavily armored hero whom the player has been controlling is revealed to be female, providing the first visible cracks to the male-hero stereotype that completely dominated games of that time.

DEFENDER OF THE CROWN (1986)

Cineware raised the stakes for visual storytelling with their series of graphics-centered games, including this title. While its gameplay, like many other of their titles, was criticized as simplistic, its use of prerendered animated scenes was so far ahead of its time that it would be another year before the term "cut-scene" would even be coined.

TECMO BOWL (1987)
[Tecmo Super Bowl, Tecmo Super Bowl II–III]

It was the port of this NES game from its arcade version that made tie-ins with real sports stars a marketing must-have. Known for its increase in realism over existing sports games, particularly those available on consoles, its success was due not only to its use of licensed NFL players but also to the inclusion of stats based on the stars' actual abilities. Its sequel, *Tecmo Super Bowl*, added 20 player rosters, editable playbooks, and team licenses, becoming the first game to include all NFL teams along with their roster of real-world players.

Pirates! (1987)
[Pirates! Gold]

Sid Meier's strategy/sim game utilized randomly generated events and dynamically adjusting systems. As a result, a great variety to the gameplay emerged that allowed the player to experience a significantly different game each time she or he played. Its innovation of a dynamic persistence within an open world helped establish Meier as one of the top game designers of our time and set a bar for all of the simulations that came after it.

Metal Gear (1987)
[Metal Gear 2, Metal Gear Solid, Metal Gear Solid 2, Metal Gear Solid: Ghost Babel]

Players have used avoidance and hiding as a strategy since the cannon in *Space Invaders* first slid behind one of its bases, but it was Hideo Kojima's game that made stealth action into a genre. Beyond a new central mechanic, the game brought with it a style of storytelling that hadn't been seen in action games to that point; its writing and emphasis on plot would go on to become a key element of the series.

Street Fighter (1987)
[Street Fighter II–III, Street Fighter II: Champion Edition, Street Fighter II: Hyper Fighting, Super Street Fighter II, Super Street Fighter II: Turbo Edition, Street Fighter Alpha, Street Fighter Alpha 2–3, Street Fighter EX, Street Fighter EX2–3, X-Men vs. Street Fighter, Marvel Heroes vs. Street Fighter, Street Fighter III: 2nd Impact, Street Fighter III: 3rd Strike]

The number of innovations that came about in this series could nearly fill a book on their own. From its early pressure-sensitive controls (a feature that would become standard on console controllers a decade later) to its now-standard six-button arcade layout, the game has become the single most iconic example of fighting games. Spawning an incredible number of sequels and variants, the series joined with Marvel Comics to produce one of the first licensing crossovers in the industry. *Street Fighter II* in particular is well known for the number of innovations it brought to fighting games; it introduced many now-standards elements of the genre including signature moves, complex undocumented button sequences, blocking, and attack combos.

EARL WEAVER BASEBALL (1987)
[Earl Weaver Baseball II, Earl Weaver Baseball II: Commemorative Edition]

Sports games were among the first to become video games but it was *Earl Weaver Baseball* that would innovate the standards that such games would follow. Though appearing to some degree in other baseball games, elements such as full team rosters of current players, statistic-based simulation, strategy-only mode, player trading, and managerial AI were all included in one game for the first time along with full-season simulation, voice synthesis, and stadium realism making their debut into sports games. The sequel pioneered a new camera system, one which would automatically follow the action.

MANIAC MANSION (1987)
[Maniac Mansion: Day of the Tentacle]

A wacky graphical adventure by Ron Gilbert and Gary Winnick, *Maniac Mansion* was a huge step forward in terms of interface design. Replacing the then-standard text parser with a GUI, it reduced the trial-and-error method forced on players and, as a result, revolutionized adventure games. It also advanced how cut-scenes were used (a term Gilbert coined) and established the importance of game engines in the streamlining of the production cycle.

FINAL FANTASY (1987)
[Final Fantasy II–X]

Final Fantasy introduced players to the rich world of RPGs with a decidedly unique take by its designer, Hironobu Sakaguchi. The series is well regarded for its use of complex stories, memorable characters, and cutting-edge graphics. Introducing standards such as side views of battles and changing classes, Square/Square Enix was the first to popularize the Japanese style of role-playing games among Western audiences.

PHANTASY STAR (1987)
[Phantasy Star II–IV, Phantasy Star Online]

Starring one of the earliest female heroes in video games, the series brought sci-fi role-playing to the public. Its integration of psuedo-3D, high frames per second, and an early save game system established its technological bona fides, but the series' use of character-driven story, cross-sequel story arch, and branching narrative also had a strong impact on games made since then. It also introduced the use of player-created macros for party AI and, most notably with *Phantasy Star Online*, pioneered the use of the Internet for console gaming.

WASTELAND (1988)
[Fountain of Dreams]

Interplay once again changed the face of RPGs when they took the genre in a new direction. Abandoning the high-fantasy world traditionally associated with role playing, the game brought a postapocalyptic America into view. It introduced gamers to a persistent world, encounters that had multiple solutions, party members with independent AI, and it replaced the traditional class-based character creation system with a more versatile skill-based approach. Though it spawned a sequel of its own, it's better known for having inspired the *Fallout* series of games, created by many of the same team members who worked on this title.

JOHN MADDEN FOOTBALL (1988)
[John Madden Football II, John Madden Football '92–'93, Madden NFL '94–'99, Madden Football 64, Madden NFL 2000–2002]

While its first version lacked any team or player endorsement, John Madden's involvement in the process brought a critical element—an intimate understanding of football's strategy and essence—that made *Madden* one of the most enduring franchises in video game history. Though originally designed for the computer, in 1990 EA released a console version of the game that introduced many of the now-standard features of football sims, such as the behind-the-QB view. As the series progressed, it mixed its strong simulation elements with arcade-style action thereby creating a unique style of play that set it apart from its competitors. It would go on to add a franchise mode and the ability to customize nearly every element of the game, cementing the game as a perennial classic.

SIMCITY (1989)
[SimCity 2000, SimCity 3000]

It took a while for Will Wright to convince anyone that his urban planning game was worth publishing. It was so innovative that no potential publisher seemed to know what to do with it. Introducing a true sandbox world, it allowed players to set their own goals and play without win and lose conditions. It spawned a slew of "Sim" titled games as the term took on a genre-defining denotation that peaked years later when Will Wright would release another game simply entitled *The Sims*.

MECHWARRIOR (1989)

[MechWarrior 2: 31st Century Combat, NetMech, MechWarrior 2: Ghost Bear's Legacy, MechWarrior 2: Mercenaries, MechWarrior 2: The Titanium Trilogy]

Bringing the large mechanical battle-crafts to the world of video games, this series combined the action of combat sims with the strategy of vehicle construction. It was *MechWarrior 2*'s utilization of hardware acceleration that helped set a new standard for graphics; it popularized the use of dedicated 3D video cards and eventually, with its *Titanium* edition, provided a showcase for the newly developed Direct3D rendering technologies. *NetMech*, released in 1996, provided an upgrade that allowed up to eight players to compete in online battles, making it one of the first games to bring combat simulation to the Internet.

HEROES OF MIGHT AND MAGIC (1990)

[King's Bounty, Heroes of Might and Magic II, Heroes of Might and Magic III, Heroes Chronicles]

Adding character-driven influences to the traditional turn-based strategy games of the time, New World Computing evolved a unique subgenre. Even in its earliest incarnation, the staples of its gameplay are there: army recruitment, selectable bonuses within the treasures, and battlefields filled with obstacles. When the series added the Might and Magic branding to its title, it went on to establish other elements as core to the genre, such as multiple heroes, experience levels, resource management, and upgradable units.

NEVERWINTER NIGHTS (AOL) (1991)

It would cost you $12 an hour to play but if you were an AOL member in the early '90s you could be one of the first persons to play a graphical MMORPG. Unrelated to the later Bioware version (the only similarity being that both were based on the same city within D&D's *Forgotten Realms* world), SSI based the online game on their Gold Box series of computer adventures utilizing the Dungeons and Dragons worlds. It remained popular throughout its life and brought success to the fledgling MMO genre.

CIVILIZATION (1991)

[Civilization II–III]

When Sid Meier took on the strategy genre, the game that resulted became a new genre in and of itself. While in hindsight there are forerunners that qualify as empire building games, it was *Civilization* that made the genre popular. The inclusion of multiple win conditions, a diplomacy system, economics, and a customizable game-state to a conquest-style game elevated it beyond what anyone else had seen and remains to this day one of the strongest icons of the genre.

DUNE II (1992)
[Dune 2000, Emperor: Battle for Dune]

Creating what is today considered the quintessential RTS style of gameplay, Westwood Studios completely altered the Dune franchise from its graphical adventure roots. In doing so, it established many of the traditions associated with the genre, such as the fog of war, structure placement, unit queuing, resource collecting, and direct squad management.

WOLFENSTEIN 3D (1992)
[Wolfenstein 3D: Spear of Destiny, Return to Castle Wolfenstein, and multiple add-on packs]

While there were shooters that utilized the first-person perspective around twenty years before this seminal title released, it is this game that truly launched the genre. John Carmack's technological improvements to the typical rendering methods used by other game engines were largely responsible for the success of this game and showed the feasibility of first-person shooters.

ALONE IN THE DARK (1992)
[Alone in the Dark 2–3, Jack in the Dark, Alone in the Dark: Ghosts in Town]

Infocom is best known for their advances in text adventure games, but lesser known is their innovations in 3D animation. Adapting early to the use of polygons over sprites, they instituted the first use of interpolated animation for this title and created one of the first non-shooter games to utilize 3D polygonal models.

MAGIC: THE GATHERING (1993)
[Beta, Unlimited, Revised, 4th–7th editions, and many expansions]

Richard Garfield created this game centered around trading and collecting cards to use within a deck. Moving card decks from their basis as a shared resource to a proprietary resource, he added desk construction as a new strategic element in games. The popularization of this collect-and-construct concept, along with the idea of assigning various degrees of rarity to pieces, would spread to many other games.

Master of Orion (1993)
[Master of Orion II–III]

Micropose's turn-based offering set many of the standards for 4X games; which makes sense as it was the first game to be so described. The variety of AI opponents, each with their own unique play styles, pushed the boundaries of what had been done in terms of balance and created a game that demanded reactionary tactics as much as pro-active ones. Providing strategic complexity without requiring excessive microman-agement, *Masters of Orion* achieved an equilibrium that many games since then have attempted to emulate but in which few have succeeded.

Myst (1993)
[Riven, Myst III]

Appearing just as graphical adventures began to wane in popularity, *Myst* became the most successful of the genre and one of the most commercially successful games of all time. Incorporating a first-person point of view with highly aesthetic graphics, it created a shift in how all games were designed. It also showed off the advantage of the recently introduced CD technology, as it was one of the first games to embrace the new form of data storage.

Doom (1993)
[Doom II: Hell on Earth, Ultimate Doom, Final Doom, Doom 64]

Very few titles have the ability to claim the amount of influence over the evolution of video games as does this series from id. A pioneer not only in the area of technology, it also distinguished the first-person shooter as its own genre, altered the marketing of games, and set new trends like LAN play. Combining many newly conceived techniques, John Carmack was able to create a pseudo-3D world unlike anything anyone had seen. It introduced full texture mapping of the entire level, varied lighting, dynamic environments, and stereo sound; all of which contributed to a level of atmosphere never before experienced in video games. Released as shareware, the game became one of the most installed pieces of software ever, with deathmatch play becoming a favorite pastime (particularly among corporate workers who were just then gaining access to networked PCs). The careful preparation and packaging of the game's assets helped legitimize modding, and its success as a third-party game engine inspired many other developers to create engines that could be expanded to other projects.

System Shock (1994)
[System Shock II]

Taking the exploding FPS genre into a new trajectory, this series by Looking Glass Studio added novel elements like story arcs, puzzle challenges, and skill development to the traditionally linear gameplay of its predecessors. Many of the modern "hybrid" shooters trace their inspiration back to this series of games.

Warcraft (1994)
[Warcraft II: Tides of Darkness, Warcraft 2: Beyond the Dark Portal, Warcraft II: Battle.net Edition]

The first multiplayer RTS, Blizzard's creation introduced to the still underdeveloped genre the elements of mission objectives, random map generation, multiple resources, and, in later incarnations, patrolling units and a persistent fog of war. Utilizing the marketing tactic of giving away a freeware version of the game (composed of its early levels), it exposed the new genre to many players. *Warcraft II* included a map editor which, while largely overlooked at the time, became a staple feature of their RTS games and eventually would break new ground for early modders.

Tactics Ogre: Let Us Cling Together (1995)

Best known for introducing many to tactical combat (later made even more popular by *Final Fantasy Tactics*), this game by acclaimed designer Yasumi Matsuno featured a story fraught with tough moral decisions amid a backdrop of ethnic cleansing. As innovative and unexpected as its story was, it is its customization and character leveling features that most impacted our current games.

Pokemon (1996)
[Pokemon Red, Green, Blue, Yellow]

Satoshi Taijiri's game combined RPG elements with concepts of a pet-sim and along the way morphed itself into a monster of a merchandising empire. Its revolutionary idea of allowing players to trade creatures with one another through the use of a linking cable created a social element that few video games up to that time had ever seen.

Resident Evil (1996)
[Resident Evil: Director's Cut, Resident Evil 2, Resident Evil 3: Nemesis, Resident Evil Code: Veronica]

The first game to be self-described as survival-horror, this game has become the poster child for the genre. The slow creeping horror, interrupted by alarming moments of terror, created a tone far different from the frantic pace standard to many games at the time. Furthermore, its cinematic nature (aided by technological advances of the newly available PlayStation) allowed for a more gruesome experience as the player navigated through the dark halls and beckoning corners. Another innovative feature of the series, introduced in the first sequel, is that the game can be played through with either one of two characters in any order, with the second scenario being affected by the events of the first.

SUPER MARIO 64 (1996)

Moving from side scrolling to free-roaming 3D environments, *Super Mario 64* quickly revolutionized platform gaming. Creating a standard for camera views and analog control, the game was an immediate hit and well received by players and critics alike. It also introduced many graphical features not yet seen on consoles; in particular its then-unique use of particles and effects.

QUAKE (1996)

[VQuake, GLQuake, WinQuake, Quake: Arcade Tournament Edition, Quake II, Quake III Arena, and multiple expansions]

Capitalizing on their success with first-person shooters, id released their first 3D game, *Quake*. Creating a true 3D engine for the game, the developers incorporated baked textures and lighting into the environment and reducing the amount of details the engine was required to render through an innovative process known as Z-buffering. Modding was actively encouraged and, as a result, *Quake* would become the first FPS with bots in the PvP environment when the modding community added them. Multiplayer gaming, something of a technical hurdle for players up till now, was greatly enhanced by the game's inclusion of an easy-to-use TCP/IP connection method, a network interface, and use of prediction code.

TOMB RAIDER (1996)

[Tomb Raider II, Tomb Raider III, Tomb Raider: The Last Revelation, Tomb Raider Chronicles]

Laura Croft, the most widely recognized female hero in video games, came in with a splash. Both hailed as a break from the male hero stereotype and criticized for reinforcing the male-fantasy stereotype of a female, the character became the iconic personification of action-adventure games. One of the earliest games to include both 3D environments and characters, it helped cement the PlayStation's dominance throughout the '90s.

TAMAGOCHI (1996)
[Tamagochi (multiple versions)]

This self-contained pet-sim device launched a craze that no likely causes parents to wince even today. A real-time AI that needed to be fed and cared for regularly, this toy brought breeding/raising games to the consciousness of children; a style of games that have risen in popularity.

DIABLO (1996)
[Diablo: Hellfire, Diablo II, Diablo II: Lord of Destruction]

Blizzard's entry into the RPG genre introduced the world to a new style of dungeon crawling. Fast paced and addictive, the game brought loot collecting to a new level. It established a new convention with items that had rarity levels, with randomly assigned effects inherent in the rarest items. Multiplayer became a phenomenon, as Blizzard launched the first integrated gaming service, Battle.net, which allowed players to join together over the Internet and play the entire game as teammates (or, due to friendly fire, as enemies). The first sequel of the series, *Diablo II,* added a pseudo-crafting element by allowing objects to be transformed into more powerful versions, a popular mechanic that many other games have since adopted.

GOLDENEYE 007 (1997)

First-person shooters were a fairly dependable standard on the PC, but early attempts to bring them to consoles had, more often than not, dismal results. Rare's release of this James Bond film adaptation changed that perception. Noted for its four-way split screen multiplayer mode, stealth aspects, and location-specific damage effects, it immediately became popular and nearly every subsequent shooter has felt its influence.

ULTIMA ONLINE (1997)
[Ultima Online and multiple expansions]

Moving from the success of his *Ultima* series, Richard Garriott brought his fantasy realm to the online world in what he termed an "MMORPG." Its success in attracting a large and dependable subscriber base provided all of the incentive other developers needed to finance their entry into the genre. Providing a robust economical foundation for its world, it became one of the first virtual societies; allowing social interaction, economic dealings, and the persistent ownership of property.

GRAND THEFT AUTO (1997)
[Grand Theft Auto: Mission Pack #1–2, Grand Theft Auto 2, Grand Theft Auto III]

Even at its inception, *Grand Theft Auto* managed to match its controversy with an equal level of innovation. While its unique combination of gameplay elements and open-world environment showed what games could be, it was its 2001 incarnation, with its adaptation to a 3D engine, that finally made sandbox-style levels a de facto standard for many in the industry.

MONSTER RANCHER (1997)
[Monster Rancher 2&3, Monster Rancher Advance]

While other breeding games preceded it, *Monster Rancher* was unique in the way it generated the player's pets. While CD scanning never caught on as a method for random generation, the idea of a video game using external sources, such as bar codes, unrelated files, or a camera to generate its data shows up from time to time in other games.

GRAN TURISMO (1997)
[Gran Turismo 2, Gran Turismo 3: A-Spec]

Providing a level of realism rarely seen in any game, this racing simulator allowed players to tweak and tune nearly every aspect of their cars. By featuring unlockable tracks, a huge variety of real-world cars, and a budget-based progression, the series became the standard by which all other racing games are judged.

STARCRAFT (1998)
[Insurrection, Retribution, Starcraft: Brood War]

Perhaps best known for elevating the online real-time strategy genre, Blizzard's game completely dominated its field for years after its release. Its uniqueness lies in providing each side with drastically different abilities while still maintaining a well-balanced game. It would also become a pioneer of pro-gaming, as corporations began to sponsor full-time players to compete in popular tournaments.

UNREAL (1998)
[Unreal: Return to Na Pali, Unreal Tournament]

Competing against the *Quake* series, *Unreal* increased the technical quality of the FPS genre with advancements like 16-bit color, bloom effects, and fog. All that was done in addition to providing a strong engine, map editor, and scripting language that brought modding to a whole new level. As the Unreal Engine became a huge success, it allowed developers to focus on content instead of technology. Creators, both professional and hobbyists, were able to design specific actions within the game without having to become programmers due to its robust scripting engine setting yet another standard for design.

HALF-LIFE (1998)
[Half-Life: Opposing Force, Half-Life: Blue Shift, Half-Life: Decay]

Valve's seminal game ushered in a new level of cinematic immersion. Allowing the player to maintain control throughout any cut-scene had never been done before and that feature, along with a strong, engrossing story, captivated players. Its ground-breaking implementation of scripted scenes and the related advancement in combat AI still to this day earn the game rave reviews.

DANCE DANCE REVOLUTION (1998)
[All Dance Dance Revolution games from 1998 to 2001 (the franchise has had many variations both as an arcade machine and as a console game, too many to list individually)]

Rhythm games, as such, were not new when Konami launched *DDR* but the dance game was the one that popularized the genre. Pioneering the concept of excer-gaming (i.e., requiring physical activity to compete within a virtual game), it brought a renewed interest in peripherals to more accurately replicate the activity being simulated.

BALDUR'S GATE (1998)
[Baldur's Gate: Tales of the Sword Coast, Baldur's Gate II, Baldur's Gate II: Throne of Bhaal]

Giving computer RPGs a fresh new life, Bioware's first-ever game introduced many players to the somewhat forgotten traditions of tabletop role-playing. Premiering a more sophisticated dialogue system than had been seen to that point, the storytelling was highly remarkable. The game's user interface, carefully constructed to fit the player's needs, proved revolutionary by being both simple and elegant. Bioware would continue to perfect both their UI and dialogue systems throughout the series and in their other games, achieving a reputation for being innovators of immersive, unhindered storylines.

EVERQUEST (1999)
[Multiple expansion packs]

It was not the first MMORPG, or even the first 3D one, but when 989 Studios' five-year project launched, it showed that the market was ready to be fully immersed into a massive real-time fantasy world. Bringing together all of the staples that we associate with the genre such as quests, con systems, guilds, loot, and raids, the game was an amazing success. Nearly every MMO throughout the next 10 years used its successes and its occasional failures as the basis for their own development.

TONY HAWK'S PRO SKATER (1999)
[Tony Hawk's Pro Skater 2–3]

It's hard to say which had more of an impact on the other: extreme sports or video games' take on them. Its impact on the games we play today, though, is much easier to determine. Besides exposing a viable market for extreme sports games, its successful merger of user control and physics formed a natural interface that quickly moved from its roots and into many other genres.

PLANESCAPE: TORMENT (1999)

When Planescape was released at the end of 1999, its graphics, tile-based layout, and standard isometric view were already on the verge of being outdated. Perhaps that is why commercial success eluded this Black Isle–developed game. But its unique take on puzzle solving, dialogue, and what exactly an RPG can be has had lasting repercussions on games today.

COUNTER-STRIKE (2000)

Proving that making a good mod can be as innovative as making a good game, this first-person shooter not only brought with it superbly crafted levels, but it introduced asymmetrical team objectives and purchasable equipment to the FPS genre. It is also largely credited with bringing teamwork to shooters. Its effect on development though is tied to its continual updating of content and balance, a move that endeared fans to the company and has since been utilized by many other developers.

DEUS EX (2000)

Open-levels and plenty of choices for the player to make made this Warren Spector game a favorite of many and its innovations were—perhaps appropriate to its conspiracy theme—both impactful and somewhat veiled. It was a first-person shooter in which not shooting was a viable strategy, a role-playing game that required quick reactions, and a stealth game that allowed you to design your character as a gun-blazing tank. Despite how much it borrowed from other genres, its gameplay was far from derivative; its true innovation can be seen in how it masterfully incorporated a balance between those different mechanics.

BLACK & WHITE (2001)

While innovative in several areas (such as the ability to zoom in and out to such extreme levels), the most notable thing about this Peter Molyneux game is the pets' advanced level of AI. The ability of the pets to learn to perform amazingly complex tasks, sometimes only through observation, changed how we think of AI. Furthermore, while ultimately not accepted at the time, its innovative use of a movement-based UI would eventually become a popular concept when consoles began to use motion-sensing controllers.

BEJEWELED (2001)

With *Bejeweled*, casual games made their mark. Unique enough in its design to stand out, but familiar enough to be accessible to millions of new players, Popcaps' seminal matching game exposed a whole new demographic to gaming and made downloading and micro-purchases popular for browsers and for mobile devices.

INDEX

Like the Book?

Let us know on Facebook or Twitter!

facebook.com/courseptr

twitter.com/courseptr